D0557031

Making Schools Work

Making Schools Work

New Evidence on Accountability Reforms

Barbara Bruns, Deon Filmer, and
Harry Anthony Patrinos

THE WORLD BANK
Washington, D.C.

© 2011 The International Bank for Reconstruction and Development / The World Bank
1818 H Street NW
Washington DC 20433
Telephone: 202-473-1000
Internet: www.worldbank.org

All rights reserved

1 2 3 4 :: 14 13 12 11

This volume is a product of the staff of the International Bank for Reconstruction and Development / The World Bank. The findings, interpretations, and conclusions expressed in this volume do not necessarily reflect the views of the Executive Directors of The World Bank or the governments they represent.

The World Bank does not guarantee the accuracy of the data included in this work. The boundaries, colors, denominations, and other information shown on any map in this work do not imply any judgement on the part of The World Bank concerning the legal status of any territory or the endorsement or acceptance of such boundaries.

Rights and Permissions
The material in this publication is copyrighted. Copying and/or transmitting portions or all of this work without permission may be a violation of applicable law. The International Bank for Reconstruction and Development / The World Bank encourages dissemination of its work and will normally grant permission to reproduce portions of the work promptly.

For permission to photocopy or reprint any part of this work, please send a request with complete information to the Copyright Clearance Center Inc., 222 Rosewood Drive, Danvers, MA 01923, USA; telephone: 978-750-8400; fax: 978-750-4470; Internet: www.copyright.com.

All other queries on rights and licenses, including subsidiary rights, should be addressed to the Office of the Publisher, The World Bank, 1818 H Street NW, Washington, DC 20433, USA; fax: 202-522-2422; e-mail: pubrights@worldbank.org.

ISBN: 978-0-8213-8679-8
eISBN: 978-0-8213-8680-4
DOI: 10.1596/978-0-8213-8679-8

Library of Congress Cataloging-in-Publication Data
Bruns, Barbara.
Making schools work : new evidence on accountability reforms / Barbara Bruns, Deon Filmer, Harry Anthony Patrinos.

p. cm. — (Human development perspectives)
Includes bibliographical references.
ISBN 978-0-8213-8679-8 (alk. paper) — ISBN 978-0-8213-8680-4
1. Educational tests and measurements—United States. 2. Educational accountability—United States. 3. Public schools—United States—Examinations. 4. School improvement programs. 5. Educational leadership. I. Filmer, Deon. II. Patrinos, Harry Anthony. III. Title.

LB3051.B78 2011
371.2'07—dc22

2010053396

Cover photos: Barbara Bruns/World Bank (sleeping teacher); Erica Amorim/World Bank (Brazilian teacher with students)
Cover design: Naylor Design

Contents

Boxes

Figures

Tables

Foreword

Very few topics command as much attention in the development field as school effectiveness. Schooling is a basic service that most citizens expect from their governments, but the quality available is quite variable, and the results too often disappointing. What will it take for schools in developing countries to deliver good quality education? *Making Schools Work: New Evidence on Accountability Reforms* seeks to answer this question.

The 2004 *World Development Report* developed a conceptual framework to analyze the kind of government and market failures in service delivery that exist in a large number of developing countries: weak accountability leading to poor motivation and inadequate incentives for performance. That report proposed a set of approaches to remedy those failures that rely on stronger accountability mechanisms. But the empirical evidence supporting those approaches was limited—and uncomfortably so.

Over several years, World Bank researchers and project staff have worked with academic researchers and their counterparts in government and civil society to remedy this evidence gap. Their studies isolate and measure the impacts of reforms and expand the evidence base on the best methods for improving school effectiveness, especially through better information, devolution of authority, and stronger incentives for teachers.

This volume is a systematic stock-taking of the evidence on school accountability reforms in developing countries. It provides a measured and insightful review and assessment of the results of a variety of approaches that developing countries are experimenting with in their quest for better schools. It is not the final word on the subject, but will hopefully contribute to better policy choices, grounded in the evidence currently available.

The Human Development Perspectives series presents research findings on issues of critical strategic importance for developing countries. Improving the effectiveness of social service delivery is clearly one such issue. *Making Schools Work* sets a standard for future efforts to assess the effectiveness of policy reforms.

Ariel Fiszbein
Chief Economist for Human Development
Chair, Editorial Board, Human Development Perspectives series
World Bank
Washington, D.C.

Elizabeth King
Director for Education
World Bank
Washington, D.C.

Acknowledgments

This study was managed by Barbara Bruns, Deon Filmer, and Harry Anthony Patrinos, who jointly authored chapters 1 and 5. Deon Filmer authored chapter 2 with inputs from Marta Rubio-Codina; Harry Anthony Patrinos authored chapter 3; and Barbara Bruns co-authored chapter 4 with Lucrecia Santibañez. The study grew out of a cross-country research program launched in 2006 with generous support from the government of the Netherlands through the Bank–Netherlands Partnership Program. That research program expanded with the launch of the Spanish Impact Evaluation Fund (SIEF) in 2007 and the establishment of a formal cluster of work on education reforms aimed at strengthening accountability. This book is above all a stocktaking of evidence emerging from the wave of new impact evaluations that the World Bank and partner countries have been able to launch thanks to this global funding support.

For the initial inspiration to step up knowledge generation from World Bank operations through rigorous evaluation, the authors are grateful to Paul Gertler, former World Bank chief economist for human development (HD). For the idea of focusing on education reforms in developing countries that tested the accountability framework of the 2004 *World Development Report*, the authors are grateful to current HD chief economist, Ariel Fiszbein.

This book is underpinned by significant contributions, including background papers, by Marta Rubio-Codina and Lucrecia Santibañez. We also thank Debora Brakarz, Katherine Conn, Margaret Koziol, and Martin Schlotter for excellent research assistance. Bruce Ross-Larsen provided excellent editorial advice. The team was guided and supervised by Elizabeth King and Ariel Fiszbein.

We also benefitted from valuable comments from our peer reviewers, Luis Benveniste, Shantayanan Devarajan, Philip Keefer, and Karthik Muralidharan, and comments from colleagues Helen Abadzi, Felipe Barrera, Nick Manning, and Halsey Rogers. Helpful guidance received at earlier stages included comments from Sajitha Bashir, Isabel Beltran, Francois Bourguignon, Jishnu Das, Pascaline Dupas, Claudio Ferraz, Francisco Ferreira, Paul Gertler, Paul Glewwe, Robin Horn, Emmanuel Jimenez, Stuti Khemani, Arianna Legovini, Reema Nayar, Ritva Reinikka, Carolyn Reynolds, Sofia Shakil, Lars Sondergaard, Connor Spreng, Miguel Urquiola, Emiliana Vegas, and Christel Vermeersch. Any and all errors that remain in this volume are the sole responsibility of the authors.

About the Authors

Barbara Bruns is lead economist in the Latin America and Caribbean region of the World Bank, responsible for education. She is currently co-managing several impact evaluations of teacher pay for performance reforms in Brazil and is lead author of *Achieving World Class Education in Brazil: The Next Agenda* (2010). As the first manager of the $14 million Spanish Impact Evaluation Fund (SIEF) at the World Bank from 2007 to 2009, Barbara oversaw the launch of more than 50 rigorous impact evaluations of health, education, and social protection programs. She has also served on the Education Task Force appointed by the UN Secretary General in 2003, co-authored the book *A Chance for Every Child: Achieving Universal Primary Education by 2015* (2003), and headed the Secretariat of the global Education for All Fast Track Initiative from 2002 to 2004. She holds degrees from the London School of Economics and the University of Chicago.

Deon Filmer is lead economist in the Research Department of World Bank. His research has spanned the areas of education, health, social protection, and poverty, and he has published extensively in these areas. Recent publications include papers on the impact of scholarship programs on school participation in Cambodia; on the roles of poverty, orphanhood, and disability in explaining education inequalities; and on the determinants of fertility behavior. He was a core team member of the World Development Reports in 1995 *Workers in an Integrating World* and 2004 *Making Services Work for Poor People*. His current research focuses on measuring and explaining inequalities in education and health outcomes and evaluating the impact of interventions that aim to increase and promote school participation among the poor (such as conditional cash or food transfers) and interventions that aim to improve education service provision (such as policies to improve the quality of teachers in remote areas). He received his Ph.D. in economics from Brown University.

Harry Anthony Patrinos is lead education economist in the Education Department of the World Bank. He specializes in all areas of education, especially school-based management, demand-side financing, and public-private partnerships. He manages the Benchmarking Education Systems for Results program and leads the Indigenous Peoples, Poverty, and Development research program. He manages impact evaluations in Latin America focusing on school-based management, parental participation, compensatory education, and savings programs. Previous books include *Indigenous Peoples, Poverty and Human Development in Latin America* (Palgrave Macmillan, 2006), *Lifelong Learning in the Global Knowledge Economy* (2003), *Policy Analysis of Child Labor: A Comparative Study* (St. Martin's, 1999), *Decentralization of Education: Demand-Side Financing* (1997), and *Indigenous People and Poverty in Latin America: An Empirical Analysis* (Ashgate, 1997). He received a doctorate from the University of Sussex.

Abbreviations

AGE	Support to School Management Program (Apoyo a la Gestión Escolar) [Mexico]
BOS	School Operational Assistance Program (Bantuan Operasional Sekolah) [Indonesia]
CERCA	Civic Engagement for Education Reform in Central America
DD	difference-in-differences [econometric method]
EDUCO	Education with Community Participation (Educación con Participación de la Comunidad)
EGRA	Early Grade Reading Assessment [Liberia]
EMIS	Education Management Information System
EQIP	Education Quality Improvement Project [Cambodia]
ETP	Extra Teacher Program [Kenya]
FUNDEF	Fund for Primary Education Development and Maintenance and Enhancement of the Teaching Profession (Fundo de Manutenção e Desenvolvimento da Educação Básica e de Valorização dos Profissionais da Educação) [Brazil]
GDP	gross domestic product
GM	grant-maintained [school-based management model, United Kingdom]
IDEB	Index of Basic Education Development (Índice de Desenvolvimento da Educação Básica) [Brazil]
IV	instrumental variables [econometric method]
NCLB	No Child Left Behind [U.S. law]
NGO	nongovernmental organization

OECD	Organisation for Economic Co-operation and Development
PDE	School Development Plan (Plano de Desenvolvimiento da Escola) [Brazil]
PEC	Quality Schools Program (Programa Escuelas de Calidad) [Mexico]
PEC-FIDE	Program of Strengthening and Direct Investment in Schools (Programa de Fortalecimiento e Inversión Directa a las Escuelas) [Mexico]
PIRLS	Progress in International Reading Literacy Study
PISA	Programme for International Student Assessment
PREAL	Partnership for Educational Revitalization in the Americas
PTA	parent-teacher association
RCT	ramdomized control trial [experimental method]
RDD	regression discontinuity design [experimental method]
SBM	school-based management
SD	standard deviation
SDMC	school development and monitoring committee [India]
SIMCE	National System for Measuring the Quality of Education (Sistema Nacional de Medición de la Calidad de la Educación) [Chile]
SNED	National System for Performance Evaluation of Subsidized Educational Establishments (Sistema Nacional de Evaluación del Desempeño de los Establecimientos Educativos Subvencionados) [Chile]
TIMSS	Trends in International Mathematics and Science Study
VEC	Village Education Committee [India]
$	All dollar amounts refer to U.S. dollars

1

Motivation and Framework

How can it be that a teacher sleeps in a classroom in the middle of a school day while students wait patiently outside? That grants intended for schools arrive with most of the funds siphoned off by intermediate layers of administration? That classrooms in slum areas teem with students, graffiti, and broken windows while schools in richer districts enjoy ample resources? That national school systems function without the periodic tests that would reveal how little students are learning over time and across districts?

These are not the only problems facing education systems in the developing world, but they are some of the most egregious—and in some sense, puzzling. While inadequate funding may be the biggest challenge that developing countries face, the proximate cause of the phenomena observed above is not a lack of resources. The teacher is in the classroom, his salary paid. The school grants program was funded by the central ministry. A fixed pot of resources may be distributed more or less equally across schools. While not simple or costless, the technology for tracking learning progress is readily available to developing countries, and many have started to implement it while others have not.

This book is about the threats to education quality that cannot be explained by lack of resources. It focuses on publicly financed school systems and the phenomenon of *service delivery failures*: cases where programs and policies that increase the inputs to education fail to produce effective delivery of services where it counts—in schools and classrooms. It documents what we know about the extent and costs of service delivery failures in public education in the developing world. And it further develops aspects of the conceptual model posited in the *World Development Report 2004*: that a root cause of low-quality and inequitable public services—not only in education—is the weak "accountability" of providers to both their supervisors and their clients (World Bank 2003).

The central focus of this book, however, is a new story. It is that developing countries are increasingly adopting innovative strategies to attack these issues. In more and more of the developing world, education results are improving because, among other reasons, education systems are becoming more accountable for results. A highly encouraging part of the new story is growing willingness by developing-country policy makers to subject new reforms to rigorous evaluations of their impacts and cost-effectiveness. Impact evaluation itself strengthens accountability because it exposes whether programs achieve desired results, who benefits, and at what public cost. A willingness to undertake serious impact evaluation is a commitment to more effective public service delivery.

In just the past five years, the global evidence base on education reforms to improve accountability has expanded significantly. While still not large, the wave of accountability-oriented reforms in developing countries that have been, or are being, rigorously evaluated now includes several different approaches and a diverse set of countries and regions. This book looks across this growing evidence base to take stock of what we now know and what remains unanswered. Although similar reforms have been adopted in many developed countries, it is beyond the scope of this book to review that policy experience in equivalent depth. Wherever possible, we do compare the emerging evidence from developing-country cases with the broader global evidence, particularly where the Organisation for Economic Co-operation and Development (OECD) experience is robust enough to support meta-evaluations and more general conclusions, or where developed-country cases appear to differ in important ways from outcomes in the developing world.

Our goal is to use evidence to distill practical guidance for policy makers grappling with the same challenges and considering the same types of reforms. In many areas, the current evidence base does not support clear answers. But by synthesizing what is supported by current evidence and by framing the issues where further research is needed, we hope to contribute to more effective policy design today and encourage further experimentation and evaluation tomorrow.

This initial chapter provides an overview and context for the rest of the book. It reviews the motivation and global context for education reforms aimed at strengthening provider accountability. It provides a rationale for the focus on the three key lines of reform that are analyzed in detail in chapters 2, 3, and 4:

- Chapter 2 drills into the global experience with *information reforms*—policies that use the power of information to strengthen the ability of clients of education services (students and their parents) to hold providers accountable for results.

- Chapter 3 analyzes the experience with *school-based management reforms*—policies that increase schools' autonomy to make key decisions and control resources, often empowering parents to play a larger role.
- Chapter 4 reviews the evidence on two key types of *teacher incentive reforms*—policies that aim to make teachers more accountable for results, either by making *contract tenure* dependent on performance, or by offering *performance-linked pay*.

The final chapter summarizes what we know about the impact of these types of reforms, draws cautious conclusions about possible complementarities if they are implemented in tandem, and considers issues related to scaling up reform efforts and the political economy of reform. Finally, we suggest directions for future work.

Service Delivery Failure in the Developing World

Between 1990 and 2010, the share of children who completed primary school in low-income countries increased from less than 45 percent to more than 60 percent (World Bank 2010)—a substantially faster rate of improvement than the standard set by the now high-income countries (Clemens, Kenny, and Moss 2007). Despite this progress, two swaths of the developing world—South Asia and Sub-Saharan Africa—will likely not achieve the United Nations Millennium Development Goal of universal primary completion by 2015. In many countries, the failure to achieve even this basic threshold of education development will come after having invested substantial national and donor resources in education—higher shares of gross domestic product (GDP) than high-income countries spent over the course of their development.

The gap in education results between developing and developed countries is even greater when measured by learning outcomes, as figure 1.1 illustrates. Among 15-year-olds tested in the OECD's Programme for International Student Assessment (PISA) in 2009, only 7 percent of Korean students and 22 percent of students across all OECD countries scored below 400 points—a threshold that signals even the most basic numeracy skills have not been mastered. Yet 73 percent of students in upper-middle-income countries and 90 percent of students in lower-middle-income developing countries performed below this level. Among the 38 developing countries participating in the Trends in International Mathematics and Science Study (TIMSS), even students in the highest-income quintile performed, on average, worse than test takers from the poorest 20 percent of OECD students.

Figure 1.1 Comparative PISA Math Proficiency, 2009
percentages of 15-year-old students scoring at "high," "average," and "below basic" levels

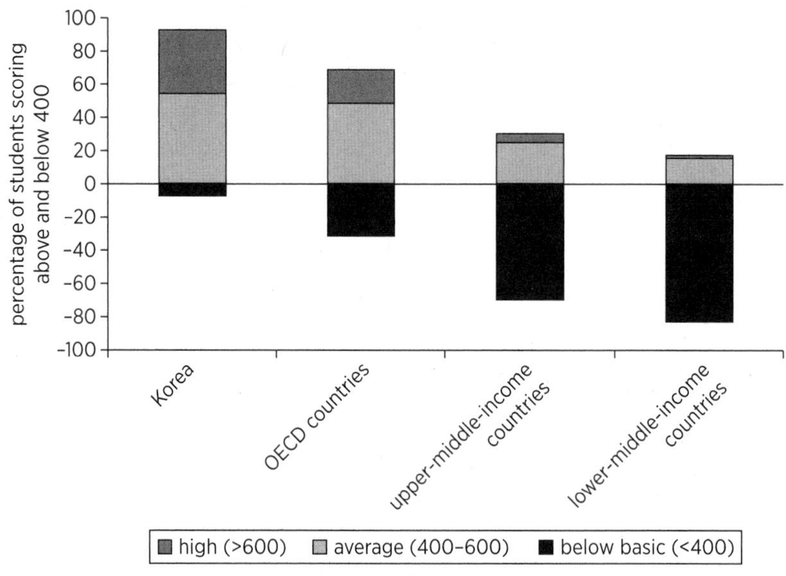

Source: OECD PISA 2009 database.

Note: OECD = Organisation for Economic Co-operation and Development. PISA = Programme for International Student Assessment. Bars are anchored to the below-400 threshold. Percentages for the three performance bands in each bar add up to 100 percent. Thresholds map to PISA standardized scores: 500 represents the mean score, and 100 points is the score associated with 1 standard deviation.

The Costs of Service Delivery Failure

The implications are serious. Researchers over the past decade have generated increasing evidence that what students actually learn—not how many years of schooling they complete—is what counts for economic growth. Moreover, in a globalizing economy, the crucial yardstick is not learning measured by national standards but learning measured in comparison with the best-performing education systems internationally.

Analyzing data on student performance on internationally benchmarked tests (such as PISA, TIMSS, and the Progress in International Reading Literacy Study [PIRLS]) from more than 50 countries over a 40-year period, Hanushek and Woessmann (2007, 2010) have demonstrated a tight correlation between average student learning levels and long-term economic growth. The relationship holds across high-income countries, across developing countries, across regions, and across countries within regions: differences in average cognitive skills are consistently and highly correlated with long-term rates of per capita income growth. While the *quantity* of education (average years of schooling of the labor force) is statistically significantly related to long-term economic growth in analyses that neglect education *quality*, the association between years of schooling and economic growth falls to close to zero once education quality (measured by average scores on internationally benchmarked tests) is introduced. It is the quality of education that counts for economic benefits from schooling.

The recent Commission on Growth and Development, which reviewed the factors associated with sustained economic growth around the world, included these two key conclusions in its 2008 report, *The Growth Report: Strategies for Sustained Growth and Inclusive Development*:

- "Every country that sustained high growth for long periods put substantial effort into schooling its citizens and deepening its human capital."
- [Rather than the quantity of education (years of schooling or rates of enrollment),] "it is the results (literacy, numeracy, and other cognitive skills) that matter to growth."

How Services Fail

Developing countries in 2010 spent an estimated 5 percent of GDP on public education. While this average obscures a slightly lower share in low-income countries and a higher share in middle-income countries, the salient point is that these levels of investment are not wildly different from average public spending on education in OECD countries, which was 4.8 percent of GDP in 2010.

Researchers have documented the weak correlation between spending and results in education that emerges from cross-country and within-country analysis—whether measured in terms of aggregate spending as a share of GDP, spending per student, or trends over time (World Bank 2003). The lack of correlation holds whether spending is compared to outputs (education attainment) or outcomes (learning), and it holds after controlling for incomes, as shown in figure 1.2a.

This pattern is not restricted to the developing world. For example, per-student U.S. spending on education doubled in real terms from 1970 to 2000 but produced no increase in student performance on benchmarked tests (Hanushek 2006). For many years, this observed "failure of input-based policies" was a core conundrum of education economics.

The *World Development Report 2004* broke new ground on this question by looking broadly at the ways in which public spending in developing countries failed to result in quality services for clients, particularly the

Figure 1.2 Correlation of Education Spending to Student Performance

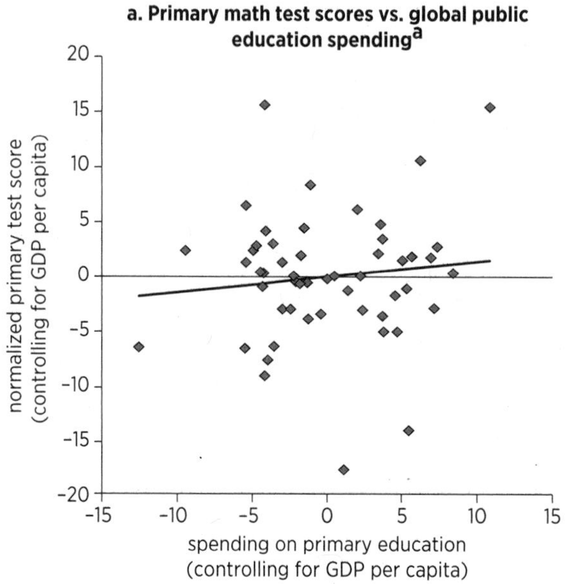

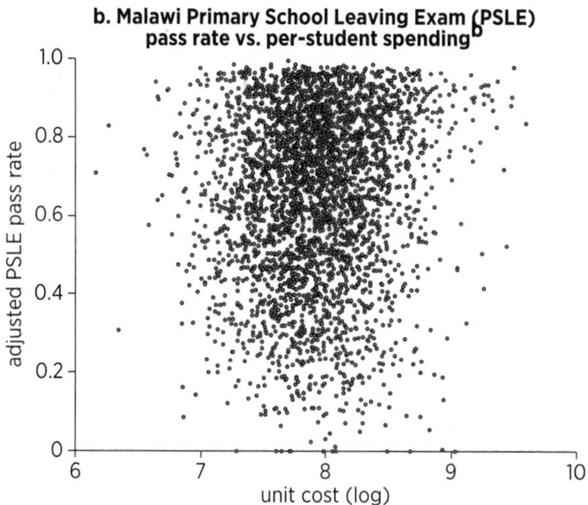

Sources: International test data for various years from Altinok and Murseli 2007; GDP per capita data from Penn World Tables (http://pwt.econ.upenn.edu); and education spending data from World Bank EdStats database. Malawi data from World Bank, UNESCO/Pole de Dakar, and Government of Malawi 2010.

a. The global figure shows deviation of normalized test scores from that predicted by GDP per capita against deviation of public spending on primary education per student (relative to GDP per capita) from that predicted by GDP per capita.

b. The Malawi figure includes only government-funded schools, and the unit cost includes teachers and book-related expenses.

poorest clients (World Bank 2003). It documented key issues in the "service delivery chain," including inequitable allocation to low-income groups, the "leakage" of funding en route from central ministries to front-line providers, and the failure of front-line providers such as teachers, doctors, and nurses to perform effectively—or even, in many cases, to show up.

Inequitable spending

The allocation of public education spending in developing countries often benefits the rich rather than the poor. Public expenditure studies in six different African countries, for example, have found that more than 30 percent of education spending benefited the richest 20 percent, while only 8 to 16 percent benefited the poorest 20 percent (figure 1.3a). But as the case of Malawi illustrates, public policy choices can transform a highly regressive pattern of expenditures into an equitable one, as that country did between 1990 and 1998, shown in figure 1.3b.

Funding leaks

Public expenditure tracking studies have documented substantial "leakage" of public funding in the flow from central ministries to the front-line providers: schools. In one well-documented case, it took concerted government action over an eight-year period to raise the share of capitation grants that actually reached Ugandan schools from less than 20 percent to 80 percent (Reinikka and Svensson 2005). Other studies have shown that "leakage" is a serious problem in many settings, as seen in table 1.1. Innovative research by Ferraz, Finan, and Moreira (2010) exploited data from randomized government audits of municipalities in Brazil to take this analysis a step further and quantify how much the leaks can matter for education quality. The 35 percent of municipalities where significant corruption was uncovered were less likely than other municipalities to have adequate school infrastructure or to provide in-service training to teachers, and their student test scores were on average a 0.35 standard deviation lower—a large disparity by global standards.

Teacher absence and loss of instructional time

The most widespread losses and abuses in education systems occur on the front lines—teachers who are absent from their posts or who demand illegal payments for services that are legally free. A study that collected estimates of teacher absenteeism in nine developing countries (using surprise visits to a nationally representative sample of schools in each country) found, on average, 19 percent of all teachers absent on any given day. The lowest rate registered was 11 percent in Peru; the highest was 27 percent in Uganda (Chaudhury and others 2006). The estimated average for India was 25 percent, but in some states, it reached 40 percent (Kremer and others 2005).

Figure 1.3 Shares of Public Education Spending Benefiting the Richest and Poorest Population Quintiles, Selected Countries

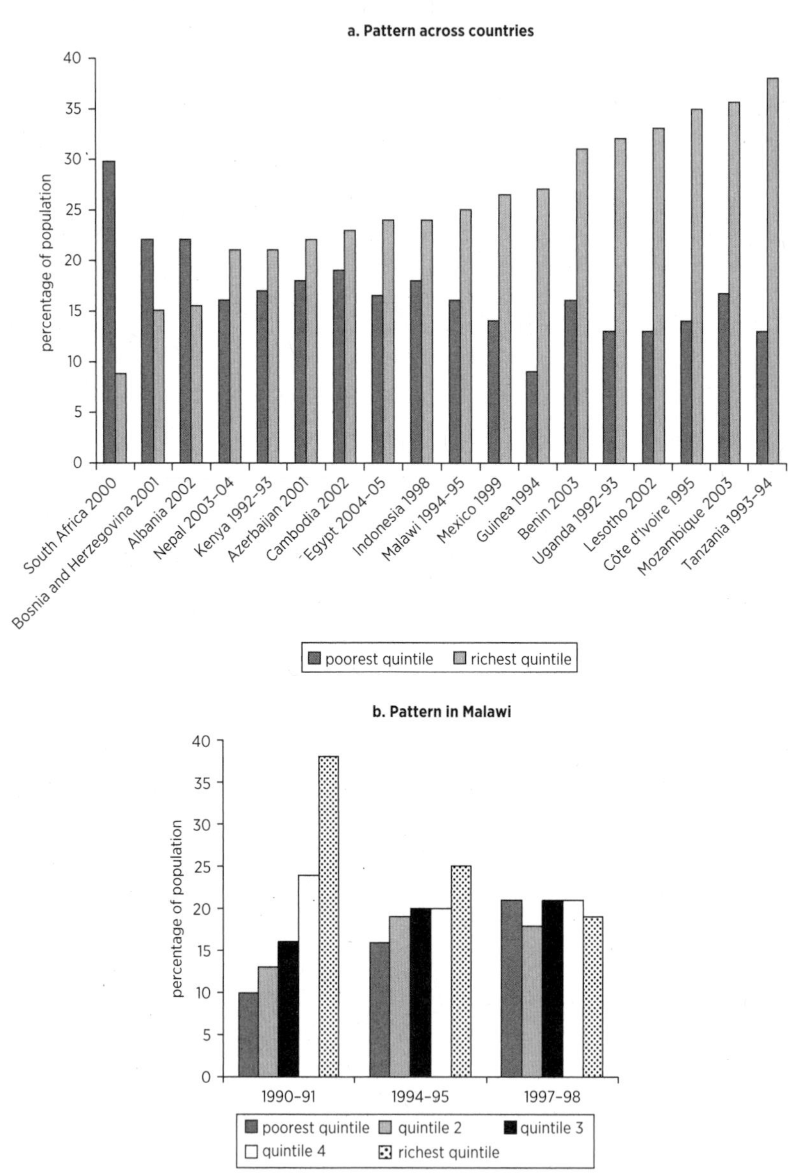

Source: Filmer and Goldstein 2010.

Table 1.1 Percentage of School Grants Reaching Schools in Selected Countries

Country and grant year(s)	Percentage received by schools
Brazil 2003 (FUNDEF capitation grant)[a]	45–87[b]
Ghana 1997–98	51
Kenya 2004 (secondary school bursary funds)	78
Madagascar 2002	88
Papua New Guinea (2001, 2002)	72, 93
Tanzania 2002–03	62
Uganda 1991–95, 2001	<20, 80
Zambia 2001 (discretion, rule)[c]	24, 90

Sources: Ferraz, Finan, and Moreira 2010 for Brazil; Ye and Canagarajah 2002 for Ghana; Republic of Kenya 2005; Francken 2003 for Madagascar; World Bank 2004 for Papua New Guinea; Ministry of Finance, Government of Tanzania 2005; Reinikka and Svensson 2005 for Uganda; and Das and others 2005 for Zambia.

a. FUNDEF = Fund for Primary Education Development and Maintenance and Enhancement of the Teaching Profession (*Fundo de Manutenção e Desenvolvimento da Educação Básica e de Valorização dos Profissionais da Educação*).

b. Range in degree of leakage found by auditors in different municipalities.

c. Discretion-based grants are determined on an ad hoc basis by the ministry; rule-based grants are determined by a funding formula.

Even when teachers are present at the schools, they are not always teaching. In India, several different studies have documented that teachers present at schools spend only half of their time teaching; the rest may be spent on administrative tasks for the local government or congregating with other teachers for tea. Standardized classroom observations have found that the significant loss of instructional time is a widespread phenomenon in the developing world (Abadzi 2009). Of every instructional hour, as figure 1.4 shows, only about 80 percent is effectively used by teachers in Lebanon, the Republic of Yemen, Lao People's Democratic Republic, and Tunisia; as little as 63 percent in Pernambuco, Brazil; and 39 percent in Ghana. (The good-practice benchmark for classroom observations in OECD countries is at least 85 percent of class time effectively used for instruction.) The implication for cost-effectiveness is staggering if the most expensive input in any education system—teacher salaries—produces learning activity only 40 percent of the time.

Why Services Fail

What explains these deep and sometimes pervasive failures of service delivery? What explains the substantial heterogeneity across settings in the extent to which education resources translate into results?

Figure 1.4 Teacher Classroom Presence and Time Spent Teaching, Selected Countries

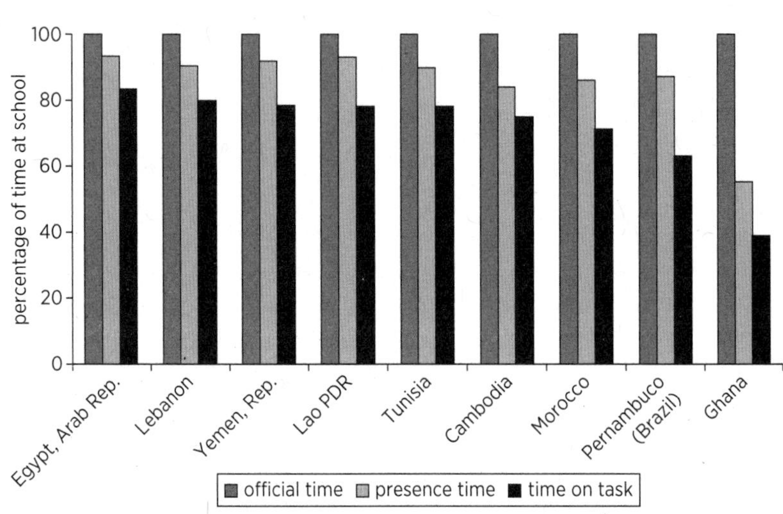

Sources: Millot and Lane 2002 for the Arab Republic of Egypt, Lebanon, and the Republic of Yemen; Abadzi 2009 for Ghana, Morocco, Pernambuco (Brazil), and Tunisia; Benveniste, Marshall, and Araujo 2008 for Cambodia; and Benveniste, Marshall, and Santibañez 2007 for the Lao People's Democratic Republic.

That the effective use of resources hinges critically on the *incentives* faced by system actors is a core insight from economics. The *World Development Report 2004: Making Services Work for Poor People* focused on the incentives faced by the various actors involved in the delivery of public services in the developing world (World Bank 2003).

Incentive systems in education face a challenge that is common to most sectors and firms: the principal-agent problem. The principal (a country's ministry of education) would like to ensure that its agents (school directors and teachers) deliver schooling that results in learning. But achieving this is complex because of the nature of the service. If education were like producing pizzas or kebabs or samosas or empanadas, the delivery process could be reduced to a set of predefined tasks that agents are instructed to carry out. Quality could be monitored by ensuring that workers follow the predefined steps.

But education services are complicated. At the point of delivery—the interaction of teachers with their students—the service provided is highly discretionary, variable, and transaction-intensive:

- *Discretionary,* in that teachers must use their own judgment to decide what part of the curriculum to deliver and how

- *Variable,* in that in a single classroom a teacher must customize services to a large number of different students with different aptitudes, motivations, and learning styles
- *Transaction-intensive,* in that producing learning results requires repeated and frequent interaction between teachers and individual students.

These features make it difficult to predefine in sufficient detail the actions teachers must take, either to specify a complete contract of what they are expected to do or to monitor that contract completely.

The principal-agent problem is further complicated because ministries of education are themselves the agents of the citizenry. If the "consumers" of education services were like restaurant patrons, repeat business and competition could be expected to ensure the restaurant's quality or it would go out of business. But governments universally mediate the market for education because the sector suffers from a set of market failures that government intervention can rectify. As a result, the users of education services—parents and children—are also principals trying to ensure that their country's ministry of education establishes a system that produces the high-quality education they demand. This sequential set of principal-agent problems demands a more complex system of incentives and accountability.

Figure 1.5 shows the set of actors and relationships that determine public sector accountability. The sequence of principal-agent problems forms a

Figure 1.5 The Accountability Framework

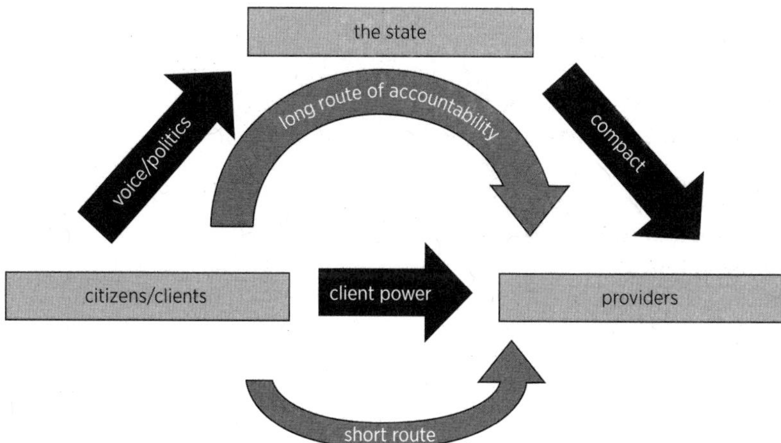

Source: World Bank 2003.

long route of accountability between the users of services and front-line providers. In a first step, the clients (parents and students) hold the state accountable. They do this by using their voice and votes, through the political process, to try to ensure that politicians and policy makers deliver the services they demand. In a second step, the state holds providers (schools and teachers) accountable for their behaviors and their results through a compact or managerial relationship. This compact can be implicit, as in most countries where schools are managed mostly within a ministry of education. But the compact can also be explicit in the case of vouchers, charter schools, and other strategies for contracting out services. When the state turns over the delivery of services to a nonstate entity, it is forced to define the terms of a specified contract.

There is also a more direct route of accountability—a short route—that runs directly from users to front-line providers. When a service is competitively provided and its quality is easy to monitor, as in a restaurant, client power is strong, and this short route is sufficient to ensure satisfactory service delivery.

In education, the short route also has an important role to play. Just as there are market failures that create the rationale for government intervention in a sector, there are also "government failures" whereby the long route breaks down, and the short route can compensate for those failures. Citizens, and poor citizens in particular, may lack the voice or the political clout to hold politicians accountable through "long-route" electoral processes. Entrenched interests, or even just the inherent difficulties of monitoring service delivery, may make it hard to define or implement an effective compact. Strengthening the short route—that is, giving parents and students a direct voice in their local school—can be an important way of improving service delivery.

Three Core Strategies for More Accountable Education Systems

Our focus on accountability is in part motivated by the theory outlined above—that education results depend on the effective resolution of a series of principal-agent problems that characterize service delivery in this sector. But the focus also has an empirical foundation. Cross-country analysis of international tests such as PISA and TIMSS shows that countries with greater local decision-making authority and greater accountability have better learning outcomes (Fuchs and Woessmann 2007; Woessmann 2003). More compelling yet is the growing set of experiments with school accountability reforms in developed and developing countries that show causal impacts on student learning.

Although a variety of accountability reform strategies have been adopted in OECD, middle-income, and low-income countries over the past two decades, this book focuses on three widely used strategies that each have a clear rationale for how reforms might translate into improved learning outcomes:

- *Information for accountability:* generation and dissemination of information about schooling rights and responsibilities, inputs, outputs, and outcomes
- *School-based management*: decentralization of school-level decision making—autonomy—to school-level agents
- *Teacher incentives:* policies that link pay or tenure directly to performance.

Information for Accountability

The notion that increased information in education can improve accountability and outcomes is not new. In the 1990s, the education sector in the United States experienced a large-scale increase in test-based accountability (Loveless 2005). By the end of the decade, most states had some form of statewide testing system in place, and this approach was entrenched at the federal level in 2001 as a part of the No Child Left Behind (NCLB) law.

Before NCLB, the implementation of school accountability systems varied extensively across states. In particular, the degree to which schools performing below standard would receive any "punishment" from state authorities varied. In some states, test-based accountability amounted to no more than information about average school (test) performance, commonly referred to as "school report cards." Studies of this U.S. experience have typically found that the impact of accountability on test scores has been positive (Carnoy and Loeb 2002; Hanushek and Raymond 2003, 2005; and Loeb and Strunk 2007). Intriguingly, the findings suggest that simply reporting information about average school test scores led to increased performance (Hoxby 2001, Hanushek and Raymond 2003), although these findings vary when alternative measures of the degree of sanction associated with accountability are used in the analysis (Hanushek and Raymond 2005).

Creating an information feedback loop to connect public service users, providers, and policy makers as a reform strategy cuts across sectors. In Bangalore, India, a civil society organization initiated the generation of "citizen report cards" that rated the quality of public services based on interviews with the users of these services (Paul 2002). These report cards were then disseminated through various media channels in ways that allowed service users to compare quality across services and across neighborhoods. This initiative has been credited with management reforms that contributed to improvements in service delivery (also see the discussion about the "right to information" movement in India in Jenkins and Goetz 1999). Similar approaches are being tried in a variety of contexts—for example, in the Ugandan health sector, where detailed "report cards" for health clinics were prepared and shared with villagers and health workers, followed by workshops to develop improvement plans for the clinics (Björkman and Svensson 2007).

When parents and students have little information about the performance of their schools or about the inputs those schools are entitled to receive, their position relative to service providers and governments is weak. They have limited ability to hold schools and teachers accountable for either effort or efficiency in the use of resources, and they have a limited empirical foundation to lobby local or national governments for greater (or better) public support to their schools. In terms of the accountability relationships illustrated in figure 1.5, lack of information weakens clients' power to hold providers directly accountable and also weakens citizens' voices relative to policy makers and politicians.

There are three main accountability channels through which information could affect learning outcomes: increasing *choice*, *participation*, and *voice*.

Increasing choice

Providing parents with hard evidence about learning outcomes at alternative schools allows parents and students to optimally go to their preferred schools. In a context where there is a choice of schools and where school-level resources are linked to attendance, the information about learning outcomes can have two effects. First, it can reduce the information asymmetry between service providers (who know substantially more about what is going on in the schools) and service users. Second, the enhanced competitive pressure induced by more effective choice can induce providers to improve quality. Both of these effects increase *client power* in the provision of services.

Increasing participation

By publicizing rights, roles, and responsibilities and by documenting service delivery shortfalls relative to other schools in the village, district, province, or country, information can be a motivator for action on the part of parents and other stakeholders. Lack of information could lead parents and other stakeholders to believe that performance is adequate—in turn leading to complacency. The provision of information can rebalance the relationship between users and providers and spur users to action, including increased or more effective oversight of schools—thereby also increasing *client power*. The logical chain is that provider effort increases as a result of this intensified oversight, thereby improving education quality.

Increasing voice

Providing credible information can allow parents and other stakeholders to lobby governments more effectively for improved policies, either at the local or national level. It provides content to feed the *voice* that citizens use to pressure governments and hold them to account. Information can expose shortcomings and biases, and its wide dissemination can overcome information asymmetries that perpetuate inequalities (Keefer and Khemani 2005; Majumdar, Mani, and Mukand 2004). Finally, information can become the basis for political competition (Khemani 2007).

School-Based Management

The highly decentralized nature of education services at the point of delivery makes them extremely demanding of the managerial, technical, and financial capacity of governments. The requirements for effective, efficient, and centrally produced and distributed education services are therefore stringent. There is an association across countries between good performance on international student achievement tests and local- and school-level autonomy to adapt and implement education content and to allocate and manage resources. Indeed, there is a trend in many countries toward increasing autonomy, devolving responsibility, and encouraging responsiveness to local needs, all with the objective of raising performance levels.

SBM defined

School-based management (SBM) is the decentralization of authority from the government to the school level. Responsibility for, and decision-making authority over, school operations is transferred to local agents. Many of these reforms also attempt to strengthen parental involvement in the schools, sometimes by means of school councils.

These aspects of SBM form two important dimensions: (1) the extent to which schools are granted autonomy over decisions—an attempt at improving the *compact* between those who oversee service provision and those who deliver it; and (2) the extent to which parents are actively encouraged to participate in the decision making—an attempt at improving the *voice* parents have in the delivery of services.

The granting of autonomy in SBM programs usually works through the establishment of a school committee (which goes by various names such as school council or school management committee). The tasks of the council or committee can vary substantially across initiatives and can include the following functions:

- Monitoring the school's performance as measured by test scores or by teacher and student attendance

- Developing curriculum
- Procuring textbooks and other education material
- Improving infrastructure and developing school improvement plans
- Hiring and firing of teachers and other school staff
- Monitoring and evaluating teacher performance and student learning outcomes
- Allocating budgetary resources
- Approving annual budgets (including the development budget) and examining monthly financial statements.

In programs that actively promote parental participation, the school committee (in the context of the figure 1.5 framework) becomes a middle point between users and front-line providers. As in the dimension of autonomy, there is a wide range in the extent to which SBM initiatives translate into effective parental involvement. In some cases, parents act merely as observers or volunteers; in others, parents take on responsibilities such as the assessment of student learning or financial management. In cases with more intensive involvement, parents are directly involved in the school's management by being custodians of the funds received and verifying the purchases and contracts made by the school.

SBM objectives

School-based management is a form of decentralization. While decentralization can involve the transfer of responsibilities from the central government to lower levels of government (such as the regional, municipal, or district levels), this book is concerned with the school as the locus of decision making. The main thrust behind SBM is that it encourages demand, ensures that schools reflect local priorities and values, and allows closer monitoring of the performance of service providers. In other words, SBM shortens *the long route of accountability*. By giving a voice and decision-making power to local stakeholders who know more about local needs than central policy makers do, it is argued that SBM will improve education outcomes and increase client satisfaction.

SBM emphasizes the individual school (as represented by any combination of principals, teachers, parents, students, and other members of the school community) as the primary unit for improving education. Its redistribution of decision-making authority over school operations is the primary means by which this improvement can be stimulated and sustained. Arguments in favor of SBM typically emphasize that it will lead to

- increased participation of local stakeholders in decision-making processes;
- more effective and transparent use of resources (because of the ability to use local knowledge in allocating resources and the increased oversight role of parents);

- more inputs and resources from parents, whether in cash or in-kind (because of the increased stake parents have in the provision of education);
- more open and welcoming school environments (because of increased parental participation and communication with school authorities); and
- higher-quality delivery of education services, ultimately improving student performance (as measured by lower repetition and dropout rates and by higher test scores).

SBM pioneers

In Australia, the 1967 Currie Report recommended the establishment of governing bodies for each school, consisting of teachers, parents, local community members, and students (Currie 1967). This report was implemented in 1974, and by the late 1990s, all eight Australian school systems had enacted legislation to introduce reforms involving SBM.

Other countries followed suit. Britain's Education Reform Act, in 1988, empowered school communities by giving public secondary schools the option of leaving local-education-authority control and becoming autonomous, grant-maintained (GM) schools. GM schools were funded by a new agency but were owned and managed by each school's governing body: a new 10- to 15-member entity composed of the head teacher and teacher and parent representatives. Control over all staff contracts and ownership of the buildings and grounds were taken from the local school districts and given to GM schools. Between 1988 and 1997, among almost 1,000 schools holding votes on the matter, most favored conversion to GM status. Elsewhere, also in 1988, boards of trustees were introduced at each school in New Zealand, and the School Reform Act instituted mandatory school councils in the United States.

In the developing world, one of the first countries to adopt SBM as part of an overall reform program was El Salvador. The reform began in 1991 under the name *Educación con Participación de la Comunidad* (Education with Community Participation, or EDUCO). EDUCO schools were publicly funded schools where parents were expected to make contributions such as providing meals or volunteering their time and labor. The distinguishing feature of EDUCO schools was their management by local Associations for Community Education (ACEs), community-elected bodies that received funds directly from the Ministry of Education. ACEs were responsible for enacting and implementing all school-level education policies, including the hiring, firing, and monitoring of teachers (Sawada and Ragatz 2005).

The main tenet of EDUCO's philosophy was the need for parents to be directly involved in their children's education. The program contributed to rebuilding the school system after a civil war and is credited with expanding preprimary and primary enrollments in rural areas, particularly in the poorest areas with little access to existing education services (Di Gropello 2006). Some evidence also shows positive effects on teacher effort, student retention, and reduced teacher absences as well as some limited evidence of improved learning outcomes (Jimenez and Sawada 1999, 2003; Sawada 1999; Sawada and Ragatz 2005).

Teacher Incentives

Many different monetary and nonmonetary factors motivate individuals to become and remain teachers, as figure 1.6 summarizes—ranging from base salaries, pensions, and benefits to the intrinsic satisfaction of helping a child to learn. Yet the phenomena described earlier in this chapter (high rates of teacher absence and persistently low learning results) attest to failures of the education system in many developing countries to create adequate incentives for teachers to deliver effective performance in the classroom.

It is not only in developing countries that policy makers wishing to recruit, groom, or motivate "great teachers" confront a political reality of recruitment and compensation systems with weak links, if any, between rewards and performance. Most education systems globally are characterized by fixed salary schedules, lifetime job tenure, and flat labor hierarchies, which create a rigid labor environment where extra effort, innovation, and good

Figure 1.6 Teacher Performance Incentives

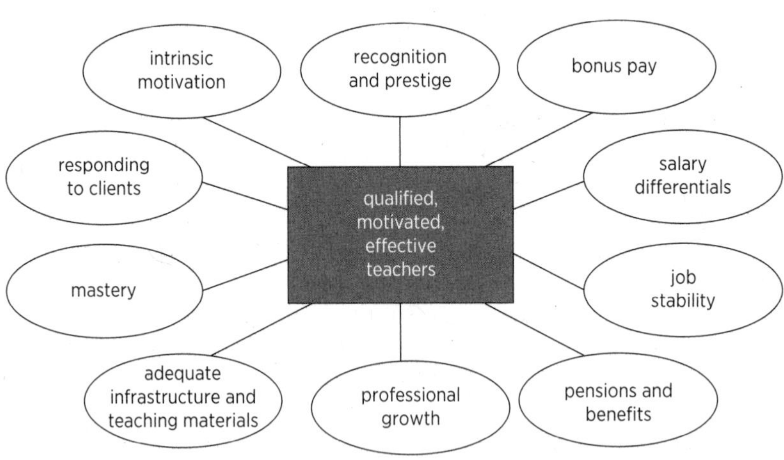

Source: Adapted from Vegas 2005.

results are not rewarded and where dismissal for poor performance is exceedingly rare (Weisberg and others 2009). Almost universally, teacher recruitment and promotion are based on the number of years of preservice training, formal certificates, and years of service. Yet an extensive body of research has documented the lack of correlation between these observable factors and teachers' effectiveness in the classroom—measured by their ability to produce learning improvements in their students (Rivkin, Hanushek, and Kain 2005).

In this context, both OECD and developing countries are increasingly experimenting with two particular teacher policy reforms that aim to strengthen teachers' accountability for performance: contract tenure reforms and pay-for-performance reforms.

In terms of the accountability triangle in figure 1.5, these reforms tighten the managerial *compact* between policy makers and providers by defining expected results with more specificity and establishing clearer rewards and sanctions. In those cases where contract teachers are directly hired and supervised by school-level committees with parent participation—a common formula—the reform also strengthens *client power* by giving parents and community members a degree of direct authority over teachers that they previously lacked. Contract tenure and pay-for-performance reforms work at the opposite ends of the incentives spectrum, one offering positive rewards and the other strengthening the threat of sanctions. But it is interesting to note that they share a political advantage: they can both be introduced alongside existing teacher policies without requiring wholesale reform of civil service rules regarding teacher salary scales, tenure, and recruitment processes.

Contract tenure reforms

Teacher recruitment under contracts that do not grant civil service status and tenure protection creates a parallel corps of "contract teachers" who work alongside the existing stream. Contract teachers are hired on fixed-term (usually one-year) contracts and, in many cases, the locus of hiring is more decentralized (to the school or community level) than under the civil service. Entry standards (education level) and salaries for contract teachers are also often different. From an incentive standpoint, the absence of job stability should make contract teachers more accountable for performance. More localized hiring also creates the potential for closer monitoring of teacher performance and additional accountability pressure.

Pay-for-performance reforms

Merit pay, performance-based pay, or teacher bonus schemes leave core salary policies intact but create an incentive at the margin with the offer of a bonus (usually an annual bonus) based on some explicit measure of teacher performance. There are many different designs, but one core distinction is *who* is rewarded: *individual* teachers or the *school as a whole* (group-based rewards). A second distinction is *what* is rewarded: bonuses can reward *inputs* (such as teacher attendance), *outcomes* (such as student learning and grade progression), or a combination. Given the expansion of standardized student testing, pay-for-performance programs are increasingly based on improvement in learning outcomes. From an incentive standpoint, pay-for-performance programs are among the strongest possible levers to strengthen accountability for specific desired results.

Accountability and Evidence

To improve student learning outcomes, school systems everywhere commonly employ a broad range strategies: teacher training, curriculum reform, textbook provision, school lunches, libraries and infrastructure, and many more. Each of these interventions has the potential to increase learning, but they typically rely on a technocratic approach to changing the level and mix of inputs. As discussed above, changing the level of inputs through increased resources is often ineffective (as figure 1.2 illustrated). Even if it is possible to establish a technically optimal mix of inputs in a given situation, the mix actually implemented is ultimately the result of accountability relationships and pressures. For example, the allocation of more resources to teacher-related inputs, as opposed to other inputs, often reflects the political voice of teachers, who are typically the most organized group of education stakeholders (see Pritchett and Filmer 1999 for a discussion and empirical illustration of this). Underlying accountability relationships have the power to shape education outcomes by affecting the level and mix of education inputs that are available in an education system as well as the effectiveness of resource use.

Among the possible strategies for strengthening accountability in education, this book focuses on information for accountability, SBM, and teacher incentives because these particular reforms are increasingly being implemented in developing countries. There is also a new wave of evidence regarding how these reforms work that has grown out of a concerted effort by the World Bank since 2005 to identify clusters of innovative developing-country reforms in these three areas and to work with partner governments to support their rigorous evaluation.[1] The three themes of this book mirror the clusters that were identified for impact evaluation support.

This book does not address two additional approaches to increasing accountability, however, and these deserve mention. The first approach involves greater use of the private sector to create a more competitive market for education—for example, through the use of vouchers or public-private partnerships. The theory of change underlying these strategies is to leverage public-private competition to induce quality improvements in the public sector. While the rigorous evidence in developing country contexts is currently limited (there has been more experience in OECD countries), it is growing, and the evidence base will be stronger in the years to come (Patrinos, Barrera-Osorio, and Guáqueta 2009).

A second approach is to strengthen the compact through administrative decentralization—reforms that shift powers or resources from the central government to the regional or district levels but do not change the degree of autonomy at the school level. These intergovernmental reforms, while they may also aim at strengthening accountability, are less amenable to the type of impact evaluation prioritized in this book. While there have been some attempts to identify impacts of these reforms using approaches that require more assumptions for identification (Galiani, Gertler, and Schargrodsky 2008; Eskeland and Filmer 2007), even these are rare. Last, to the extent that these decentralization reforms merely shorten the long route of accountability (by replacing the "state" with "local government" in the figure 1.5 framework), basic accountability problems on the front lines of service delivery may remain (Khemani 2001).

Accountability Reforms in Context

Accountability-oriented reforms in education or in any other sector take place in a broader context of public sector policies and management. They are influenced by, and interact with, this context in several ways.

Context of broad public sector reform

First, there can be a direct link between broader public sector reform efforts and specific applications in education. In Australia and New Zealand in the late 1980s, for example, information and SBM reforms similar in design and spirit to the cases reviewed in this book were implemented as part of high-profile, government-wide efforts to make the public sector more results-focused, transparent, and responsive to citizens. A more recent case, the 2008 teacher pay-for-performance reform adopted in the state of Minas Gerais in Brazil (which closely parallels one of the cases discussed in this book) was an explicit part of a broad, statewide "management shock program" (*choque de gestao)* aimed at making the public sector more results-focused and efficient.

Context of public sector dysfunction

Second, dysfunctions in the broader public sector context can create the latent or explicit demand for education accountability reforms. If schools are not functioning because of a breakdown of the state, as in civil-war-torn El Salvador in the early 1990s or Nepal in 2001, bottom-up demands from parents can generate a radical model of locally managed schools in response. If constrained public sector resources cannot finance universal primary schooling at the prevailing civil service teacher wage, local hiring of lower-wage contract teachers may emerge as an official or unofficial education system response, as occurred in many parts of Africa and India in the 1990s. Indeed, as noted earlier, it is likely no coincidence that the two specific approaches to teacher incentive reforms reviewed in this book (contract tenure and pay-for-performance reforms) are attracting increasing interest from developing-country policy makers. Both can inject flexibility into otherwise rigid civil service rules governing teachers' pay levels and accountability for performance without requiring across-the-board reforms of those rules that would be resisted by teachers' unions, or the civil service as whole.

Context of political power

Third, the broader political context can delimit or undermine the impact of reforms adopted in the education sector to improve accountability. The power of a reform that gives parents information about school outcomes to promote systemwide improvement will be constrained if the ethnic minorities or low-income communities whose schools are most disadvantaged are underrepresented in the political process.

Context of influence on public sector accountability

Fourth, and conversely, accountability reforms in education also have the potential to wedge open a political space for broader public sector management reforms. Increasing the information available to all stakeholders—the users of services, the overseers, and the providers—could change the debate about overall public sector effectiveness. Access to information can also provide tools for various stakeholders to hold each other to account. Likewise, SBM could change the relative power of the different stakeholders, with spin-off effects for performance management. And increasing the role of performance evaluation in the career management of public sector teachers could set the stage for more generalized public-sector pay reforms. From this perspective, each of these smaller-scale reforms may not be an end in itself but rather a contribution to a dynamic process that ultimately produces larger-scale change.

Use of Impact Evaluations

This book synthesizes results from 22 recent, high-quality impact evaluations of accountability-focused reforms in 11 developing countries. These evaluations represent only a small subset of the available studies on these topics, but they merit special attention because they meet a high bar for methodological rigor. In almost all cases, the studies were prospectively designed impact evaluations whose goal was to establish attribution: that the size and nature of the impacts observed were *directly caused* by the program.

This focus on the identification of causal impacts is one of the hallmarks of rigorous impact evaluation. Rather than being satisfied with correlations—for example, that schools with management committees tend to have better learning outcomes—rigorous impact evaluations aim to quantify the extent to which observed increases in learning outcomes were the *result* of school committees, excluding the possible role of other observed and unobservable factors.

Rigorous impact evaluations quantify causal effects by comparing what happened *with* the program to a credible estimate of what would have happened *without* it. The most robust method for this is a randomized control trial (RCT). When programs are implemented so that beneficiaries (be they schools, communities, or individual students) are randomly selected from a larger group of potential beneficiaries, the "treatment" and "comparison" populations will be statistically identical—in both observable and unobservable ways. Under these conditions, the impacts of a program on its beneficiaries can be directly compared with the outcomes experienced by nonrecipients. The use of random assignment minimizes the threat of selection bias—that is, that the individuals benefiting from a program are in some way different from those who do not benefit and that these inherent differences, rather than exposure to the program, explain the different results.

Evidence from RCT evaluations of accountability-oriented reforms figures prominently in this book because these evaluations typically achieve the highest internal validity—or standard of proof that the observed results are attributable to the program. Fifteen of the 22 cases reviewed in this book are pilot programs whose experimental design was expressly developed to establish rigorous evidence of impact. They constitute excellent tests of the efficacy of a new reform or program because they demonstrate whether the program can work under carefully controlled conditions and the size of the impacts that can result.

While RCTs are often implemented on a pilot scale, it is relatively rare to find systemwide reforms implemented through random assignment.[2] But pilot programs are not necessarily a window into the reality of how these kinds of reforms would gestate or be implemented in a nonexperimental context or at scale. As such, they raise questions of the external validity of the results: to what extent can we expect the same impacts if these programs are implemented in different settings or systemwide?

Therefore, while evaluations that rely on quasi-experimental approaches such as regression discontinuity design (RDD) or difference-in-differences analysis (DD) require somewhat more stringent assumptions to generate credible estimates of causal impacts, they can play a valuable role in deepening our understanding of how reforms work at larger scale. In this spirit, we also review studies that have been carried out with careful, nonexperimental designs that attempt to overcome problems in causal inference by using statistical approaches such as instrumental variables (IV) or by controlling for observable characteristics through the use of regression or matching techniques. When carefully done, these studies can provide a window into the impacts of a reform program implemented at large scale and under real-world political and technical conditions.

The availability of a critical mass of studies that rely on rigorous impact evaluation methods allows findings in this book to be implicitly weighted. Evaluations with the highest internal validity weigh heavily in our overall conclusions, but we also consider external validity important. Results from a study that is well designed from a statistical standpoint but whose results are valid for only a small—and possibly unrepresentative—population may be of limited value for education policy makers. Evaluation results from a program that has been carefully monitored and "tended" but has little resemblance to what could be implemented on a large scale may also be less relevant than evaluations of programs implemented systemwide. Our synthesis attempts to balance these considerations.

The central research question in all 22 of the studies we review was "how much does the accountability-linked reform cause student learning to improve?" Thus, valid measurement of student learning was a key concern across the studies. In the experimental-design (RCT) studies, student learning was measured by learning assessments specifically designed for the evaluation. In some cases, these instruments included innovative features, such as the effort of researchers in Andhra Pradesh, India, to apply both a standard math and literacy test and "conceptual tests" that challenged students to apply the same material in new ways. The objective was to identify whether students' improvements reflected true mastery of concepts or intensified memorization and "teaching to the test."

In other contexts, such as the evaluations in Brazil and Mexico, learning was measured by national assessments that can be linked to international assessments. Across programs and evaluations of this degree of heterogeneity, the only way to describe learning impacts in a uniform way is to present them in terms of standard deviations of the administered tests.

It is important to keep in mind that a 1.0 standard deviation increase in learning measured on one test will not reflect the same amount of actual learning improvement as a 1.0 standard deviation increase on another test.

What underlies the measure of a 1.0 standard deviation improvement in learning outcomes will differ across these studies. Yet the language and framework of what is evaluated remains comparable. In each setting, the student assessment instrument was devised to capture the range of learning performance that is appropriate and expected for children of that age and grade in that schooling context. In every context, a 0.3 standard deviation improvement in outcomes will represent significant progress relative to the order of magnitude of learning improvements more typically observed in the education evaluation literature, in which a 0.2 standard deviation improvement is generally considered robust. Thus, with the caveat in mind that we cannot translate the actual content of a 0.2 standard deviation improvement in learning from one country context to another, we can certainly learn from the comparative evaluation of programs that aim to generate impacts of this size. The following chapters review this evidence and its implications for the design of accountability-based reforms to improve education results.

Notes

1. This comparative research program would not have been possible without the generous support of the Bank-Netherlands Partnership Program (BNPP) and the Spanish Impact Evaluation Fund (SIEF).
2. A notable exception is Mexico's *Progresa-Oportunidades* conditional cash transfer program, rolled out to the universe of eligible low-income districts over a five-year period, in which the order of districts' incorporation in the program was randomly assigned.

References

Abadzi, Helen. 2009. "Instructional Time Loss in Developing Countries: Concepts, Measurement, and Implications." *World Bank Research Observer* 24 (2): 267–90.

Altinok, Nadir, and Hatidje Murseli. 2007. "International Database on Human Capital Quality." *Economics Letters* 96 (2): 237–44.

Benveniste, Luis, Jeffery Marshall, and M. Caridad Araujo. 2008. *Teaching in Cambodia*. Washington, DC: World Bank and Royal Government of Cambodia.

Benveniste, Luis, Jeffery Marshall, and Lucrecia Santibañez. 2007. *Teaching in Lao PDR*. Washington, DC: World Bank and Lao People's Democratic Republic. http://siteresources.worldbank.org/INTLAOPRD/Resources/Teaching_In_LaoPDR_Eng.pdf.

Björkman, Martina, and Jakob Svensson. 2007. "Power to the People: Evidence from a Randomized Field Experiment of a Community-Based Monitoring Project in Uganda." Policy Research Working Paper 4289, World Bank, Washington, DC.

Carnoy, Martin, and Susanna Loeb. 2002. "Does External Accountability Affect Student Outcomes? A Cross-State Analysis." *Educational Evaluation and Policy Analysis* 24 (4): 305–31.

Chaudhury, Nazmul, Jeffrey Hammer, Michael Kremer, Karthik Muralidharan, and F. Halsey Rogers. 2006. "Missing in Action: Teacher and Health Worker Absence in Developing Countries." *Journal of Economic Perspectives* 20 (1): 91–116.

Clemens, Michael A., Charles J. Kenny, and Todd J. Moss. 2007. "The Trouble with the MDGs: Confronting Expectations of Aid and Development Success." *World Development* 35 (5): 735–51.

Commission on Growth and Development. 2008. *The Growth Report: Strategies for Sustained Growth and Inclusive Development.* Washington, DC: World Bank.

Currie, George. 1967. "An Independent Education Authority for Australian Capital Territory: Report of a Working Party (Currie Report)." Department of Adult Education, Australian National University, Canberra.

Das, Jishnu, Stefan Dercon, James Habyarimana, and Pramila Krishnan. 2005. "Teacher Shocks and Student Learning: Evidence from Zambia." Policy Research Working Paper 3602, World Bank, Washington, DC.

Di Gropello, E. 2006. "A Comparative Analysis of School-based Management in Central America." Working Paper 72, World Bank, Washington, DC.

Eskeland, Gunnar, and Deon Filmer. 2007. "Autonomy, Participation, and Learning in Argentine Schools: Findings, and Their Implications for Decentralization." *Education Economics* 15 (1): 103–27.

Ferraz, Claudio, Frederico Finan, and Diana B Moreira. 2010. "Corrupting Learning: Evidence from Missing Federal Education Funds in Brazil." Discussion Paper 562, Pontifícia Universidade Católica do Rio de Janeiro (PUC-Rio) Department of Economics, Rio de Janeiro, Brazil.

Filmer, Deon, and Markus Goldstein. 2010. "The Expenditure Incidence of Public Spending on Health and Education: An Update." Unpublished manuscript, World Bank, Washington, DC.

Francken, Nathalie. 2003. "Service Delivery in Public Primary Schools in Madagascar: Results of a Budget Tracking Survey." Public Expenditure Tracking Survey (PETS) study report, Madagascar Country Office, World Bank, Antananarivo, Madagascar.

Fuchs, Thomas, and Ludger Woessmann. 2007. "What Accounts for International Differences in Student Performance? A Re-Examination Using PISA Data." *Empirical Economics* 32 (2–3): 433–64.

Galiani, Sebastian, Paul Gertler, and Ernesto Schargrodsky. 2008. "School Decentralization: Helping the Good Get Better, but Leaving the Poor Behind." *Journal of Public Economics* 92 (10–11): 2106–20.

Government of Tanzania. 2005. Public Expenditure Tracking Survey (PETS) study report for the Ministry of Finance, Dar es Salaam, Tanzania.

Hanushek, Eric. 2006. "School Resources." In Vol. 1 of *Handbook of the Economics of Education,* ed. Eric Hanushek and Finis Welch, 866–908. Amsterdam: North Holland.

Hanushek, Eric, and Margaret Raymond. 2003. "Lessons about the Design of State Accountability Systems." In *No Child Left Behind? The Politics and Practice of*

Accountability, ed. Paul Peterson and Martin West, 127–51. Washington, DC: Brookings Institution Press.

———. 2005. "Does School Accountability Lead to Improved Student Performance?" *Journal of Policy Analysis and Management* 24 (2): 297–327.

Hanushek, Eric, and Ludger Woessmann. 2007. "The Role of Education Quality for Economic Growth." Policy Research Working Paper 4122, World Bank, Washington, DC.

———. 2010. "Education and Economic Growth." In *Economics of Education*, ed. Dominic J. Brewer and Patrick J. McEwan, 60–67. Amsterdam: Elsevier.

Hoxby, Caroline. 2001. "Testing Is about Openness and Openness Works." *Hoover Daily Report*, July 30.

Jenkins, Rob, and Anne Marie Goetz. 1999. "Accounts and Accountability: Theoretical Implications of the Right-to-Information Movement in India." *Third World Quarterly* 20 (3): 603–22.

Jimenez, E., and Y. Sawada. 1999. "Do Community-Managed Schools Work? An Evaluation of El Salvador's EDUCO Program." *World Bank Economic Review* 13 (3): 415–41.

———. 2003. "Does Community Management Help Keep Kids in Schools? Evidence Using Panel Data from El Salvador's EDUCO Program." Center for International Research on the Japanese Economy (CIRJE) Discussion Paper F-236, University of Tokyo, Japan.

Keefer, Philip, and Stuti Khemani. 2005. "Democracy, Public Expenditures, and the Poor: Understanding Political Incentives for Providing Public Services." *World Bank Research Observer* 20 (1): 1–28.

Khemani, Stuti. 2001. "Decentralization and Accountability: Are Voters More Vigilant in Local than in National Elections?" Policy Research Paper 2557, World Bank, Washington, DC.

———. 2007. "Can Information Campaigns Overcome Political Obstacles to Serving the Poor?" In *The Politics of Service Delivery in Democracies. Better Access for the Poor*, ed. Shantayanan Devarajan and Ingrid Widlund, 56–69. Stockholm: Ministry for Foreign Affairs, Sweden. http://citeseerx.ist.psu.edu/viewdoc/download?doi=10.1.1.133.7367&rep=rep1&type=pdf.

Kremer, Michael, Nazmul Chaudhury, F. Halsey Rogers, Karthik Muralidharan, and Jeffrey Hammer. 2005. "Teacher Absence in India: A Snapshot." *Journal of the European Economic Association* 3 (2–3): 658–67.

Loeb, Susanna, and Katharine Strunk. 2007. "Accountability and Local Control: Response to Incentives with and without Authority over Resource Generation and Allocation." *Education Finance and Policy* 2 (1): 10–39.

Loveless, Tom. 2005. "Test-Based Accountability: The Promise and the Perils." *Brookings Papers on Education Policy* (2005): 7–45.

Majumdar, Sumon, Anandi Mani, and Sharun Mukand. 2004. "Politics, Information and the Urban Bias." *Journal of Development Economics* 75 (1): 137–65.

Millot, Benoit, and Julia Lane. 2002. "The Efficient Use of Time in Education." *Education Economics* 10 (2): 209–28.

OECD PISA (Organisation for Economic Co-operation and Development Programme for International Student Assessment) 2004 Database. http://pisa2006.acer.edu.au/.

Patrinos, Harry Anthony, Felipe Barrera-Osorio, and Juliana Guáqueta. 2009. *The Role and Impact of Public-Private Partnerships in Education*. Washington, DC: World Bank.

Paul, Samuel. 2002. *Holding the State to Account: Citizen Monitoring in Action*. Bangalore, India: Books for Change.

Pritchett, Lant, and Deon Filmer. 1999. "What Education Production Functions Really Show: A Positive Theory of Education Expenditures." *Economics of Education Review* 18 (2): 223–39.

Reinikka, Ritva, and Jakob Svensson. 2005. "Fighting Corruption to Improve Schooling: Evidence from a Newspaper Campaign in Uganda." *Journal of the European Economic Association* 3 (2–3): 259–67.

Republic of Kenya. 2005. "Public Expenditure Tracking Survey (PETS) 2004: Preliminary Report." Ministries of Planning and National Development, Finance, Health, and Education Science and Technology, Republic of Kenya.

Rivkin, Steven G., Eric A. Hanushek, and John F. Kain. 2005. "Teachers, Schools, and Academic Achievement." *Econometrica* 73 (2): 417–58.

Sawada, Y. 1999. "Community Participation, Teacher Effort, and Educational Outcome: The Case of El Salvador's EDUCO Program." Working Paper 307, William Davidson Institute, University of Michigan, Ann Arbor.

Sawada, Y., and A. B. Ragatz. 2005. "Decentralization of Education, Teacher Behavior, and Outcomes." In *Incentives to Improve Teaching: Lessons from Latin America*, ed. E. Vegas, 255–306. Washington, DC: World Bank.

Vegas, E., ed. 2005. *Incentives to Improve Teaching: Lessons from Latin America*. Washington, DC: World Bank.

Weisberg, D., S. Sexton, J. Mulhern, and D. Keeling. 2009. "The Widget Effect: Our National Failure to Acknowledge and Act on Differences in Teacher Effectiveness." 2nd ed. Report of The New Teacher Project, Brooklyn, NY. http://widgeteffect.org/downloads/TheWidgetEffect.pdf.

Woessmann, Ludger. 2003. "Schooling Resources, Educational Institutions, and Student Performance: The International Evidence." *Oxford Bulletin of Economics and Statistics* 65 (2): 117–70.

World Bank. 2003. *World Development Report 2004: Making Services Work for Poor People*. Washington, DC: World Bank.

———. 2004. "Papua New Guinea: Public Expenditure and Service Delivery (PESD)." PESD study report, World Bank, Washington, DC. http://siteresources.worldbank.org/INTPUBSERV/Resources/PNG.PESD.Education.Final(G).jun.2004.pdf.

———. 2010. *World Development Indicators 2010*. Washington, DC: World Bank.

World Bank, UNESCO/Pole de Dakar, and Government of Malawi. 2010. *The Education System in Malawi—Country Status Report*. Working Paper 182, World Bank, Washington, DC.

Ye, Xiao, and Sudharshan Canagarajah. 2002. "Efficiency of Public Expenditure Distribution and Beyond: A Report on Ghana's 2000 Public Expenditure Tracking Survey in the Sectors of Primary Health and Education." Africa Region Working Paper 31, World Bank, Washington, DC.

2

Information for Accountability

Recent decades have seen an exponential growth in the availability and use of information in the education sector. At the global level, data such as those compiled by the United Nations Educational, Scientific, and Cultural Organization (UNESCO) Institute for Statistics (UIS) are covering a greater number of countries with regular updates; coverage of 283 indicators compiled by the UIS increased from 45 percent in 1990 to over 64 percent in 2009 (Porta Pallais and Klein 2010).

Countries are increasingly carrying out national learning assessments, and more countries are participating in regionally and internationally benchmarked learning assessments. The number of low- and middle-income countries participating in the Trends in International Mathematics and Science Study (TIMSS) increased from 15 to 38 between 1995 and 2011, and the number participating in the Programme for International Student Assessment (PISA) increased from 18 to 37 between 2000 and 2009. At the same time, Education Management Information Systems (EMISs) are becoming commonplace and are being used for planning and for programmatic purposes in many countries.

All of these data have the potential to be turned into information—information that can be used to leverage change for improved service delivery and better learning outcomes. A direct way that information can be used is as an input into management decisions, both at a national level and at the level of a particular school. An alternative approach—using information for accountability—aims to change the relationships of accountability among the various actors in the education system to change behaviors and thus improve outcomes.

While some approaches focus on generating national-level data to spur debate and motivate change (as described in box 2.1), this chapter focuses on approaches that have attempted to use information for accountability at the school level. These approaches include reforms or interventions that generate information on roles and responsibilities, school inputs, outputs, or outcomes and disseminate that information to local-level stakeholders. In the cases to date, there have been variants along a number of dimensions: the content, the level of aggregation, the data collection and compilation, and the way the information is disseminated. The interventions, however, also have common elements: they involve collecting representative data, compiling and analyzing those data, and disseminating them.

The information disseminated varies from simply reporting test scores to more comprehensive reporting of students' socioeconomic characteristics; other measures of performance; students' and parents' satisfaction with the school; school financing; audit findings; and the school's record of inputs, or expenditures. This information may be combined in different ways to produce a school report card, a ranking of schools within a geographic area, a regional or national report card, or simply an article in the newspaper. Some approaches have focused on simple, easy-to-understand measures, while others have tried to adjust for socioeconomic or other factors.

Once compiled, information can be disseminated directly through meetings with parents and parent and teacher associations; through notes and reports sent to parents' homes or, more broadly, through public events with the relevant government officials; and through public media (radio stations and newspapers, for example).

To date, the specific purpose and audience for information campaigns have varied—with the concomitant variation in content, style, and channels of dissemination. The main stated goals typically have been to stimulate parental involvement and citizen demand for school performance and to motivate education reform at multiple levels—school, community, region, and country (Winkler and Sevilla 2004).

An important defining feature of information-for-accountability interventions is that they focus on the use of information, in and of itself, as the instrument of change. This focus stands in contrast to approaches that use information as an input into a system of official rewards and sanctions in an incentive-based scheme. These incentives systems are discussed at more length in chapter 4, "Making Teachers Accountable." This chapter focuses instead on approaches that leverage information to affect the behavior of households, teachers, and school and local government officials directly.[1]

BOX 2.1

Using Aggregated Data for Accountability

Central and Latin America: National and Regional Report Cards

In 2001, the Partnership for Educational Revitalization in the Americas (PREAL) launched a report card initiative in several Central and Latin American countries (Ortega 2006). PREAL report cards use country-level data on key education indicators and regional aggregates to provide reliable and detailed information on the state and progress of education in a country (or region) as a whole. The purpose is to remind governments that their work in education is being monitored and reported to leaders outside the education sector; to give more control over education to civil society and create a demand for information; and to foster dialogue, set priorities, and identify and evaluate policies to improve schools.

PREAL report cards are short, nontechnical summaries that present information under three headings: results, reforms, and recommendations. The report cards present data in ranked order and include statistical annexes with supplementary information. In addition, PREAL uses radio and television to disseminate findings more widely and to reach parents and school staff outside main cities. PREAL currently produces a Latin American report card, a Central American report card, and national-level report cards in 10 countries. Common parameters are established for all report cards to ensure comparability. Anecdotal evidence suggests that the PREAL report cards have increased public awareness about the performance of their countries' education systems.

Southern and Eastern Africa: Consortium for Monitoring Educational Quality

In the mid-1990s, the International Institute for Education Planning (IIEP) and a number of ministries of education in southern and eastern Africa launched an initiative known as the Southern and Eastern Africa Consortium for Monitoring Educational Quality (SACMEQ). The purpose was to build the capacity of organizational providers and policy makers to monitor and evaluate basic education systems. Activities have concentrated on providing hands-on experience in applying modern survey research methodologies, collecting and analyzing data, producing data archives, and preparing and disseminating national evidence-based education policy reports. To date, three large-scale, cross-national studies have been produced. Findings have been widely disseminated among policy makers in the member countries. The

(continued next page)

BOX 2.1 *continued*

reports have played an important role in national debates concerning policies to improve the quality of education. Moreover, SACMEQ has become an important source for training in quantitative research methods in the region (Ross 2006).

International Comparisons: TIMSS, PIRLS, and PISA

Over the past decades, a series of international assessments has been developed to allow participating nations to compare students' education achievements across borders and, hence, quality differentials across education systems worldwide. The International Association for the Evaluation of Educational Achievement (IEA) administers two of these standardized assessments: the Trends in International Mathematics and Science Study (TIMSS), which tests knowledge of fourth- and eighth-grade students in math and science, and the Progress in International Reading Literacy Study (PIRLS), which tests reading achievement of fourth graders. TIMSS was first administered in 1995 and conducted every four years thereafter, whereas PIRLS was first administered in 2001 and conducted every five years thereafter. Having their basis in the curricula of schools in tested countries, these tests aim to investigate three aspects: the intended curriculum, the implemented curriculum, and the achieved curriculum.

A similar exercise, which emphasizes problem-solving skills rather than curriculum, is the Programme for International Student Assessment (PISA). PISA was first carried out in 2000 by an international consortium of research and education institutions led by the Australian Council for Educational Research (ACER). Since then, it has continued to be implemented every three years by the Organisation for Economic Co-operation and Development (OECD). The subject of focus in PISA is rotated in each cycle: first, reading literacy; next, math and problem solving; and finally science literacy. Nevertheless, in each round, tests are administered in all subjects.

Outputs of these assessments are rankings of aggregate country performance and a series of reports, which typically receive considerable attention in the media and among educators and researchers. Overall, standardized international assessments provide an empirical base to hold organizational providers and policy makers accountable, as they present the relative performance of the education system they manage over time and with respect to other countries. As a result, the assessments increase transparency and give more control over education to citizens/clients.

How Information Can Increase Accountability—and Outcomes

When parents and students have little information about the performance of the schools they have access to, or when they have little information about the inputs that schools are responsible for using, their position relative to service providers is weak. They have limited basis for selecting between schools; they have limited ability to hold schools and teachers accountable for either effort or efficiency in the use of resources; and they have limited empirical foundation to lobby governments, both national and local, for improvements in public support to their schools. In the terminology of the *World Development Report 2004*, lack of information weakens *client power* (to hold providers accountable), and it weakens citizens' *voice* (relative to policy makers and politicians) (World Bank 2003). Figure 2.1 illustrates the accountability framework based on this dynamic.

There are three main accountability channels through which information can be expected to affect learning outcomes: increasing *choice, participation,* and *voice*. An alternative channel for information to affect outcomes is through its use in *management*.

Increasing Choice

In many—although certainly not all—school systems, students face a choice of schools. This choice may be between public schools, but it is often between public and private schools. Indeed, in some countries such as

Figure 2.1 The Role of Information in the Accountability Framework

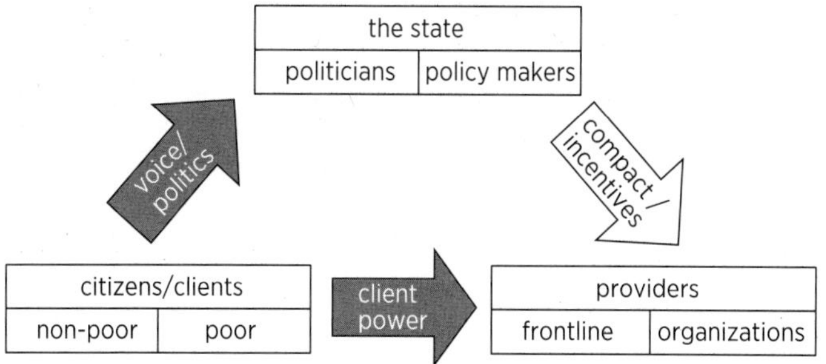

Source: World Bank 2003.

Note: Arrows outlined in gray designate where information-based interventions affect relationships of accountability in education.

Chile, Pakistan, and Zimbabwe, more than 50 percent of primary students attend private schools (Glewwe and Kremer 2006). When school performance information was provided to low-income parents in one U.S. setting, parents used this information to select higher-performing schools when faced with a choice of schools—and that translated into higher student test scores (Hastings and Weinstein 2008). The extent to which such information is a factor will crucially depend on the degree of effective school choice in any particular setting.

In addition to optimal student-school matching, in contexts with school choice, information may work to increase competition among schools. To the extent that funding follows students—either through public funding formulas or through private fees—schools may compete to attract students.[2] Therefore, by making information readily available, schools may work to improve quality to draw in more students and thereby boost income. This improved quality would then be reflected in measures of learning outcomes.

Increasing Participation

School choice is only one mechanism by which information for accountability could lead to improved outcomes. Lack of knowledge about school performance may cause parents to believe that performance is adequate and prevent them from demanding improvements (Winkler and Herstein 2005). By revealing shortfalls—relative to other schools in the village, district, province, or country—information can be a motivator for action on the part of parents and other stakeholders. Indeed, some information-for-accountability interventions include social mobilization efforts to leverage the information for closer monitoring of school performance and service delivery.

One of the crucial roles for information in this channel is providing credible evidence on school performance. This evidence can underpin pressure for improvements in school quality and be one source of information for monitoring that quality. Parent participation and oversight potentially enables closer monitoring of resource allocation—ensuring alignment between what parents want (which may include higher test scores) and the way resources are deployed. Participation also enables closer monitoring of effort on the part of teachers and other educators.[3] Both of these results—better deployed resources and greater effort—are, in turn, inputs into higher learning outcomes.

There are also "softer" reasons why information might positively affect school processes and outcomes. Because information-for-accountability campaigns may promote dialogue and consultation among all actors, they can potentially alleviate information asymmetries and promote discussion and communication, all of which might result in an environment more conducive to learning.

Increasing Voice

In the context of decentralized service delivery, the idea of access to information as a critical element to reduce the extent to which the rich can "capture" services (that is, structure delivery systems such that the rich benefit disproportionately) and thereby improve delivery for the poor has strong theoretical foundations (Bardhan 2002; Bardhan and Mookherjee 2000, 2005). Information provides transparency to government actions and the political process, and that transparency may promote better policies and improve outcomes.

But there is a more general way in which information can work through local (and even national) governments to improve learning outcomes. By providing credible evidence, information could allow parents and other stakeholders to effectively lobby governments for improved policies. It provides content to the voice that citizens might use to pressure governments and enables them to hold those governments to account. While we focus in this chapter on school- and local-level approaches, one can also interpret national-level information generation and dissemination as a way of leveraging information for accountability by strengthening voice.

Internationally, regionally, or even nationally benchmarked assessment systems—such as PISA, TIMSS, the Southern and Eastern Africa Consortium for Monitoring Educational Quality (SACMEQ), or the U.S. National Assessment of Educational Progress (NAEP) all provide aggregate assessment data that can be used to promote the public accountability of education systems. Likewise, internationally comparable national "report cards" such as those developed in Latin America by the Partnership for Educational Revitalization in the Americas (PREAL) have leveraged summaries of a variety of data to promote debate and pressure for reform, as described in box 2.1.

In addition to empowering citizens' voice, information can be leveraged for political change through a competitive electoral process. Indeed, the political "market" is characterized by incomplete information, and the generation and provision of information can fill that void (Keefer and Khemani 2005). Moreover, systematic bias in the availability of information (for example, better information in urban areas than in rural areas) can lead to systematic bias in the provision of public services (Majumdar, Mani, and Mukand 2004). To the extent that local (or even national) politicians might run on a platform of service delivery performance, credible information can potentially drive the political debate. Improvements in indicators thereby become both the basis for political argument and a measure of administrative performance (Khemani 2007).

Using Information for Management

The focus in this chapter is on the use of information *per se* as an accountability tool. However, perhaps one of the more straightforward uses of information is to enable better decision making by managers. In information-poor environments, access to better information could help direct resources where they are most needed and enable managers to better understand whether the allocations they are making are achieving desired results. Being effective in this context does not involve information to leverage accountability but rather information to be used as an input into technocratic decisions. Box 2.2 discusses two recent evaluations that tested whether school-level and school-specific information provided to school administrations affected outcomes—with modest impacts in one case (Madagascar) and no impacts in another (Andhra Pradesh, India).

Another way that information can be used for management is as an input into a strong accountability system. As discussed in more detail below, this is the way that information is used in the U.S. model under the No Child Left Behind Act (NCLB). In that system, detailed, school-specific information on the performance and performance gains of students and subgroups of students is measured. Schools that fail to meet performance targets are subject to various sanctions, depending on how far short of the targets they fall and how long they have failed to meet them. Sanctions range from a requirement to develop a school reform plan, to a requirement to allow students to transfer to other schools, to a requirement to completely restructure (that is, to close and reopen under new management and staff). Information in this type of system is not being used for its intrinsic contribution to the promotion of accountability but rather as part of a strategy of incentives.

From Information to Outcomes

Even though education interventions are typically justified on the basis of just one of these channels leading from information to outcomes (increasing choice, participation, or voice), any specific intervention probably works through multiple channels. For example, school-specific information may promote more informed choice—but could also enable more, or more effective, participation and monitoring on the part of parents. Or credible information may enable parents to effectively pressure both schools and local governments.

BOX 2.2

Using Information for Management

This chapter focuses on interventions that have aimed to leverage information for accountability, for change, and for improved outcomes. But another approach would be to view information as a management tool—as an input into school-level decision making without bringing to bear the accountability aspect. Two new field experiments have evaluated the potential for this approach, with mixed findings.

The first study is in Madagascar, where a set of tools was distributed to 909 randomly selected schools, including 303 randomly selected control schools (Lassibille and others 2010). The intervention consisted of a management toolkit and guides, training, and "report cards" for school directors and subdistrict- and district-level officers. The intervention ran for two school years, 2005 to 2007, and baseline and follow-up data were collected, including test scores from standardized tests in three subjects. The program showed quite large impacts on behaviors: the share of teachers who completed all "key" tasks increased from 42 percent to 63 percent, and the share of schools in which all teachers performed all "key" tasks rose from 22 percent to 43 percent. In addition, there were statistically significant, albeit small, impacts on student attendance and repetition. However, the impact on student learning was small and not statistically significant.

A second study focused on diagnostic feedback to teachers and low-stakes monitoring of classroom processes in the Indian state of Andhra Pradesh (Muralidharan and Sundararaman 2010).[a] A set of 100 schools were randomly selected to receive the treatment, which consisted of the following:

- An independently administered baseline test
- A detailed, written diagnostic feedback report on the performance of students at baseline
- A note on how to interpret the feedback report along with benchmarks
- An announcement that students would be retested at the end of the year to monitor progress
- Six low-stakes monitoring visits during the year to observe teaching processes and activity.

An additional set of 300 schools were randomly selected to serve as control schools. These control schools received one unannounced visit during the school year in which data on teacher absenteeism

(continued next page)

BOX 2.2 *continued*

and classroom behavior were collected. To minimize the potential for contamination, these schools received only one week's notice before endline testing occurred in those schools. The study found substantial impacts on behaviors—as observed during the visits—in the treatment schools: teachers were more likely to be observed actively engaged in teaching, using textbooks, engaging students, and using the blackboard. In addition, they were more likely to assign homework and to provide guidance on that homework. However, students in these schools did no better on independently administered tests than students in schools that did not receive the program.

a. This study was a corollary to a teacher incentives and school grant study, which is described in more detail in chapter 4, "Making Teachers Accountable."

Information for Accountability in High-Income Countries

Reforms in the United States

In the 1990s, the education sector in the United States experienced a large-scale increase in test-based accountability in which school- and teacher-level incentives were based on pupils' test scores (Loveless 2005). By 2001, only two states did not have any measurement or accountability system in place in the education sector (Hanushek and Raymond 2003). Seventeen states had report cards at the school or district level, which provided limited information on school performance. The remaining states had implemented systems with simple performance measures that rated performance as acceptable or unacceptable. In many states, these data systems were accompanied by explicit sanctions or rewards, but the extent to which schools performing below standard would receive any sanction from state authorities varied. In some states, the model was close to what is being described here as information for accountability—commonly referred to as "school report cards" in the U.S. system.

These early accountability systems paved the way for passage of federal legislation, the No Child Left Behind Act, in 2001. NCLB solidified both the test-based information systems and the strong accountability measures that flowed from them. The Act mandated state-approved student assessment in mathematics and reading skills as well as the production and distribution of school-level reports—broken down by student sociodemographic background.

Much of the work on the effectiveness of these test-based accountability approaches is based on the cross-state variation that existed before NCLB. Some national-level studies have found significant improvements in student outcomes as a result of standardized-test-based accountability (Carnoy and Loeb 2002; Hanushek and Raymond 2005), although the limited number of observations these studies are based on introduces some uncertainty. State-specific analyses produce ambiguous results. While some analyses document positive short-run effects of accountability on student math scores (Figlio and Rouse 2006; West and Peterson 2006; Chakrabarti 2006), other results have been less compelling (Clark 2003; Haney 2000, 2002).

Intriguingly, from the perspective of purely information-based approaches, some findings suggest that simply reporting information about average school test scores led to increased performance (Hoxby 2001, Hanushek and Raymond 2003). The results, however, are sensitive to how sanctions are measured and are not robust across specifications (Hanushek and Raymond 2005).

More recent work has begun to assess the impact of NCLB itself. Anecdotal reports have suggested that the NCLB report cards raise public awareness and civic involvement when schools fall into one of the several "watch list" categories (Loveless 2005). More systematic work (based on national data exploiting the fact that some states in which NCLB was implemented already had similar programs in place whereas others did not) has documented significant gains in math test scores (Dee and Jacob 2009). A recent paper that investigated principals', teachers', and students' behavioral responses to the pressures introduced by Florida's education accountability system showed that schools focused on low-performing students by reorganizing teachers' and students' time and increasing the learning resources available to teachers (Rouse and others 2007). These responses have resulted in test score gains in reading and math.

Reforms in the United Kingdom

In the United Kingdom, the government introduced greater accountability into the government-funded school sector in 1988. Schools are required to publish information about their students' performance on national test assessments at different ages in primary and secondary school. For example, public junior high schools are required to make available the proportion of students achieving a certain number of exam passes at a certain level. These data are compiled and published by the government and are also used by the media to rank schools in nationally published school "league tables."

These rankings are then used by central government to sanction poorly performing schools. This sanction takes the form of "naming and shaming" but can also involve the replacement of school management—or even school closure, in extreme situations. In addition, the information can be used by parents in choosing a school for their child. Poorly performing schools may lose students (which leads to a reduction in resources because, to an extent, public funds follow the students), while high-performing schools may gain pupils.

Moreover, since the early 1990s, all English state schools have been inspected by an independent government agency, the Office for Standards in Education (Ofsted). There have been two rounds of inspection over the course of the first 10 years of this policy, through which most schools have been inspected. Starting in 2000, Ofsted produced ratings of schools consisting of two elements: (1) test scores combined with background characteristics and (2) qualitative evidence from the inspector reports. A school report for each school is also produced and publicly released immediately after the inspection.[4] If a school fails the Ofsted standards, the local education authority can apply sanctions. These schools are also subject to repeat inspections and greater scrutiny. In turn, the governing board of the school can remove the school principal.

Assessments of the impact of these reforms suggest improvement in raw exam scores. However, it is not clear to what extent such apparent improvements are due to a change in performance as opposed to either changes in the difficulty of the tests (Goldstein 2001; Tymms and Fitz-Gibbon 2001) or other schools' responses (some perhaps salutary such as extra focus on students with difficulties, some detrimental such as excluding weak students from examinations). Evaluation is also hampered by the fact that other reforms were implemented simultaneously, and it has been difficult to isolate which elements of the set of reforms introduced have had an impact on outcomes (Bradley and others 2000).

One study that has attempted to address these issues focuses on the impacts of the accountability measures on the distribution of student achievement within schools (Burgess and others 2005). The analysis found that the performance of marginal students (those on the threshold of meeting the performance benchmark that feeds into the information system) improved but only when schools faced competition for students. When there was no competition, these marginal students appeared to do no better. Worryingly, the study found that low-ability students fared particularly badly under the reform, especially when a large number of students were on the margin of meeting the threshold. While the magnitude of the effects was small, the authors concluded that schools did react in the short run to the incentives created by accountability measures—although not always to the benefit of all students.

Reforms in New Zealand

New Zealand has introduced large institutional reforms to promote information for accountability. To make sure that front-line providers and decision makers act on the information generated, the government established an independent body: the Education Review Office (ERO). The ERO assesses individual schools approximately once every three years unless the performance of a school or service is so poor that it places the education or safety of the students at risk.[5] Reports on individual schools are freely available to the public: they are either posted online or on the school walls, or they are distributed in the school. The focus of the assessments is on school improvement and on making recommendations to individual boards of trustees concerning what they are doing well and where they need to improve.

The focus of the school reforms in New Zealand was on empowering school boards and providing them with information for management as well as introducing school choice into the education system. One assessment found that most schools did actively share the information with stakeholders (ERO 2007). While there have been assessments of the perceptions of the reforms on stakeholders (for example, Wiley 1999 on information and Ladd and Fiske 2003 on choice), there have been no studies evaluating the reforms' overall effect on test scores.

Information for Accountability in Middle- and Low-Income Countries

The accountability reforms in high-income countries, often accompanied by information-for-accountability campaigns, provide insights into the issue for middle- and lower-income countries. However, there are two main shortcomings that these experiences have for illuminating the issue in the developing-country context. First, these campaigns were typically embedded in larger, multifaceted reform efforts. For example, the experience in those U.S. states that implemented low-stakes school report cards come closest to the notion of information for accountability that is the focus here. However, these initiatives were soon overtaken by events, in the form of the high-stakes national NCLB reform. Of course, a more generic concern is the extent to which lessons from such different contexts might be relevant for substantially poorer countries.

There have been attempts to generate and disseminate information to improve the quality of service provision in developing countries. Often, these efforts outside of the education sector have explicitly aimed at mobilizing social action through the use of "citizen report cards," as discussed further in box 2.3. Only recently has there been a systematic approach to evaluating the impact of those interventions using an experimental or quasi-experimental counterfactual. Before turning to the more rigorously evaluated cases (in the later section about impact evaluations), this section focuses on descriptive accounts of interventions that have been tried in developing countries. The discussion is organized around three main approaches to the use of information: school-level report card programs, test-based score rankings, and participatory public expenditure or input-tracking interventions.

School-Level Report Cards

When thinking about information for accountability, school-level "report card" interventions come closest to the notion of creating and generating information that can be used by parents to make better choices and can empower them to participate more effectively in school management or lobby local governments for action. This section describes five cases in which such an approach was used.

Brazil: Paraná state school report card

Perhaps one of the most concrete and clear examples of a large-scale information-for-accountability intervention in education in a developing country was in the Brazilian state of Paraná, which experimented with school report cards between 1999 and 2002 (Winkler 2005; Brooke 2005). The stated goals of the initiative were to increase parental knowledge about the quality of instruction in schools and to raise parents' voice in school matters at the school council and state levels. The initiative also aimed to increase awareness among school personnel about their schools' instructional quality and academic performance.

The report cards combined the following school data:

- Test-based performance (fourth- and eighth-grade test scores)
- Student flows (promotion, retention, and dropout rates)
- School characteristics (average class size and teachers' qualifications)
- Parental opinion and satisfaction with several aspects of the school (facilities, security, teaching practices, quality of education, and parental involvement)
- Parental opinion on the availability of information on school performance and activities.

The cards also contained comparative municipal and state averages for most of the key indicators so that parents and teachers could compare the

BOX 2.3

Citizen Report Cards

The notion of creating an information feedback loop—connecting the public service users, providers, and public-policy principals—cuts across sectors.

India: Citizen Report Cards in Bangalore

In 1994, a small nongovernmental organization (NGO) group launched a survey to gather feedback on several public services, including education, in Bangalore (Paul 2002; Bures 2003). Data on service quality, corruption, and satisfaction with public services were collected from nearly 1,200 middle- and low-income households and structured into a "report card." The report card gave low ratings to all major service providers and showed high levels of client dissatisfaction with staff behavior in the provider agencies. It also showed that clients had to incur high direct costs (bribes) and indirect costs (individual investments) to compensate for missing or unreliable services. The findings of the report card were widely publicized through the press and discussed with the service providers, which created a sense of shame. Some of the providers acknowledged problems and took corrective action. Moreover, the growing public interest in the initiative led to the constitution of a nonprofit body, the Public Affairs Center (PAC), to manage and expand the report card initiative and provide advice to service providers on ways to improve. In 1999, a second PAC report card indicated mild improvements in services but also an increase in corruption. In the education sector, for example, while 30 percent of the households noted an improvement in school infrastructure, another 50 percent felt that school facilities, materials, and equipment had not changed. This time, the findings from the report card were first shared with management teams from selected agencies and then disseminated in public discussions involving citizen groups, the media, and leaders and staff of all the service providers. In these meetings, the heads of the agencies explained their plans to deal with the reported problems. These events and the report card findings were also covered in the news media. Another report card in 2004 revealed substantial improvement in citizen satisfaction in almost all services and some decline in corruption.

Following the Bangalore experience, citizen report cards have evolved into a widely used tool for improving service delivery. They have been scaled up to cover urban and rural services in 24 states in India and have also spread to several cities in Albania, Kenya,

(continued next page)

BOX 2.3 *continued*

Mozambique, the Philippines, South Africa, Uganda, Ukraine, and—on a pilot basis—Vietnam.

Ukraine: Ternopil and Ivano-Frankivsk Citizen Report Cards

In the Ukrainian cities of Ternopil and Ivano-Frankivsk, the People's Voice Project started in 1999 to promote public participation to build an open, accountable, and effective local government in several cities (Bures 2003). Household and entrepreneur surveys revealed widespread dissatisfaction with service quality. However, only 93 percent of the citizens had ever filed a complaint because they believed that doing so would be futile. Dissemination and public discussion of the survey findings led citizens, NGOs, and public officials to engage in several actions to improve public services. In the area of education—identified as a primary concern area—yearly education plans and education advisory councils were established to create an action plan for further education reforms.

The Philippines: Pro-Poor Services Report Cards

Governments can also use report cards to bring citizens directly into the budget allocation process. For example, the Philippine government used findings from the Report Card on Pro-Poor Services to develop new poverty alleviation strategies and programs (Bhatnagar and others 2003; Bures 2003). The survey was conducted in 2000 by the World Bank in collaboration with Social Weather Stations, an independent survey research organization in the Philippines. The survey included 1,200 households across four regions. It collected data on awareness, access, use, and satisfaction related to public services in five areas: health care, primary education, housing, water, and subsidized rice distribution. On education, the report card collected and disseminated data on school enrollment, dropout rates, perceived quality, tuition fees, class size, textbook availability, and parent-teacher associations. The feedback showed a high degree of dissatisfaction with the education system among the poor, resulting in relatively low enrollment in primary school (90 percent for 7- to 12-year-old children) and substantial dropout rates.

Uganda: Health Citizen Report Cards

In Uganda, citizen report cards focused on health service delivery were randomly assigned to 50 rural communities across nine districts. In 25 treatment communities, the quantitative information collected in the health citizen report cards was disseminated together with practical

(continued next page)

BOX 2.3 *continued*

information on how to best use this information in meetings between users and providers. A separate set of communities served as control areas. Impact estimates of treatment show that the intervention improved average health care use, increased infant weight, and reduced child mortality among children under five (Björkman, Reinikka, and Svensson 2006; Björkman and Svensson 2007). The studies also found evidence that staff in treatment communities increased efforts in health provision as a result of the increased community monitoring. In particular, staff in treatment clinics began to share information about treatment practices, availability of drugs, and service delivery in general. There was no evidence of increased government funding (financial or in-kind) or investments.

performance of their schools with that of neighboring schools. This relatively simple, three-page summary of indicators was disseminated to parents and teachers through various local-level workshops. Results were also published in the state education secretariat's monthly newsletter and widely disseminated through press releases and press conferences.

While no rigorous evaluations of this experiment exist, anecdotal evidence suggests positive effects. Parents engaged in discussions with teachers about how they might improve school performance and, through school councils, increased their voice in policy debates about education (Winkler 2005). The report cards also acted as a management tool at the school level and as a driver of wider education reforms (Winkler and Sevilla 2004). One of the key aspects highlighted in reviews of the intervention is that the low-stakes nature of the report cards helped make them politically feasible despite a strong teachers' union (Winkler 2005; Brooke 2005). Nevertheless, a change of state government at the end of 2002—when a new state secretary for education was inaugurated—led to abandoning the innovation.

Central America: CERCA school report cards

More recently, starting in 2004, the Civic Engagement for Education Reform in Central America (CERCA) began implementing a school-level report card model that combines information reporting with a proactive participatory approach to school priority setting (Flórez, Chesterfield, and Siri 2006). Elected representatives of various stakeholders, parents, teachers, principals, students, and community leaders were involved in collecting data and producing the school report card using simple indicators on school characteristics, coverage, efficiency, quality of teaching, and learning. Subsequently, the group was tasked with a self-assessment exercise to analyze the report card and to develop, implement, and monitor actions to improve learning outcomes.[6] The school report card and action plan were then disseminated and discussed within the entire school community.

The model was implemented on a small scale—36 schools in poor and mostly rural areas of the Dominican Republic, El Salvador, Guatemala, Honduras, and Nicaragua. Again, the lack of a carefully constructed counterfactual and, in this case, the small scale of the intervention make it hard to draw strong conclusions. The anecdotal reports from the case studies state that, compared with nonparticipating schools with similar profiles, participating schools experienced higher involvement of community members in school activities. CERCA-participating schools were also more likely to have developed and implemented an action plan, and parents became more engaged in promoting reading and writing, even when they were illiterate themselves (Flórez, Chesterfield, and Siri 2006). Those who reviewed the intervention also highlighted its low cost and potential for sustainability (Flórez, Chesterfield, and Siri 2006).

Sub-Saharan Africa: School Profiles, Report Cards, and Self-Assessments

The approach of collecting information and disseminating it to parents as a way of promoting their participation in school-level decision making has been tried in several Sub-Saharan African contexts. The following describes just three of these interventions.

School profiles in Uganda. Uganda's Ministry of Education reforms, launched in 2001, included the overhaul of its Education Management Information System. One reform was to provide feedback from EMIS in the form of "school profiles." These profiles were reported to have been well received by headmasters and to have provided useful input in the headmasters' discussions with parent-teacher associations and elected officials. The profiles have also been credited with positively altering the community mind-set regarding education provision. Additionally, school profiles were intended to reassert a form of soft vertical accountability by signaling to schools how much the central government knew about them (Cameron, Moses, and Gillies 2006).

School report cards in Kano State, Nigeria. Communities in Kano State received school report cards that included basic information about their schools (Winkler and Herstein 2005). The reports included easy-to-interpret graphs that showed how school-specific indicators compared with local-area and statewide data. The dissemination included radio debates in which specialists discussed the indicators and what they meant. Anecdotal reports suggest that the information was being used by stakeholders and increased transparency in the management of the system. It also helped strengthen the almost nonexistent accountability links between the communities and schools as well as between the central and local governments.

A school self-assessment system in Namibia. Another experience in six northern regions of Namibia involved parents and school councils in the writing of their own report cards and school improvement plans (Gillies 2004). The system was designed to foster school-level discussion on school climate, management and planning, teacher attitudes, availability of inputs, continuous assessment, parental activities, and school support for parental involvement. A team of inspectors used the same indicators to provide an alternative assessment. The school report cards were disseminated to a school management team made up of teachers, parents, and supervisors. Findings from the school assessment were also summarized at the regional levels and used as a diagnostic tool for management at these levels. Anecdotal reports suggest that the initiative succeeded in mobilizing parents, communities, and schools to participate in the work and management of their schools. It also helped contribute to the creation of meaningful and common standards of performance and expectations.[7]

Test-Based Rankings

While ranking schools based on test scores, as an accountability measure, originated largely in the United States, two developing countries have tried to use a similar approach: Brazil and Chile (the latter discussed in the section below about impact evaluations).

Ceará state's new millennium school prize

Since 1992, the Brazilian state of Ceará has publicly rewarded the best-performing schools with its New Millennium School Prize (Brooke 2005). All schools in the state are ranked according to the raw average performance of their fourth- and eighth-grade students in math and Portuguese standardized tests—an approach that does not account for variations in student background. While awards are given to both school personnel and the best-performing students, the main stated goal is to promote public recognition of high-performing schools. To date, there has been no rigorous evaluation of whether the program has been effective.

Rio de Janeiro state's new school program

The state of Rio de Janeiro, since 2000, has attempted to build on this approach with its New School Program (Brooke 2005). Longitudinal data on students' test scores in math and Portuguese and on students' characteristics are used to construct a measure of individual value-added performance, conditional on observable indicators. An aggregate school efficiency index is constructed by combining this information with data on student flows (such as progression rates and age-grade distortion rates) and school management. Within homogenous socioeconomic groups—based on students' mean family income—schools are ranked. Teachers and principals in the highest-ranked schools receive monetary rewards. No evaluation of this program has occurred.

Public Expenditure and Input Tracking

The discussion and cases so far have focused on approaches built around information about school-level performance. Another way that information has been used to increase accountability—with the goal of increasing learning outcomes—is through its role in promoting public resource tracking. Leaks in the flow of funds or in-kind resources—such that little reaches front-line service providers—have been documented in many settings (World Bank 2003). Publicly disseminating school-specific information on what resources to expect—thereby mobilizing communities to monitor the resource distribution—has been tried as an approach to reducing these leaks. Two notable experiences with this approach occurred in the Philippines and Uganda (the latter discussed below in the section below on impact evaluation).

The Philippines: Textbook Count 1-2-3

The Textbook Count 1-2-3 program in the Philippines was instituted to combat corruption that had been documented at various levels of the Philippine education sector at the end of the 1990s (Leung 2005; van der Linden 2007). Basic inputs, such as textbooks, were not reaching students—resulting in serious shortages at the school level—and those textbooks that were delivered were of substandard quality. According to some studies, bribes in the provision of learning materials ranged from 20 percent to 65 percent of the value of the contracts. Contractors were alleged to be charging the Department of Education for nonexistent deliveries of books and then splitting payments with the officials who approved the invoices.

Following a change in government in 2001, the school textbook provision system was reformed. Starting in 2003 and for three years thereafter, the Textbook Count 1-2-3 program published a detailed list of when textbooks were going to be delivered in each province. These lists were widely published in newspapers and "socialized" through meetings with teachers, government officials, and NGOs. The meetings covered the numbers and quality of textbooks, the specific delivery methods, and the schedules, which took into account the geographical peculiarity of each area—an important consideration given the nature of the country as an archipelago. In addition, the initiative engaged and trained a variety of organizations such as parent-teacher associations and local NGOs to verify and report on the delivery of the textbooks.

Although no systematic data have been gathered on the process and final outcomes, anecdotal evidence suggests that the program was successful in reducing corruption. By 2005, all textbooks produced were delivered (compared with an estimated loss of 40 percent in 2001), textbook prices were reduced, and quality standards reportedly improved. Recent efforts to institutionalize and sustain the initiative have included creating a legal framework, ensuring its financial sustainability, and expanding it to other procurement areas such as school buildings and furniture.

Evaluating the Impact of Information-for-Accountability Interventions

Most of what we know about the impacts of information-for-accountability reforms in developing countries comes from small pilots and case studies, such as those described above. This largely qualitative and anecdotal evidence suggests that information-for-accountability reforms might have positive impacts: greater collaborations and better communications between parents and teachers, improved parental participation in school matters, better and more frequent data reporting mechanisms, better resource flows, and some suggestion of improved education outcomes.

Evaluation Analysis to Date

However, these descriptive analyses and case studies fall short of what one would want as an evidence base for strongly advocating these types of reforms, for the following reasons:

- Each intervention has been custom-designed for the specific setting. This is obviously appropriate; it would be unreasonable to apply a standardized approach. But site-specificity makes it is hard to draw any general conclusions.
- Many of the interventions have been implemented on a small scale—for example, the CERCA school report cards implemented in 36 schools in Central America.
- The indicators used vary substantially—from self-assessments in the Namibia case to sophisticated institutionalized assessment systems in Brazil.

- None of these cases attempts to establish a rigorous counterfactual—what would have happened in the absence of the intervention. Without such a counterfactual, it is impossible to attribute changes in outcomes to the interventions themselves.[8]

Two existing studies have tried to establish causality using nonexperimental approaches: evaluations of Chile's test-based school rankings and of Uganda's newspaper campaign.

Chile: School rankings

Chile has a long-standing history of publishing average test scores by school, a practice that has established the country as a regional leader in the application of standardized achievement tests and the dissemination of their results. Moreover, Chile has one of the most liberalized school markets in the world since the introduction of a series of school finance reforms in 1981—the best-known of which is an extensive education voucher system.

In 1988, the *Sistema Nacional de Medición de la Calidad de la Educación* (National System for Measuring the Quality of Education, or SIMCE) was established and, since the mid-1990s, its results have been widely disseminated, in part through newspaper listings of schools' rankings. The motivating idea was that a ranking of schools, along with linking school funding to the number of students at each school, would stimulate competition that would, in turn, improve school quality. The government also began to use SIMCE results to allocate resources. Various commentators (notably Mizala, Romaguera, and Urquiola 2007) have pointed out that simple school rankings from repeated cross-sections using SIMCE largely capture students' socioeconomic status and are not a good reflection of school effectiveness.[9]

The approach was subsequently revised, resulting in an approach that used data on school type, location, and characteristics, and flows and data on student socioeconomic characteristics, test score levels, and intercohort gains to rank schools within a predetermined "homogenous" group of schools in each administrative region. The goal was for this *Sistema Nacional de Evaluación del Desempeño de los Establecimientos Educativos Subvencionados* (National System for Performance Evaluation of Subsidized Educational Establishments, or SNED) to be an index that would compare only schools serving students of similar backgrounds. Since 1996, the system has identified "outstanding schools," which became eligible for financial awards, every two years. During the two years the award is in force, SNED-winning schools receive two rewards: (1) an annual bonus for teachers, and (2) public identification as a high-performing school. (See chapter 4 on teacher incentives for a discussion of the impact of the SNED teacher bonuses.) The publicity happens through press releases, newspapers, parent-teacher association meetings, the Ministry of Education's website and, in some municipalities, through banners posted on winning schools.

Mizala and Urquiola (2007), using a regression discontinuity design, analyzed the extent to which parental choices, and therefore school markets, respond to signals of school effectiveness. The identification of impact comes from the fact that the cutoff for being identified as a well-performing school is clear: within the groups of schools serving students from similar socioeconomic backgrounds, the top 25 schools are selected for the award in each round. Intuitively, schools just above and just below the cutoff within each group are virtually identical—except for the fact that those above the cutoff receive the award. A comparison of differences in outcomes across the cutoff therefore provides an estimate of the impact of the program.[10] The study captured the impact on the education market through three sets of indicators: (1) enrollments in first and ninth grade, (2) the probability and amount of school fees, and (3) the heterogeneity of schools' populations as given by a vulnerability index, household income, and parent education.

None of the outcome measures showed any sensitivity to the availability of information—a result that is robust to restricting the sample to schools operating in the same market, to parents of high socioeconomic status (who might be more sensitive to information), and to secondary schools (at which level students are more mobile). As a possible explanation, the authors suggested that SNED might not have sufficiently registered with parents (despite its decade-long existence). Another possibility is that, even if parents were familiar with SNED and valued its effectiveness, their choices might have been based on other characteristics of the school, such as proximity or peer quality.[11]

Uganda: Newspaper campaign

One well-discussed example of information-for-accountability interventions is the large-scale public information campaign around a capitation grant to schools instituted in Uganda in the mid-1990s. The capitation grant, financed and run by the central government and using provincial and district offices as distribution channels, was disbursed to public primary schools to cover nonwage expenditures. The information campaign involved publishing budget flows to districts, including amounts and dates, in national newspapers—including local-language editions. Monitoring of districts by the central government was also strengthened.

This intervention has been credited with increasing the share of public spending allocated to schools that actually reached schools from 20 percent in 1995 to around 80 percent in 2001 (Reinikka and Svensson 2006). It has also been credited with improving total enrollment in the schools where expenditure shares increased (Reinikka and Svensson 2005). In addition, Björkman (2006) argues that students in areas with high exposure to newspaper circulation scored better in the Primary Leaving Exam than students in districts with less exposure—with the channel for the impact being the increased resources that reduced leakage enabled. Going from "low" to "high" newspaper access was associated with an improvement of about a 0.4 standard deviation on the exam—equivalent to an 11 percent increase in the test scores of the average student in Uganda.

The identification of impacts in these analyses rests on differential exposure to newspapers—newspaper outlets and newspaper circulation in the two studies, respectively. The intuition is that the availability of newspapers affected the information acquired, which affected behavior, which led to improved resource flows, which in turn affected outcomes. The results from these studies are striking: information access substantially reduced leakage, increased enrollment, and led to an increase in test scores.

A key assumption in this instrumental variables approach is that the availability of newspapers is not related to outcomes through any other channel besides its effect through information. Since the approach assesses difference-in-differences and therefore controls for fixed location-specific attributes, these effects would need to be dynamic to undermine the validity of the instrument. Specifically, time-varying factors related to newspaper access that also affect outcomes would undermine identification. The arguments marshaled by the authors are compelling: newspaper access is related to knowledge about the grant program but not to knowledge about political matters and is therefore unlikely to be picking up an ability to lobby politicians for resources. Newspaper access was not related to leakage before the information campaign and is therefore unlikely to be picking up an unobserved factor related to leakage. Last, newspaper access has an effect over and above that of income and remoteness, so it is not simply a proxy for these variables. Nevertheless, the extent to which one believes that the impacts can be attributed to information access is dependent on one's acceptance of these arguments.

Evidence from Four New Field Experiments

Four more recent interventions were designed with the specific goal of evaluating the impact of information on behaviors and outcomes. Through careful pre- and postintervention data analysis, combined with randomized allocation of information dissemination, the studies enable substantial new insights into the potential for information as a tool for promoting accountability—and outcomes. Nevertheless, the small number of studies and the location-specific nature of the findings suggest that there is substantial scope for further work.

Pakistan: Report cards

The education system in Pakistan is characterized by a vibrant private sector—one 2007 estimate put the share of students at the primary and secondary levels at 31.2 percent and 31.4 percent, respectively.[12] Providing information about school performance in such an environment has the potential to especially affect outcomes through competition between private schools and between the public and private sector. A large-scale study of the education system in three districts of Pakistan's Punjab Province sought to evaluate what the effects of such an intervention would be (Andrabi, Das, and Khwaja 2009).[13]

The specific sites of the information intervention were 112 randomly selected villages within the three districts. Only villages with at least one private school were included in the sample frame, corresponding to about 50 percent of villages overall. In total, the study covered 823 public and private schools—on average, 7.3 schools per village. The study schools included roughly 9,900 students. Half of the villages in each district were assigned "treatment" status, and half served as a control group, with the intervention running two years.

The intervention itself consisted of a set of report cards distributed to parents and teachers. The content of the cards was based on the results from a set of tests in English, mathematics, and Urdu—the local language. Parents received two report cards: (1) The first card included the child's individual score in each subject, his or her quintile rank across all tested students, and the average scores for the child's school and for his or her village as well as the quintile rank for each of these. (2) The second card included the average scores for each school in the village, its quintile rank, and the number of students tested. Teachers received an additional card that included a disaggregation of the scores across subtopics—for example, word recognition and sentence building in English.[14]

The cards were delivered through discussion groups in which most of the time was spent explaining how to interpret the cards. The approach intentionally avoided providing advice to parents or schools; the goal was merely to ensure that the participants could understand and interpret the content.[15] Families and schools received no financial benefits (for example, household transfers or school grants) for their participation in this program.

A key feature of this intervention is that the investigators intended for it to be a villagewide intervention. All schools in all villages were a part of the study. The information campaign was intended to affect the whole market for education in the village—not just one (public) school.

India: Jaunpur district in Uttar Pradesh

A different approach was taken in a field experiment of alternative approaches to promote community engagement and improve learning outcomes in the Jaunpur District of the Uttar Pradesh state of India (Banerjee and others 2008). This large state—with a population roughly the size of Mexico's—has economic and social indicators that are roughly in line with the rest of the country. Teacher absenteeism, estimated at 26.3 percent based on a survey in 2003, is likewise similar to the national average of 24.8 percent (Kremer and others 2005).

Three approaches were designed to build on an existing institution for community engagement in education, the village education committee (VEC). While VECs exist in a *de jure* sense, a baseline survey found them to be all but nonfunctional: a survey of 1,029 VEC members (identified as such by school principals) revealed that only 38 percent spontaneously self-identified as members, and only 25 percent responded that they were members when asked directly. VEC members, as well as parents of school-age children in the study villages, knew little about the VEC's roles and responsibilities. These roles include both indirect authority—by monitoring school performance, reporting to higher authorities, and requesting additional resources—and direct authority by supervising the hiring and firing of community-based contract teachers and allocating additional resources to the school from a government-run program (the *Sarva Shikha Abhiyan* [Education for All program]).

This lack of engagement was concomitant with low indicators of learning achievement: 15 percent of village children ages 7–14 could not recognize a letter, 38 percent could not recognize numbers, and only 39 percent could read and understand a simple story. At the same time, parents systematically overestimated their children's abilities.

The three interventions also built on the experience of the collaborating NGO (Pratham, a large Indian NGO focused on education improvement) with improving education outcomes. The first approach was based largely on explaining and publicizing the role of the VEC—both to VEC members and to the community at large. Through a series of small group meetings, culminating in a large village meeting, NGO facilitators held discussions about the structure and organization of local service delivery, with an emphasis on the role and activities of the VEC. Facilitators were tasked with ensuring that specific facts about the public education system and the VEC's roles and responsibilities were conveyed. After the two-day intervention, pamphlets outlining these roles and responsibilities were left with each VEC member.

The second approach built on the first. In addition to group discussions, local volunteers were trained in simple reading, writing, and math assessment tools. They were tasked with administering these tests to school-age villagers and, in collaboration with parents and other community members, were supposed to convert these test results into village "scorecards." These scorecards then became inputs into the village meetings, helping to steer the discussion toward learning outcomes.

The third approach added one more dimension. Local volunteers were sought to receive training in reading instruction. These trained volunteers then held remedial reading classes, known as "reading camps," after school hours. NGO staffers provided ongoing support to the program in these villages through periodic visits; an average village received seven of these visits.

Each approach was implemented in 65 villages, with an additional 85 villages serving as a control group. The 280 study villages were randomly selected from four blocks within the Jaunpur district, and allocation into each treatment approach was randomized within each block. Baseline data were collected in March and April 2005, with follow-up data collected one year later. The interventions were implemented from September through December 2005. Data were collected from 2,800 households, 316 schools, and more than 17,500 school-age children (ages 7–14).

India: Three-state study

The third new information-for-accountability field experiment is similar to the simplest of the Uttar Pradesh approaches, although the intervention differed in important respects. This intervention was carried out in 12 districts across three Indian states: Uttar Pradesh (again), Madhya Pradesh, and Karnataka (Pandey, Goyal, and Sundararaman 2009, 2010).[16]

Indicators of service delivery are similar in the three states, with teacher absenteeism estimated at 26.3 percent in Uttar Pradesh, 17.6 percent in Madhya Pradesh, and 21.7 percent in Karnataka in 2003 (Kremer and others 2005). In general, however, Karnataka typically stands out as having higher economic and social indicators. Indeed, in the baseline survey for this experiment, teacher attendance was 67 percent and 65 percent in Uttar Pradesh and Madhya Pradesh, respectively, while it was 88 percent in Karnataka. At the time of the unannounced visit at baseline, 31 percent and 27 percent of teachers, respectively, were actively engaged in teaching in Uttar Pradesh and Madhya Pradesh, while 68 percent were doing so in Karnataka.

Baseline indicators for the districts in this intervention also suggest a lack of knowledge and engagement by the formally established bodies supposed to oversee education matters: VECs in Uttar Pradesh, parent-teacher associations (PTAs) in Madhya Pradesh, and school development and monitoring committees (SDMCs) in Karnataka. Levels of learning (tested in second-to-fourth-grade students in public schools) were extremely low in Uttar Pradesh and Madhya Pradesh: only about 14 percent of students at baseline could read a sentence in these states, and only about 16 percent could correctly perform the addition tasks on the test. In Karnataka, the levels of learning at baseline were substantially higher: 46 percent of students could read a sentence, and 75 percent could do the basic addition problems correctly.

The intervention in this study consisted of a set of information dissemination tools delivered repeatedly to selected villages. The tools consisted of a six-minute film shown on a mobile screen, a set of posters, a large wall painting, take-home calendars, and a learning assessment booklet. The goal was to convey, in a systematic way and to a broad audience, the roles and responsibilities of the relevant school oversight committees as well as a series of facts about the rules, rights, and organization of those committees. The information was delivered in two rounds: September 2006 to January 2007 and August 2007 to January 2009. In each case, the campaign was carried out three times, separated by a period of two to three weeks. Each campaign consisted of up to three community meetings in various neighborhoods of the gram panchayat (the local-government unit of intervention, consisting of approximately three villages) in which the film was shown, posters displayed, the mural painted, and the take-home materials distributed.

The intervention was implemented in randomly selected gram panchayats in each district, stratified by block (an intermediate administrative level). The evaluation was based on a baseline survey carried out February–March 2006, a first follow-up survey carried out February–April 2007, and a second follow-up survey carried out February–April 2009. By the second follow-up, therefore, exposure to the program was on the order of two years.

The initial baseline survey was implemented in one public school in each gram panchayat. In Uttar Pradesh and Madhya Pradesh, 15 students from each second-, third-, and fourth-grade class were tested. In Karnataka, 15 students from each fourth- and fifth-grade class were tested. The associated school oversight committee members were then interviewed. At follow-up, fresh cohorts of third- and fourth-grade students were tested in Uttar Pradesh and Madhya Pradesh, and fresh cohorts of fourth- and fifth-grade students were tested in Karnataka. In Uttar Pradesh and Madhya Pradesh, the initial second-grade cohort was retested when the students would have been in fifth grade if they had proceeded at the expected pace.

Liberia: Early grade reading assessment

The fourth information intervention with a rigorous evaluation was carried out in Liberia as a part of an Early Grade Reading Assessment (EGRA) exercise (Piper and Korda 2010). The setting is characterized by low school participation rates and extremely low levels of learning. The evaluation sought to study the impact—beyond the simple EGRA measurement—of three versions of follow-on activities:

- In a first group of schools, the EGRA exercise was implemented, but the results were not publicized or disseminated. This served as the control group for the evaluation.
- In a second group of schools, a "light" intervention was implemented. In these schools, parents and community members were provided with the results of the literacy assessment and were informed that the tests would

be repeated. Teachers in these schools were trained in how to prepare student report cards and instructed to distribute these four times a year.

- In the third group of schools, a "full" version of the intervention was implemented. In these schools, teachers received intensive training on reading instructional strategies, over and above the "light" treatment interventions.

The baseline EGRA was carried out in November 2008 and covered 2,957 second- and third-grade students from 176 schools. Assignment to control, light, and full treatment was done randomly, with geographic clustering, targeting 60 schools in each group. A follow-up EGRA was administered in June 2009, and a final assessment was carried out in June 2010. The results discussed here are from the final assessment. Notably, this was a study of sequential cohorts of students rather than a longitudinal study of the same students over time (that is, in each assessment, a new group of second- and third-grade students was selected).

EGRA assessed students on a variety of reading tasks: letter-naming fluency, phonemic awareness, familiar word fluency, unfamiliar word fluency, connected-text oral reading fluency, reading comprehension, and listening comprehension. In addition, an Early Grade Math Assessment (EGMA) was administered individually and orally, covering basic mathematical skills. Neither the "light" nor the "full" interventions was geared toward math, but the rationale for including the math assessment was to see whether there could be spillover effects from reading to math.

Impact on Learning Outcomes

Pakistan: Report cards

The evaluation strategy in Pakistan exploited the randomized design: test score gains in the treatment and control villages could be compared after either one or two years of exposure to the intervention. Because treatment occurred at the village level, much of the analysis was carried out on average village test scores, although the results were not sensitive to whether village- or student-level data were used in the empirical analysis.

The main result was that average test scores increased in the villages where the report cards were distributed: in those villages, test scores were 0.10–0.15 of a standard deviation higher than in the control villages. The results were sustained after two years of the program. Gains were especially big in private schools that had low test scores to begin with (increasing by more than a 0.3 standard deviation); gains were moderate in government schools (increasing by about a 0.1 standard deviation); and gains were small to insignificant in the private schools that had high scores at baseline.

India: Jaunpur District in Uttar Pradesh

The Uttar Pradesh study found little impact on learning outcomes. The impacts of the interventions that focused on raising awareness about the VEC's roles and responsibilities and on self-assessment of learning achievements through the use of community scorecards were estimated to be small and statistically insignificantly different from zero. For example, 85.5 percent of children could read at least letters at baseline; at follow-up, 89.2 percent of the children in the control group could do so, while 89.6 percent of the children in the VEC awareness and scorecard intervention villages could do so. Similarly, 32.7 percent of children could subtract or divide at baseline, while at follow-up, 39.7 percent in the control group could do so, compared with 40.3 percent in the scorecard intervention villages.

The study did find, however, that the reading clubs led to improvements in reading ability—especially for children who could not read at baseline. In villages where this intervention was implemented, children who could not read at baseline were almost 8 percentage points more likely to be able to read letters at follow-up than children in the other villages. Children who enrolled in the reading clubs saw large reading gains: among those who had not previously been able to read, attending the classes made them 60 percentage points more likely to be able to read at follow-up.[17]

India: Three-state study

Unlike the Jaunpur District intervention in Uttar Pradesh, the three-state village information campaign intervention did lead to measurable impacts on learning outcomes. In Uttar Pradesh, the third- and fourth-grade students scored about 16 percent at baseline in mathematical addition tasks, and the impact of the treatment was to raise that score by about 5 percentage points more than the control group.[18] Similar impacts were found for the other math competencies. At baseline, about 14 percent of these students could read a sentence and words, and the impact of the treatment was to raise that by 4 percentage points more than the control group.

In Madhya Pradesh, the impact of the program appears in the test scores of the fifth-grade students who were followed from the initial cohort of second-grade students. Among this group, the impact of the program was to raise math scores by 4 percentage points above the counterfactual performance.

In Karnataka, the impact of the program on fourth- and fifth-grade students was also large in math. For example, at baseline, about 28 percent could perform division, and the intervention raised that competency by 7 percentage points more than the control group.

Liberia: Early grade reading assessment

Despite the randomized control design of the study, some (small) statistically significant differences at baseline led the researchers to adopt a difference-in-differences approach to estimating impact. That is, they studied the difference after the intervention after subtracting out the differences before the intervention.

The information-only intervention—that is, the "light" intervention—increased only one of the seven indicators used in EGRA: the measure of letter fluency.[19] The test scores for this indicator increased by a 0.24 standard deviation as a result of the program. During the mid-term assessment, the "light" intervention also showed impacts on oral reading fluency, reading comprehension, and listening comprehension. However, after the two years of the program had run their course, none of the indicators other than letter fluency was affected by this intervention.

On the other hand, the "full" intervention—which included the information dissemination as well as the teacher training components—had statistically significant impacts on *all* the indicators measured. The effect sizes were estimated to be large, from a 0.38 standard deviation in listening comprehension to 1.40 standard deviations for unfamiliar word decoding.

Intriguingly, of the nine mathematics indicators included in EGRA, six were statistically significantly positively increased by the "full" intervention (three were statistically significantly positively increased by the "light" intervention).[20]

Channels of Impact

Pakistan: Report cards

The Pakistan case is somewhat atypical in that it focused on all schools—both public and private—in a setting where private schools were a strong presence and there was a substantial amount of school choice. Nevertheless, the study found little in the way of switching between schools. Public distribution of test scores and rankings via report cards did alter parents' perceptions of school quality: ex post perceptions were more aligned with test scores than ex ante perceptions. Enrollment in government schools appears to have increased somewhat at the expense of private schools with low initial test scores (which were more likely to close). However, there was substantial stability across time regarding which schools individual students attended. The study found little impact of the intervention on other measures of household behavior; there was no change in parental time spent on education with children, no change in time spent on school work outside of school, and no change in education expenditures (excluding school fees).

The study documents that while there was no learning impact in private schools that had high test scores at baseline, school fees in these schools fell. The authors argue that both high-quality and low-quality private schools were adjusting to align the price-adjusted quality of schooling that they were offering: low-quality schools responded by increasing quality, while high-quality schools responded by reducing price (in part because there may be diminishing returns to investments in quality). This latter adjustment was especially large in schools where the "cost-per-test score" was highest before the intervention.

All of these findings are consistent with the increased competition that information is introducing into the market. It is harder to use these competitive forces to explain the change in government schools. Indeed, despite the fact that there appears to have been limited direct competition for students between public and private schools (at least over the relatively short period of the program implementation), public schools in villages that received report cards posted gains in test scores of slightly less than a 0.1 standard deviation.

The study also offers some insights into how schools increased test scores. In villages that received report cards, schools were more likely to have textbooks and more likely to have more of them. In addition, schools appear to have devoted more time to teaching and learning; the time spent on breaks was between 14 and 23 minutes less on average per day as a result of the intervention. This corresponds to a reported increase in the time that households reported that children spent in school, which increased by an average of 37 minutes per day as a result of the intervention.

India: Jaunpur District in Uttar Pradesh

The awareness-building and community mobilization interventions that were implemented in the Jaunpur District of Uttar Pradesh did indeed raise the level of knowledge among the various stakeholders. VEC members were more likely to know about the VEC's responsibilities and rights. In addition, VEC members became much more aware of the state of education in the village. Knowledge among parents, however, did not increase by much. While the impacts were statistically significantly different from zero, they were small. Even in treatment villages, barely 7 percent of parents reported being aware of the VEC after the interventions.

Likewise, behaviors were not much affected by the information interventions. VECs in treatment villages did not report having complained to higher authorities any more than those in control villages, nor were they more likely to have requested more resources—either in the form of grants or in the form of extra contract teachers. Similarly, parents did not engage any more in school activities as a result of the interventions; they did not visit schools any more, they did not volunteer any more time, and there were no additional school meetings organized.

India: Three-state study

Consistent with the estimated impacts on learning, the three-state study in India found impacts on behavioral change and knowledge. In Uttar

Pradesh—where engagement was lowest at baseline—the intervention led to more meetings, more participation in inspections, and greater knowledge about school matters (such as school accounts) as well as the roles and responsibilities of the VECs. In Madhya Pradesh, PTA members reported more inspections, and greater participation in those inspections, although impacts on reported knowledge were not statistically significantly different from zero. In Karnataka, the impacts were detected most in the area of knowledge—about school accounts and the role of the SDMCs.

The impacts appear to have been mostly concentrated among the more elite members of the school committees—that is, non-Scheduled Caste members. Moreover, in Uttar Pradesh and Madhya Pradesh, the impacts were concentrated in villages with low proportions of Scheduled Caste or Scheduled Tribe populations—that is, relatively better-off villages. These are presumably villages where literacy levels and other social and economic indicators are higher. Of particular note, in Karnataka there was evidence that school committees took action as a result of the information: the program resulted in school committees letting go of contract teachers who had high absenteeism.

Similarly, the study found impacts on teacher effort in the two states where it had been especially low at baseline: Uttar Pradesh and Madhya Pradesh. In both states, the intervention led to an increase in teacher attendance (of between 6 and 8 percentage points), and in Madhya Pradesh to an increase of teacher activity conditional on attendance (of 8 percentage points). All of this effect comes from an impact on civil service teachers as opposed to contract teachers, for whom impacts were not statistically significant.

Liberia: Early grade reading assessment

Interpreting the Liberia results is made somewhat complicated for two reasons:

First, the "light" treatment was especially light compared with the full treatment. In particular, teachers in the "full" treatment received ongoing support and supervision. However, the communities in the "light" program only received one-time information feedback from EGRA, with teachers being shown how to prepare report cards, and there was no verification of whether they actually distributed report cards.

Second, the impacts went beyond reading—that is, math tests were affected by the "full" intervention. There are two potential explanations for this: (1) possible spillover effects from reading to math (indeed, the ability to decode and interpret written material may well affect math scores); and (2) the possibility that the ongoing support and engagement provided to the schools, even though focused on reading, changed the motivation and effort of teachers in a way that affected math scores.

Nevertheless, the impacts of the "full" intervention are striking. The large effect sizes are greater than those typically found in the evaluations of other education interventions, where an effect size of 0.2 is considered large.[21] Given the study design, it is impossible to know whether the teacher training and support, without the public information disseminated through the EGRA feedback and report cards, would have had an impact. Given the frequently disappointing results with teacher training programs (see World Bank 2003 for a discussion), it is likely that the combination of the two did make a difference. Without the incentive to *implement* what they have learned in the classroom, teachers often fall back on familiar teaching methods. In this case, however, it is possible that the effect of the information was to give teachers an additional incentive to make that transition. Further research would be needed to validate this conjecture.[22]

What Have We Learned?

The evidence to date clearly presents a mixed set of results about the potential of information for accountability to improve learning outcomes. Consistent with the analyses of the U.S. experience with report-card-like accountability interventions, the developing country examples of interventions with rigorous impact evaluation show similarly varied results. Table 2.1 summarizes the features and impacts estimated by these studies.

Assessing the Evidence

The interventions and findings share some similarities. All of the interventions are of the "weak accountability" nature: no explicit sanctions are associated with poor performance. All of the interventions appear to have affected awareness and knowledge, with various actors typically becoming more able to convey information about school quality in their localities as well as the material specifically disseminated through the information campaigns (for example, in the India studies, information about the roles and responsibilities of the school oversight committees).

However, the dissimilarities are a more prominent feature of these evaluation studies. The nature of the interventions varied substantially—from externally provided information about performance to the provision of self-assessment tools; from media-based public dissemination of information to in-depth sustained community meetings to help explain the information and help stakeholders to process it; from exposures as short as three to six months to those as long as four years.

While most of the studies used information to enhance *client power* relative to front-line providers, one of the programs (the Uganda newspaper

Table 2.1 Impact Evaluation Studies of Information-for-Accountability Interventions

Program	Nature of intervention	Impact summary	Exposure duration	Evaluation strategy
Chile: school rankings	Publicizing top schools in comparison with schools that serve similar populations	No impact on learning outcomes or behaviors	2 and 4 yrs.	RDD
Uganda: newspaper campaign	Publicizing through the media the amounts and timing of capitation-grant distribution to districts	Reduced leakage in the flow of resources; increased enrollment and learning	More than 2 yrs.	IV
Pakistan: report cards	Detailed information of externally collected data on performance, intensively disseminated to parents, teachers, and school administrators	Increased learning outcomes in public schools and initially poor-performing private schools; reduced fees at initially high-performing private schools	1 and 2 yrs.	RCT
India: Jaunpur District, Uttar Pradesh	Promoting awareness about roles, rights, and responsibilities of school oversight committees; creating self-assessment tools and village-specific scorecards; contracting remedial teachers for reading instruction	Slightly increased awareness of roles, rights, and responsibilities; no impact on behaviors; no impact on learning outcomes in "information-only" interventions	3–6 mos.	RCT
India: three-state study	Promoting awareness about roles, rights, and responsibilities of school oversight committees	Increased awareness of roles and responsibilities, especially in higher socioeconomic groups; impacts on learning outcomes detected	3–6 mos., 2 yrs.	RCT
Liberia: Early Grade Reading Assessment (EGRA)	Disseminating EGRA results to communities; training teachers in reading instruction techniques	Large impacts of the two programs combined (limited to no impact of "information-only" intervention)	2 yrs.	RCT, DD

Sources: Mizala and Urquiola 2007 for Chile; Reinikka and Svensson 2005, 2006, and Björkman 2006 for Uganda; Andrabi, Das, and Khwaja 2009 for Pakistan; Banerjee and others 2009 for Jaunpur District, India; Pandey, Goyal, and Sundararaman 2009, 2010 for India Three-State Study; Piper and Korda 2010 for Liberia.

Note: RDD = regression discontinuity design. IV = instrumental variables. RCT = randomized control trial. DD = difference-in-differences analysis.

campaign) aimed to rebalance power between clients and politicians or policy makers, thereby affecting client *voice*. The variability across these evaluation studies reflects the broader variability in the approaches used to promote information for accountability. Nevertheless, all of these variations make it difficult to draw too many strong general conclusions from these studies about the impact of information for accountability.

One primary goal of impact evaluation studies is to investigate "proof of concept"—that is, to answer the question of whether an intervention, or a type of intervention, *could* have an impact on outcomes. The studies to date suggest that the answer to this question is *yes,* information for accountability can improve outcomes. The examples of India (the three-state study), Liberia, Pakistan, and Uganda show that, under some configurations, information can be leveraged for change—change that results in increased learning outcomes. In addition, the programs appear to be quite cost-effective, as box 2.4 explains.

Notably, each of these interventions was positioned to leverage change in different ways. In Uganda, the goal was to provide information that allowed stakeholders to hold local administrative units (districts) accountable for the funds that they received. In Pakistan, the goal was to provide information to reduce asymmetric information within a vibrant local education market. In the India three-state study, the goal was to provide

BOX 2.4

Cost-Effectiveness of Information Interventions

Generating and disseminating information, if effective, should improve learning at a relatively low cost. Hoxby (2002) discussed the low relative cost of generating and disseminating information about inputs, outputs, and especially outcomes in the United States.

For the Pakistan report card impact evaluation, the authors calculated that the total cost of compiling and disseminating the report cards for the entire population was roughly equal to the fee reduction in the initially well-performing schools (Andrabi, Das, and Khwaja 2009).

The India three-state study benchmarked the cost of the information campaign against the benefit reaped solely in terms of days worked by teachers. The study's authors showed that the effective gain in the use of public resources (that is, the value of the increase in teacher attendance due to the project) was between 20 and 35 *times* the cost of the program (Pandey, Goyal, and Sundararaman 2010).

information to empower local education bodies to exercise their rights of oversight and to empower parents to be aware of their direct role in monitoring schools. In Liberia, information appeared to leverage parent engagement to make teacher capacity-building effective. This variation suggests that all four of these channels may be potential avenues for leveraging change through information.

One feature of these interventions that appears to be associated with success was the clarity and authority associated with the information disseminated. The newspaper campaign in Uganda disseminated readily understood information—dates and amounts of disbursements. The report cards in Pakistan disseminated simple, externally validated indicators of school performance, which were then carefully explained to the target audiences. The three-state study in India emphasized the systematic nature of the information campaign; used creative approaches; repeated visits to ensure that the messages "stuck"; and left behind posters, murals, and take-home materials to ensure that the information dissemination outlasted the visit from outsiders.

Another feature that should be borne in mind when assessing the strength of the evidence is the exposure time. Short exposure times are common in impact evaluation analysis, with potentially noxious impacts on the validity of the findings (King and Behrman 2009). Learning outcomes are slow to change, and therefore it is perhaps unrealistic to expect to see impacts in as short a period as three months.

But these features are not panaceas. Clear, externally validated information that is widely disseminated for a long period of time will not always lead to salutary impacts. The Chilean SNED example shows that well-understood information about schools' relative performance, widely publicized through media and at schools, was insufficient to change education markets—even after two or four years of exposure. By contrast, the India study in the Jaunpur District, Uttar Pradesh, showed that remedial reading lessons were able to increase reading abilities in a short time frame.

In summary, these evaluation studies answer one big question—finding that, yes, information appears to have the potential to leverage change for improving learning outcomes—but they also raise many additional questions. Further research is likely needed to establish, more consistently and clearly, when and how information can be used most effectively.

Designing an Information-for-Accountability System

One important aspect of information is that, once it has been created and disseminated, it can be used by all—and one person's use does not reduce another person's use. It has the attributes of what, in economics, is termed a public good. Public goods face the problem that since no one person or entity reaps the full returns, there will be less than optimal investment in their creation. If information is to be leveraged for outcomes, it is therefore likely that its collection and dissemination will need to be subsidized and supported.

The limited evidence on information for accountability to date suggests that it is perhaps too soon to try to identify which specific aspects of the approach may ensure the largest impact. As described above, there is a great deal of heterogeneity across the cases described here regarding (a) which information was disseminated and how that information was presented, and (b) the extent to which the information was accompanied by capacity-building efforts to ensure that the information was understood. Despite the limited information base, some principles do emerge from the cases so far.

Which information to disseminate and how to present it?

First, simplicity is an important goal to strive for. The report card intervention in Pakistan provides a model that shows substantial promise; the information in the report cards was straightforward and related to an outcome of overarching interest—learning. As figure 2.2 illustrates, each parent was informed about their child's performance in math, Urdu, and English, with these scores rated from "needing a lot of work" to "very good." The equivalent information for the child's school and village was also provided (left panel of figure 2.2). A separate card provided to parents listed average results for each school in the village (right panel of figure 2.2).

In Paraná State, Brazil, which implemented a school report card between 1999 and 2002, the information distributed was likewise kept simple, although it went beyond learning outcomes and included information about student flows and the numbers of teachers and students. In addition, it included feedback from a set of surveys carried out at the school level with responses from parents and students to questions about various aspects of school functioning, as figure 2.3 shows.

The additional information included in the Paraná report cards is of two types: (1) data available from regular data gathering sources such as EMIS, including information on students, student flows, and teachers as well as on infrastructure and the availability of certain types of resources at the school level; and (2) data from specialized surveys, such as those collecting information about parents' perceptions of the schools.

The issue to address with the first type of data is where to draw the line: how much is too much? EMIS typically collect a large set of data, much more information than could be used in a report card exercise. To the extent that report cards are a tool for *mobilizing* parents and stakeholders, including these data is probably of limited use. If report cards are to be used as management and planning tools, however, then detailed information of

Figure 2.2 Report Cards Given to Parents in Pakistan

a. Child information
performance in three subjects (math, Urdu, English)

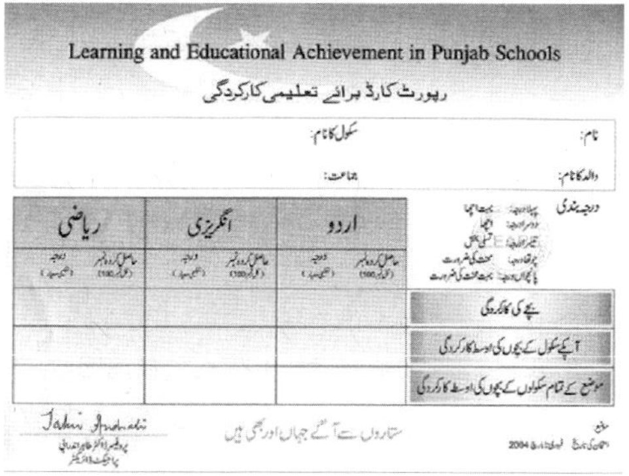

Learning and Educational Achievement in Punjab Schools

رپورٹ کارڈ برائے تعلیمی کارکردگی

ریاضی		انگریزی		اردو		

b. Village schools information
performance of all primary schools in villlage

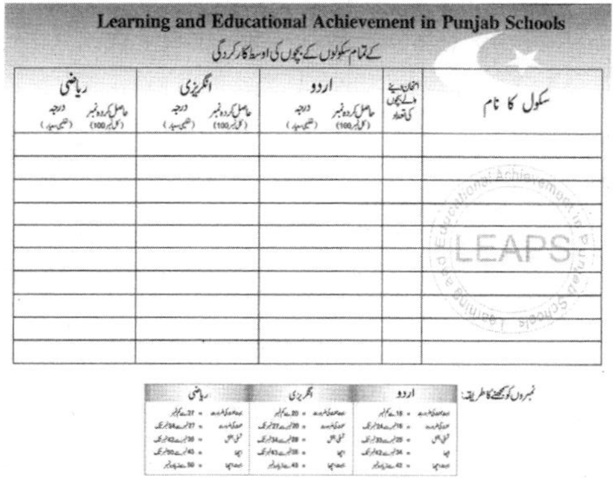

Learning and Educational Achievement in Punjab Schools

ریاضی		انگریزی		اردو			سکول کا نام

LEAPS

(English translation)

a.

Mathematics		English		Urdu		
actual score	quintile	actual score	quintile	actual score	quintile	
						child's performance
						average performance of children in your school
						average performance of children in your village

b.

Mathematics		English		Urdu		No. of children tested	Name of school
actual score	quintile	actual score	quintile	actual score	quintile		

Source: Andrabi, Das, and Khwaja 2009.

Note: Quintile descriptions range from "needing a lot of work" to "very good."

Figure 2.3 Report Card in Paraná State, Brazil, 1999–2000

a. Original (Portuguese)

AVALIAÇÃO DO RENDIMENTO ESCOLAR 2000

		Esta Escola						Outras Escolas no Município		Paraná	
		Média	Alunos Avaliados	Alunos Nível I	Alunos Nível II	Alunos Nível III	Alunos Nível IV	Média	Alunos Avaliados	Média	Alunos Avaliados
Língua Portuguesa	4ª	*						250	480	250	39.239
	8ª	275 ▲	43	5%	21%	19%	56%	255	282	250	31.125
Matemática	4ª							251	465	250	38.441
	8ª	263 ◆	48	13%	21%	23%	44%	252	276	250	31.007
Ciências	4ª							258	469	250	38.033
	8ª	261 ◆	47	15%	26%	26%	34%	251	266	250	31.125

Fonte: SEED/NIE – AVA 2000

Nota: 1 Veja o encarte para a descrição dos quatro níveis de desempenho.
2 — o número de alunos é insuficiente para apresentar o resultado.
* a escola (ou município) não ofereceu (ou teve avaliado) esse nível de ensino.
** a escola (ou município) não participou da AVA 2000.
*** nenhuma outra escola no município participou da AVA 2000.
■ dados insuficientes para estimar a média corrigida.
▲ média acima do esperado em função do perfil dos alunos avaliados.
▼ média abaixo do esperado em função do perfil dos alunos avaliados.
◆ média aproximadamente igual ao esperado em função do perfil dos alunos avaliados.

APROVAÇÃO, REPROVAÇÃO E ABANDONO[1]

	Esta Escola			Município			Paraná		
	Ensino 1ª a 4ª	Ensino 5ª a 8ª	Ensino Médio	Ensino 1ª a 4ª	Ensino 5ª a 8ª	Ensino Médio	Ensino 1ª a 4ª	Ensino 5ª a 8ª	Ensino Médio
Aprovação	*	90%	74%	88%	83%	71%	89%	81%	75%
Reprovação		8%	10%	11%	13%	12%	9%	13%	10%
Abandono		2%	16%	1%	4%	17%	2%	6%	15%

Fonte: MEC/INEP/SEEC – Censo Escolar 2002 (Resultados Preliminares)

Nota: 1. Dados referem-se ao ano escolar de 2001 da rede pública de ensino regular.
2 * a escola (ou município) não ofereceu esse nível de ensino.

PROFESSORES E ALUNOS[1]

		Esta Escola			Município			Paraná		
	Total[2]	Ensino 1ª a 4ª	Ensino 5ª a 8ª	Ensino Médio	Ensino 1ª a 4ª	Ensino 5ª a 8ª	Ensino Médio	Ensino 1ª a 4ª	Ensino 5ª a 8ª	Ensino Médio
Alunos	2.091	*	950	1.141	8.046	7.455	4.257	825.853	737.602	408.020
Tamanho médio de turma			38	38	29	35	36	27	34	37
Professores			40	74	355	407	285	39.255	37.464	22.938
Professores com nível superior			100%	100%	59%	100%	100%	46%	97%	97%

Fonte: MEC/INEP/SEEC – Censo Escolar 2002 (Resultados Preliminares)

Nota: 1 Dados da rede pública de ensino regular.
2. Total de alunos no ensino fundamental e médio.
3. * a escola (ou município) não oferece esse nível de ensino.
4 O critério do Estado para ocupação de salas, em função de sua área, é de no mínimo 25 alunos e no máximo 30 para o ensino de 1ª a 4ª; de 30 a 40 alunos para 5ª a 8ª séries e, de 30 a 45 alunos para o ensino médio.

Secretaria de Estado da Educação

b. Translation (English)

School Performance Assessment, 2000

		This School						Other Schools in Your Municipality		Paraná	
		Mean	Number of Pupils Assessed	Pupils at Level I	Pupils at Level II	Pupils at Level III	Pupils at Level IV	Mean	Number of Pupils Assessed	Mean	Number of Pupils Assessed
Portuguese	4th	*						257	7,232	250	39,239
	8th	258 AP	61	16%	25%	25%	34%	263	4,852	250	31,125
Math	4th	*						255	7,101	250	38,441
	8th	262 AC	56	23%	11%	27%	38%	261	4,710	250	31,007
Science	4th	*						254	7,055	250	38,033
	8th	251 AB	63	19%	30%	25%	25%	260	4,743	250	31,125

Source: SEED/NIE, AVA 2000

Note: School Effects:
AC Average above the expected mean, given the profile of pupils assessed.
AB Average below the expected mean, given the profile of pupils assessed.
AP Average roughly equal to the expected mean, given the profile of pupils assessed.

Promotion, Repetition, and Dropout

	This School			Other Schools in Your Municipality			Paraná		
	Grade 1-4	Grade 5-8	Secondary Education	Grade 1-4	Grade 5-8	Secondary Education	Grade 1-4	Grade 5-8	Secondary Education
Promotion	*	67%	78%	95%	79%	71%	89%	81%	75%
Repetition	*	33%	20%	4%	16%	13%	9%	9%	10%
Dropout	*	0%	2%	2%	5%	15%	2%	2%	15%

Source: MEC/INEP/SSEC, Censo Escolar 2002 (*Resultados Preliminares*).

Note: Data refer to the 2001 school year for public schools in formal education.
* The school (or municipality) did not offer this level of education.

Teachers and Students

		This School			Other Schools in Your Municipality			Paraná		
	Total	Grade 1-4	Grade 5-8	Secondary Education	Grade 1-4	Grade 5-8	Secondary Education	Grade 1-4	Grade 5-8	Secondary Education
Pupils	2,192	*	1,381	811	113,573	100,754	65,965	825,850	737,602	408,020
Average class size		*	37	39	30	35	38	27	34	37
Teachers		*	47	34	6,048	4,193	2,765	39,255	37,464	22,938
Teachers w/ higher education		*	100%	100%	67%	98%	98%	46%	97%	97%

Source: MEC/INEP/SSEC, Censo Escolar 2002 (*Resultados Preliminares*)

Note: *Data from Public schools: total pupils in primary and secondary education.*
* The school (or municipality) did not offer this level of education.
The state government standard for pupil class ratio varies from aminimum of 25 to a maximum of 30 pupils per class for 1st to 4th grade, 30–40 pupils per class for 5th to 8th grade, 30–45 pupils per class for secondary education.

a. Original (Portuguese)

Opiniao dos pais de alunos desta escola sobre...

A qualidade do ensino

142 dos 145 pais (98%) estão satisfeitos com a qualidade do ensino que seu(s) filho(s) recebe(m).
140 dos 144 pais (97%) acham que as instalações da escola são bem conservadas.
138 dos 144 pais (96%) acham que as instalações da escola são apropriadas às atividades de ensino.
139 dos 145 pais (96%) reconhecem que os professores da escola são dedicados ao trabalho.
134 dos 143 pais (94%) estão satisfeitos com a assiduidade dos professores.

O envolvimento dos pais

121 dos 137 pais (88%) gostariam de ter um envolvimento maior nas atividades da escola.
132 dos 140 pais (94%) acham que o diretor da escola favorece a participação de todos nos trabalhos da escola.
39 dos 47 pais (83%) indicam que a escola promoveu atividades voltadas ao envolvimento dos pais em assuntos de ensino.
30 deles participaram dessas atividades.
37 dos 53 pais (70%) indicam que a escola promoveu atividades voltadas ao envolvimento dos pais na administração da escola.
21 deles participaram dessas atividades.

A troca de informação

101 dos 147 pais (69%) indicam que a escola promoveu reuniões regulares entre pais e mestres.
132 dos 145 pais (91%) dizem que existe um sistema regular de comunicação com os pais.
130 dos 144 pais (90%) dizem que os professores mandam tarefas à casa que promovem o interesse dos pais na educação dos filhos.
118 dos 142 pais (83%) dizem que recebem informações a respeito das lições favorecendo o seu acompanhamento.

Segurança

138 dos 141 pais (98%) se sentem confiantes em mandar seus filhos para esta escola.
65 dos 139 pais (47%) acham que esta escola apresenta problemas disciplinares.
37 dos 134 pais (28%) acham que esta escola apresenta problemas internos de segurança.
70 dos 137 pais (51%) acham que esta escola é sujeita a problemas de segurança de sua vizinhança.

Nota da escola

9,0 média atribuída por 148 pais

Perfil dos pais

5 dos 140 pais (4%) pais indicaram fazer parte do Conselho Escolar.
7 dos 142 pais (5%) pais indicaram ser membros da diretoria da APM.
34 dos 138 pais (25%) pais indicaram ser voluntários nesta escola.
51 dos 146 pais (35%) tem mais de 1 filho(a) nesta escola.

Fonte: Questionário submetido aos pais e responsáveis na Semana da Família na Escola, entre 20 e 28 de abril de 2002.
Nota 1. Somente escolas com mais de 160 alunos responderam ao questionário.
2. Os resultados apresentados representam apenas as opiniões daqueles que responderam ao questionário, e não necessariamente representam a opinião de todos os pais desta escola.
3. Os resultados são baseados no total de respostas válidas e não no número de questionários recebidos.
4. Os resultados baseados em menos de cinco respondentes são representados pelo símbolo —
5. O símbolo * indica que a escola não retornou questionários.

Núcleo de Informações Educacionais – NIE

b. Translation (English)

Parents' opinions about this school regarding . . .
Education quality
59 out of 70 parents (84%) are satisfied with the quality of education their children receive.
43 out of 68 parents (63%) believe the school buildings are well maintained.
63 out of 69 parents (91%) believe the school infrastructure is appropriate to educational activities.
50 out of 69 parents (72%) believe that school teachers are dedicated to teaching.
57 out of 71 parents (80%) are satisfied with teachers' punctuality.
Parental involvement
65 out of 69 parents (94%) would like to have greater involvement in school activities.
64 out of 68 parents (94%) believe that the head teacher favors participation of the school community in school activities.
50 out of 71 parents (70%) indicate that the school promoted parental involvement in education issues. 31 of them participated in such activities.
47 out of 68 parents (69%) indicate that the school promoted parental involvement in school administration issues. 23 of them participated in such activities.
Information dissemination
48 out of 72 parents (67%) report that the school promoted regular meetings between parents and teachers.
55 out of 68 parents (81%) say a regular communication system with parents has been established.
58 out of 65 parents (89%) say that teachers assign homework tasks that promote parents' interest in their children's education.
47 out of 69 parents (72%) report receiving information about their children's homework so they could follow up on it.
Security
51 out of 72 parents (71%) feel safe sending their children to school.
47 out of 67 parents (70%) believe the school has discipline problems.
47 out of 68 parents (69%) believe the school has internal security problems.
60 out of 69 parents (87%) believe the school is subject to security problems in the neighborhood.
School grade
7.8 (mean attributed by 68 parents).
Parent profile
5 out of 70 parents (7%) reported participating in the School Board.
7 out of 69 parents (10%) reported being members of the Parents and Teacher Association Secretariat.
14 out of 68 parents (21%) reported being a volunteer at this school.
22 out of 69 parents (32%) have more than one child at this school.

Source: Survey submitted to parents during School Family Week, April 20–28, 2002.
Note: Only schools with more than 160 pupils responded to the survey.
The results reported represent only the opinions of those parents who answered the questionnaires and not those whose children attend this school.
The results are based on the total number of valid responses and not the total number of questionnaires received.

(continued next page)

Figure 2.3 Report Card in Paraná State, Brazil, 1999–2000 *(continued)*

a. Original (Portuguese)

O ALUNO DESTA ESCOLA DIZ QUE ...

	4ª série	8ª série
seu responsável sempre lê seus boletins escolares	*	74%
seu responsável sempre vai à escola quando chamado		73%
seu responsável sempre ou quase sempre comparece às festas escolares		18%
nunca foi reprovado		85%
pelo menos um dos pais tem ensino médio completo		45%
tem computador em casa		23%
tem automóvel em casa		70%

	4ª série Língua Portuguesa	4ª série Matemática	4ª série Ciências	8ª série Língua Portuguesa	8ª série Matemática	8ª série Ciências
sempre ou quase sempre requer orientação em seus deveres de casa				21%	29%	24%
gosta muito da maneira de seu professor ensinar				51%	64%	59%
gosta do livro didático adotado				53%	54%	57%
não teve dificuldades para aprender				37%	21%	30%

Fonte: SEED/NIE – AVA 2000: Questionário do Aluno
Nota: 1 — o número de alunos é insuficiente para apresentar o resultado
* a escola não ofereceu (ou teve avaliado) esse nível de ensino.
** a escola não participou da AVA 2000

A DIREÇÃO DESTA ESCOLA DIZ QUE...

- durante a sua gestão, o diretor dedicou a maior parte de seu tempo ao acompanhamento do trabalho pedagógico dos professores.
- nas reuniões gerais da escola em que todos os pais foram convocados, os resultados da avaliação do rendimento dos alunos foi o tema mais abordado. Em média, essas reuniões contaram com a presença de 75% dos pais.
- nas reuniões gerais da escola em que todos os professores foram convocados, o projeto pedagógico da escola foi o tema mais abordado. Em geral, essas reuniões contaram com a presença de quase todos ou todos os professores.
- o Conselho Escolar reúne-se quando necessário e atuou predominantemente em decisões sobre o processo educativo.

Fonte: SEED/NIE – AVA 2000: Questionário da Escola
Nota: 1. ** a escola não participou da AVA 2000

b. Translation (English)

The pupils in this school say that . . .	4th Grade			8th Grade		
His/her parents always read his/her school reports.	*			74%		
His/her parents always go to the school when requested.				66%		
His/her parents always or almost always attend school events.				15%		
He/she has never failed.				59%		
At least one of his/her parents has completed secondary education.				35%		
He/she has a home computer.				21%		
He/she has a car.				63%		
	Portuguese	Math	Science	Portuguese	Math	Science
He/she always or almost always required guidance with his/her homework.				27%	29%	38%
He/she enjoys very much the way his/her teacher teaches.				68%	37%	42%
He/she likes the textbook used.				27%	44%	43%
He/she did not have trouble learning.				42%	25%	19%

Source: SEED/NIE, AVA 2000: *Questionário do Aluno.*
Note: * The school did not offer (or had not assessed) this level of education.

The school head teacher says that . . .
During his/her administration, the head teacher dedicated most of his/her time to the organization of the school management structure.
During the general school meetings to which all parents were invited, the educational projects for the different periods of the school year were discussed. On average, parental attendance at these meetings was 75%.
The School Board met every two months.

Source: SEED/NIE, AVA 2000: *Questionário do Escola.*

Sources: Original Portuguese version from Vasconcelos 2003; translation from Winkler and Sevilla 2004.

this type is likely to be useful. There is no one-size-fits-all approach, but in a given situation it is probably useful to separate out the management and planning aspects of the report cards and provide those data to the school through a separate feedback method, as box 2.2 discussed above. This separation would allow the report cards to be simpler and more focused on selected indicators.

The issue with data on stakeholder perceptions is different. Some report-card interventions have included *only* this type of feedback—indeed, the multisectoral "Citizen Report Cards" in Bangalore, India, (as box 2.3 described) included only perceptions and no "factual" data on learning or other school information. Collecting data about perceptions involves the fielding of a survey to representative samples of parents and students at each school, which could be costly and hard to replicate on a regular basis. Of course, collecting information on learning outcomes could be costly as well, but that kind of data gathering is narrowly focused on students in the classroom, can be done in the context of regular classroom activities, and does not require tracking back to the students' households to interview parents.

The apparent success of the Pakistan intervention suggests that the extra EMIS or perception-related information is not necessary to generate impact. The two India cases that included no learning information as a part of the feedback showed mixed results. While it is substantially too soon to draw too many conclusions based on a limited number of cases, this pattern does suggest that careful thought needs to be put into which information should be included in each particular situation. The priority should be on simple indicators that parents care about, that they understand, and that are likely to *motivate* them to action. The indicators are likely to differ depending on the socioeconomic context (in particular, the literacy level of the parents) and the specifics of the education market (recall that Pakistan had a particularly vibrant private sector). Piloting various approaches should precede any scale-up of a report card exercise.

How much "socialization" do the report cards need?

The notion that simply introducing information into a system is sufficient to upset an equilibrium—and lead to a stronger set of accountability relationships—is an attractive one. If such an intervention has an impact, its cost-effectiveness would be large, as box 2.4 discusses.

The studies reviewed here show a big range in the extent to which information was accompanied by additional interventions to ensure that it was being understood and to maximize the chance that it would be acted on. At one extreme is the Uganda case, where it was simply newspaper availability that identified the impact. At the other extreme are the Pakistan and India three-state studies, which had more in-depth, community-based dissemination strategies. Impacts of the campaigns were therefore found at both extremes. While a relatively hands-off approach may work for some situations, the case of Chile suggests that it is not always enough. The comparison between the two India-based studies suggests that, at least for the community mobilization efforts, a more sustained and comprehensive approach might have been necessary. The India three-state intervention involved more frequent visits and provided more subsequent follow-up visits—which seem to have translated into greater impact.

Björkman and Svensson (2007) described an intervention in Uganda that provided information about health service delivery and local health outcomes along with an intensive community mobilization campaign that included the development of action plans. The authors estimated that this approach had a large impact on improving service delivery and reducing infant mortality.

It is likely that there are many settings in developing countries where the current equilibrium is that parents and local stakeholders feel disengaged from the education system (and perhaps disempowered from it). Simply making information available may not be enough to change that status quo—at least in the initial phases of a report card scheme. Complementary activities might include community meetings at which the results of the report cards are described item by item (such as in the Pakistan case). They might also include approaches that ensure that the stakeholders have a framework within which to channel their input into schools (such as in the Ugandan health sector example). More-intensive interventions are likely to be costlier—both in financial and human terms—and less easy to scale up than less-intensive ones—but little is known about the tradeoff between these approaches. Again, piloting alternative approaches within a given setting would be important before large scaling up of activities.

Downsides of Information for Accountability

It is hard to argue against greater access to accurate information. Nevertheless, it is important to keep in mind that the approach has several potential shortcomings. Much of the research on potential downsides has focused on the distortions that strong accountability approaches can engender.

First, they could lead to strong opposition to reform—as discussed in the case of Brazil (Brooke 2005). Second, they could have unintended consequences—many of which undermine the validity of the exercise itself. Strategic behavior on the part of schools undergoing an assessment was found in the Chicago school system when a strong accountability system was introduced—from outright cheating on the part of teachers (Jacob and Levitt 2003) to more subtle effects such as excluding students from the testing; retaining students in grades that were not subject to testing; or reducing the scope of subjects taught, or the curriculum itself, away from nontested subjects (Jacob 2005). While these effects have been documented, Loveless (2005) concludes that the "harms" described to date appear temporary and malleable.

Elite capture is another potential problem with information campaigns that rely on written communication, which is more likely to be understood by educated parents. The India three-state study suggests that the potential for elite capture is real. Moreover, when combined with other interventions, information can have the potential to aggravate inequalities even further. In Chile, vouchers provided to promote school choice, combined with information, facilitated an increase in the stratification of schools—with students of high socioeconomic status going to good schools and students of low socioeconomic status going to the lower-quality schools (Hsieh and Urquiola 2006). Contreras, Flores, and Lobato (2004) argue that the Chilean SNED system exacerbated socioeconomic inequalities—with larger learning gains associated with higher baseline household income and parental education levels.

Yet another potential pitfall of information-for-accountability interventions that rely on test scores relates to measurement issues. Test scores measure a variety of factors. While teachers and schools matter, the role of the innate endowments of students, their socioeconomic backgrounds, and the level of support they receive from their families for education are all important. To the extent that test-score-based campaigns do not take those factors into consideration, they may be misleading. While such variables could be taken into account to some extent—as was done in Chile and Pakistan—the measurement issues related to test scores can be quite problematic. Kane and Staiger (2002) describe the properties of school test score measures and forcefully argue that they are less reliable than commonly recognized. In particular, the small samples underlying average test scores for a grade from a particular school make that average a noisy measure—even (or perhaps especially) if adjusted for previous-year scores or observed characteristics. Mean reversion in test scores—the fact that positive (or negative) school-specific shocks in one year will be reversed in the subsequent year—will lead to misguided interpretation of the role of information based on test scores or the interventions based on them (Chay, McEwan, and Urquiola 2005). Kane and Staiger (2002) argue for the use of test scores averaged over time—an approach available only if there is frequent testing.

Conclusion: Beyond Proof of Concept

Despite the theoretical appeal of information for accountability, the experience to date suggests that it does not offer a silver bullet for solving issues of service delivery. But that is probably too tall an order for any single approach. The evidence to date in developing countries—which is admittedly thin—suggests that information *can* lead to improvements in outcomes. This happened because information promoted effective choice and competition, because it enabled more effective participation in school oversight and management, and because it enabled citizens to hold local governments accountable.

Many questions remain open—for example, on the most effective ways to design information programs, or on the factors that enable or disable impacts on learning outcomes, or on the way to collect and disseminate information. Given the cost-effectiveness of the information-for-accountability approach, research into these areas is likely to be valuable. Priority areas for research include those discussed in this concluding section.

What Is the Best Target Audience—and How Is Information Interpreted?

The cases to date suggest variability in the extent to which target populations "absorb" information that is being disseminated. This variability could occur for various reasons. For example, if the information provided is not additional—in the sense that it merely confirms people's prior beliefs—then one might expect minimal impact. This is consistent with the Chile SNED results, although the study in Pakistan found that the information was instrumental in narrowing the range of opinions about the quality of schools and, in so doing, reduced the "noise" of people's prior perceptions. The issue that deserves more attention, therefore, is the extent to which information is merely confirmatory or whether it alters beliefs in a way that may motivate action.

This is not to say that confirmatory information would not necessarily be value added. One of the hypotheses behind information as an accountability tool is that externally validated performance indicators provide parents and other community stakeholders the basis for lobbying and monitoring schools and local governments. Even merely confirmatory information could still perform this function. The Pakistan study suggests that this may be occurring (as one explanation for the impacts found in public schools), but there are other explanations as well. Understanding more about this potential role of information would provide insights into the channels through which it could improve outcomes.

An additional dimension in the targeting of information campaigns relates to the potential "capture" of the information. One of the general fears about decentralization efforts is that they result in elite capture—the use of the new powers by local populations who have power to further their own objections, sometimes at the expense of the less well-off (Bardhan and

Mookherjee 2000, 2005). Information may have a heterogeneous impact on stimulating choice, participation, or voice in a way that disproportionately benefits the already advantaged, thereby aggravating inequalities.

The results from the studies to date provide contrasting results on that score. The results from the Uganda newspaper campaign showed that the schools with the least political power benefited the most from the new transparency in terms of reduction in leakage (Reinikka and Svensson 2004). On the other hand, the results from the India three-state study showed that the non-Scheduled Caste and non-Scheduled Tribe members of the school oversight committees showed the greatest change as a result of the intervention. Moreover, the impacts found in the latter study were largest in villages with low shares of Scheduled Caste and Scheduled Tribe members in the population—suggesting some degree of elite capture. The extent to which the nature of the information, its packaging, and dissemination strategies might mitigate or exacerbate this effect is something important to find out.

Another way in which the nature of the information and the characteristics of the target population interact is the extent to which information is provided into a setting where education is valued. The low levels of popular engagement and knowledge about VECs documented in the Jaunpur District of Uttar Pradesh attest to a disconnect between the population and the education system. The interventions in India were all aimed at raising that engagement, through awareness and knowledge building. But if the perceived value of education is low—or low relative to the opportunity cost of the time required to participate in school activities, monitor teachers, or organize and lobby governments—then it should not be surprising if information has no impact. Likewise, if people have become conditioned to have low expectations for service delivery and do not believe their actions will change the behavior of providers, they might not be willing to make the effort to bring about that change since it is perceived as futile.

How Does Information Interact with Collective Action?

Some of the rationales for information campaigns depend on the ability of parents and potentially other community members to undertake collective action. Information is an input into processes of participation and voice, which require groups of people to coordinate their actions to influence front-line providers and local governments. But collective action is not automatic and depends, among other things, on the characteristics of the population involved—for example, its heterogeneity.

In addition, the nature of the information and the way it is disseminated matters. Information that enables private action—such as the report cards in Pakistan—might have more impact than information that is geared primarily toward facilitating collective action. In discussing their study results from the Jaunpur District of Uttar Pradesh, India, the authors attributed the impact of the reading classes versus the nonimpact of the information campaigns to this effect (Banerjee and others 2008). The former was a largely private endeavor that provided private benefits, while the latter requires coordination, for which there are large externalities to any individual behavior.

What Information Has the Most Impact?

As described above, the studies so far are quite different in terms of the types of information disseminated. In Chile and Pakistan, the emphasis was on externally validated and verified data on learning outcomes. Both of those studies, however, were quite different from the scorecard approach used in the India examples. In India, villagers were provided with the tools to assess learning levels, but these were meant to be self-assessment tools (that is, not externally validated), with no comparators available or provided. In the Jaunpur District in Uttar Pradesh, India, the self-assessment tool appeared to provide no benefit over and above the information on rights, roles, and responsibilities. In the India three-state study, it was not possible to disentangle these effects. Understanding the importance of the credibility and external validation of information on learning outcomes would be important for policy development.

The different cases have also highlighted alternative ways of presenting information on learning outcomes. In Chile, SNED built on an earlier effort based on "raw" scores (SIMCE) and combined test scores with other indicators, such as the socioeconomic background of the school's students, to determine school performance. In Pakistan, the data were presented raw, with village- and district-level comparators provided to give context.

More generally, the extent to which raw or value-added scores would be the most effective is unknown ("value added" being defined either as over time for the same students, for the same schools, or in terms of performance over and above what is predicted by observed characteristics). While greater sophistication in the way data are manipulated may serve to convey their meaning more accurately, this sophistication must be weighed against the extent to which the target audience understands and interprets the data. The cases to date provide little guidance on how to make this tradeoff.

Is There a Role for Strong Accountability in Developing Countries?

One of the features of the evaluation studies in developing countries is the lack of strong accountability models. All of the approaches rely only on information itself as a tool for accountability rather than on any explicit sanctions or rewards associated with it. The studies of strong accountability in the United States suggest that such measures can have strong impacts on outcomes, albeit with potentially distortionary impacts, as previously discussed. Indeed, Winkler and Sevilla (2004) point to the lack of sanctions and rewards related to performance as one of the salient factors of accountability systems in developing countries.

While no evidence suggests that strong accountability is an appropriate strategy for developing countries (although chapter 4 provides evidence that incentives can affect teacher behavior), the lack of studies suggests that this is a potential area for further research.

What Can Providers Do with the Information, or the Pressure, They Receive?

The extent to which schools can respond to information, to competitive pressures, or to parent participation will determine the extent to which one should expect any impacts. Indeed, if schools have no (or extremely limited) decision-making authority, then it would not be surprising to find limited impact. The Pakistan study showed that *private* schools were the ones most affected by the intervention—either by increasing quality or reducing fees (an option not open to public schools, which are free in Pakistan). One might expect that the ability of schools to realign expenditures and efforts to improve quality would matter in determining the potential for impact. None of the studies to date can shed much light on the extent to which information acts only as a complement to school autonomy (consistent with the choice and participation channels for change) or whether it can be, to some extent, a substitute.

A related issue is that, even if schools have the authority and the ability to make decisions, schools and teachers may not know how to improve quality. School administrators may be resistant to change because they don't know any other way of acting. Teachers may be reluctant to change teaching methods. There is undoubtedly some truth to this—if it were easy to improve quality, it would likely have already happened. But the cases so far suggest that schools, even in these poor settings, were able to make relatively easy adjustments that are associated with improvements in quality. In Pakistan, the effective school day increased by about 30 minutes in initially low-performing private schools. In the India three-state study, teacher attendance and teacher activity conditional on attendance (that is, the likelihood of a teacher being engaged in teaching activities at the time of the unannounced visit) increased substantially in the two states where teacher attendance and activity were initially lowest (Uttar Pradesh and Madhya Pradesh). In Liberia, the explicit teacher training that was overlaid on top of the information intervention yielded dramatic impacts on reading (and measurable impacts on math) ability.

These issues—the extent to which information can feed into decision making at the school level and the degree to which schools know which changes to make—are taken up more explicitly in the next chapter, devoted to the evidence on school-based management.

Notes

1. Another aspect of the use of information not discussed here is the use of information as a tool to stimulate demand. For example, the perceived return to education was low among youth in the Dominican Republic (Jensen 2010). When information about average rates of return was made available to a randomly selected group of youths, they ultimately completed between 0.20 and 0.35 more years of schooling. Other studies of the impact of information about the costs or benefits of education have shown consistent results (Nguyen 2008; Dinkelman and Martinez 2010).
2. Friedman (1955), advocating the use of vouchers to promote money-follows-the-student school choice, is largely credited with framing the notion of school choice as a way to improve outcomes. See Hoxby (2003) for a more recent review of the issues related to school choice in the United States.
3. An example of the impact of oversight is in Jimenez and Sawada (1999), which studied the impact of El Salvador's *Educación con Participación de la Comunidad* (Education with Community Participation, or EDUCO) "community-managed" school program. In that case, student test scores were higher, in part because of greater teacher effort (Sawada 1999).
4. These reports, along with performance tables, can be accessed from http://www.dcsf.gov.uk/performancetables/.
5. See http://www.ero.govt.nz/ for more details.
6. Action plans included activities such as involving parents and older students in tutoring activities, teachers following up more closely with students with difficulties, organizing classrooms into smaller groups, and addressing child labor activities that are incompatible with schooling.
7. In addition to these experiences, EMIS-based report cards have been implemented in Benin, Madagascar, Niger, and Togo more recently. These exercises have aimed at increasing accountability at the school level through public display of the information and by helping management—for example, through the determination of school grants or the prioritization of schools for inspection.
8. Flórez, Chesterfield, and Siri (2006) assessed the impact of CERCA schools by comparing outcomes in these schools to those in "similar" nonparticipating schools. However, the authors were not specific about how this comparison group was selected, nor did they document how similar or dissimilar the groups were in terms of observable (and potentially unobservable) characteristics.
9. These findings are similar to those in Kane and Staiger (2001, 2002) using U.S. data.

10. The authors argue that the potentially confounding fact that teachers in award-winning schools also received a bonus would have relatively small impact on the results. They argue that, if anything, the potential bias would be upward as higher teacher salaries might make schools more attractive to parents. Other analysts have focused on the teacher incentive aspect of the program and argue that this has indeed generated returns in the form of increased test scores (see the discussion in chapter 4 about teacher accountability).
11. Contreras, Flores, and Lobato (2004) evaluated the impact of the SNED teacher bonuses on testing achievement. They showed that there is a positive and significant correlation between winning the award and subsequent student performance. Primary schools that received an award in 2002 had higher math scores in 2004, even after controlling for mothers' schooling and household income and for homogenous group dummies and testing performance in the previous two years for which scores were available. The data suggested similar conclusions for secondary schools.
12. Based on EdStats "Country Trends and Comparisons," available at http://go.worldbank.org/ITABCOGIV1.
13. The evaluation summarized here was a part of a broader effort to "understand how much learning is taking place and to identify what factors determine the quality of the education children receive" (Andrabi, Das, and Khwaja 2009). Details of the broader effort are at http://www.leapsproject.org.
14. The cards in the second year of the program included information based on learning gains between the first and second years.
15. There was an additional protocol for distributing cards to the relatively small share of parents who did not attend the meetings.
16. Districts included in the study were Sitapur, Pratapgargh, Hathras, and Kanpur Dehat in Uttar Pradesh; Dhar, Guna, Katni, and Raisen in Madhya Pradesh; and Bellary, Gulberga, Kolar, and Chikmagalur in Karnataka.
17. The study computes this by using exposure to the intervention as an instrument for class participation in an instrumental variables analysis of the impact of reading clubs.
18. "Score" refers to the percentage of students who can perform a competency correctly.
19. The seven indicators used were letter fluency (per minute), phonemic awareness (of 10), familiar words (per minute), unfamiliar words (per minute), oral reading fluency (per minute), reading comprehension (%), and listening comprehension (%).
20. The nine indicators were number identification, quantity discrimination (per minute), missing number, addition 1 (per minute), addition 2 (per minute), subtraction 1 (per minute), subtraction 2 (per minute), multiplication, and fractions (%).
21. It is possible that the narrow nature of the indicators measured—letter fluency, unfamiliar word decoding—as opposed to a broad-based index contributed to these large effect sizes.
22. Li and others (2010) document how parental communication works as a complement to tutoring in improving learning outcomes in a randomized field experiment in China.

References

Akyeampong, Kwame. 2004. "Whole School Development in Ghana." Background paper for the *Education for All Global Monitoring Report 2005: The Quality Imperative*, UNESCO, New York. http://unesdoc.unesco.org/images/0014/001466/146616e.pdf.

Andrabi, Tahir, Jishnu Das, and Asim Khwaja. 2009. "Report Cards: The Impact of Providing School and Child Test Scores on Educational Markets." Unpublished manuscript, World Bank, Washington, DC.

Banerjee, Abhijit V., Rukmini Banerji, Esther Duflo, Rachel Glennerster, and Stuti Khemani. 2008. "Pitfalls of Participatory Programs: Evidence from a Randomized Evaluation in Education in India." Policy Research Working Paper 4584, World Bank, Washington, DC.

Bardhan, Pranab, and Dilip Mookherjee. 2000. "Capture and Governance at Local and National Levels." *American Economic Review* 90 (2): 135–39.

———. 2002. "Decentralization of Governance and Development." *Journal of Economic Perspectives* 16 (4): 185–205.

———. 2005. "Decentralizing Antipoverty Program Delivery in Developing Countries." *Journal of Public Economics* 89 (4): 675–704.

Bhatnagar, Deepti, Animesh Rathore, Magüi Moreno Torres, and Parameeta Kanungo. 2003. "Empowerment Case Studies: The Filipino Report Card on Pro-Poor Services." Case study commissioned by the World Bank, Washington, DC. http://siteresources.worldbank.org/INTEMPOWERMENT/Resources/14875_FilipinoReportCard-web.pdf.

Björkman, Martina. 2006. "Does Money Matter for Student Performance? Evidence from a Grant Program in Uganda." Working Paper 326, Institute for International Economic Studies (IIES), Stockholm University, Sweden.

Björkman, Martina, Ritva Reinikka, and Jakob Svensson. 2006. "Local Accountability." Seminar Paper 749, IIES, Stockholm University, Sweden.

Björkman, Martina, and Jakob Svensson. 2007. "Power to the People: Evidence from a Randomized Field Experiment of a Community-Based Monitoring Project in Uganda." Policy Research Working Paper 4289, World Bank, Washington, DC.

Bradley, Steve, Robert Crouchley, Jim Millington, and Jim Taylor. 2000. "Testing for Quasi-Market Forces in Secondary Education." *Oxford Bulletin of Economics and Statistics* 62 (3): 357–90.

Brooke, Nigel. 2005. "Accountability educacional en Brasil, una vision general." Document 34, Partnership for Educational Revitalization in the Americas (PREAL), Santiago, Chile.

Bures, Laura. 2003. "Empowerment and Poverty Reduction: A Sourcebook." PREM Tools and Practices 16, World Bank, Washington, DC. http://siteresources.worldbank.org/INTEMPOWERMENT/Resources/486312-1098123240580/tool16.pdf.

Burgess, Simon, Carol Propper, Helen Slater, and Deborah Wilson. 2005. "Who Wins and Who Loses from School Accountability? The Distribution of Educational Gain in English Secondary Schools." Centre for Market and Public Organization Working Paper Series 05/128, University of Bristol, England.

Cameron, Laurie, Kurt Moses, and John Gillies. 2006. "School Report Cards: Some Recent Experiences." EQUIP2 Policy Brief, U.S. Agency for International Development. Washington, DC. http://www.equip123.net/docs/e2-ReportCards_WP.pdf.

Carnoy, Martin, and Susana Loeb. 2002. "Does External Accountability Affect Student Outcomes? A Cross-State Analysis." *Educational Evaluation and Policy Analysis*. 24 (4): 305–31.

Chakrabarti, Rajashri. 2006. "Vouchers, Public School Response and the Role of Incentives: Evidence from Florida." Working paper, Federal Reserve Bank of New York.

Chay, Kenneth Y., Patrick J. McEwan, and Miguel Urquiola. 2005. "The Central Role of Noise in Evaluating Interventions that Use Test Scores to Rank Schools." *The American Economic Review* 95 (4): 1237–58.

Clark, Melissa. 2003. "Education Reform, Redistribution, and Student Achievement: Evidence from The Kentucky Education Reform Act." PhD dissertation chapter, Economics Department, Princeton University.

Contreras, Dante, Lorena Flores, and Felix Lobato. 2004. "Monetary Incentives for Teachers and School Performance: Evidence for Chile." Unpublished manuscript, Universidad de Chile, Santiago.

Dedu, Gabriel, and Gibwa Kajubi. 2005. "The Community Score Card Process in Gambia." Participatory and Civic Engagement Social Development Note 100, World Bank, Washington, DC.

Dee, Thomas, and Brian Jacob. 2009. "The Impact of No Child Left Behind on Student Achievement." National Bureau of Economic Research Working Paper 15531, NBER, Cambridge, MA. http://www.nber.org/papers/w15531.pdf.

Dinkelman, Taryn, and Claudia Martinez. 2010. "Investing in (Secondary) Schooling in Chile." Unpublished manuscript, Princeton University and Universidad de Chile.

EdStats (database). World Bank, Washington, DC. http://go.worldbank.org/ITABCOGIV1.

ERO (Education Review Office). 2007. "The Collection and Use of Assessment Information in Schools." ERO, New Zealand. http://www.ero.govt.nz.

Figlio, David, and Cecilia Rouse. 2006. "Do Accountability and Voucher Threats Improve Low-Performing Schools?" *Journal of Public Economics* 90 (1–2): 239–55.

Flórez, Ana, Ray Chesterfield, and Carmen Siri. 2006. "The CERCA School Report Card: Communities Creating Education Quality. Final Report." Academy for Education Development, Global Education Center, Washington, DC.

Friedman, Milton. 1955. "The Role of Government in Education." In *Economics and the Public Interest*, ed. R. A. Solo. Piscataway, NJ: Rutgers University Press.

Gillies, John. 2004. "Strengthening Accountability and Participation: School Self-Assessment in Namibia." EQUIP2 Policy Brief. U.S. Agency for International Development, Washington, DC. http://www.equip123.net/docs/e2-AcctParticipation_Policy%20Brief.pdf.

Glewwe, Paul, and Michael Kremer. 2006. "Schools, Teachers, and Education Outcomes in Developing Countries." In *Handbook of the Economics of Education, Vol. 2*, ed. Eric A. Hanushek and Finis Welch, 946–1017. Amsterdam: North Holland.

Goldstein, Harvey. 2001. "Using Pupil Performance Data for Judging Schools and Teachers: Scope and Limitations." *British Educational Research Journal* 27 (4): 433–42.

Hamilton, Laura, and Daniel Koretz. 2002. "Tests and Their Use in Test-Based Accountability Systems." In *Making Sense of Test-Based Accountability in Education,* ed. Laura Hamilton, Brian Stecher, and Stephen Klein, 13–49. Santa Monica, CA: RAND.

Haney, Walt. 2000. "The Myth of the Texas Miracle in Education." *Education Policy Analysis Archives* 8 (41).

———. 2002. "Lake Woebeguaranteed: Misuse of Test Scores in Massachusetts, Part I." *Education Policy Analysis Archives* 10 (24).

Hanushek, Eric, and Margaret Raymond. 2003. "Lessons about the Design of State Accountability Systems." In *No Child Left Behind? The Politics and Practice of Accountability,* ed. Paul Peterson and Martin West, 127–51. Washington, DC: Brookings Institution Press.

———. 2005. "Does School Accountability Lead to Improved Student Performance?" *Journal of Policy Analysis and Management* 24 (2): 297–327.

Hastings, Justine S., and Jeffrey M. Weinstein. 2008. "Information, School Choice and Academic Achievement: Evidence from Two Experiments." *The Quarterly Journal of Economics* 123 (4): 1373–1414.

Hoxby, Caroline. 2001. "Testing Is about Openness and Openness Works." *Hoover Daily Report,* July 30. http://www.hoover.org/news/daily-report/24960.

———. 2002. "The Cost of Accountability." National Bureau of Economic Research Working Paper 8855, NBER, Cambridge, MA.

———. 2003. *The Economics of School Choice.* Chicago: University of Chicago Press.

Hsieh, Chang Tai, and Miguel Urquiola. 2006. "The Effects of Generalized School Choice on Achievement and Stratification: Evidence from Chile's School Voucher Program." *Journal of Public Economics* 90 (8–9): 1477–1503.

Jacob, Brian. 2005. "Accountability, Incentives and Behavior: The Impact of High-Stakes Testing in the Chicago Public Schools." *Journal of Public Economics* 89 (5–6): 761–96.

Jacob, Brian, and Steven D. Levitt. 2003. "Rotten Apples: An Investigation of the Prevalence and Predictors of Teacher Cheating." *The Quarterly Journal of Economics* 118 (3): 843–77.

Jenkins, Rob, and Anne Marie Goetz. 1999. "Accounts and Accountability: Theoretical Implications of the Right-to-Information Movement in India." *Third World Quarterly* 20 (3): 603–22.

Jensen, Robert. 2010. "The (Perceived) Returns to Education and the Demand for Schooling." *The Quarterly Journal of Economics* 125 (2): 515–48.

Jimenez, Emmanuel, and Yasuyuki Sawada. 1999. "Do Community-Managed Schools Work? An Evaluation of El Salvador's EDUCO Program." *World Bank Economic Review* 13 (3): 415–41.

Kane, Thomas, and Douglas Staiger. 2001. "Improving School Accountability Measures." National Bureau of Economic Research Working Paper 8156, NBER, Cambridge, MA.

———. 2002. "The Promise and Pitfalls of Using Imprecise School Accountability Measures." *Journal of Economic Perspectives* 16 (4): 91–114.

Karim, Shahnaz. 2004. "Transparency in Education: Report Card in Bangladesh." International Institute for Education Planning Report, UNESCO, Paris.

Keefer, Philip, and Stuti Khemani. 2005. "Democracy, Public Expenditures, and the Poor: Understanding Political Incentives for Providing Public Services." *World Bank Research Observer* 20 (1): 1–28.

Khemani, Stuti. 2007. "Can Information Campaigns Overcome Political Obstacles to Serving the Poor?" In *The Politics of Service Delivery in Democracies: Better Access for the Poor*, ed. Shantayanan Devarajan and Ingrid Widlund. Stockholm: Expert Group on Development Issues Secretariat, Ministry for Foreign Affairs. http://citeseerx.ist.psu.edu/viewdoc/download?doi=10.1.1.133.7367&rep=rep1&type=pdf.

King, Elizabeth M., and Jere R. Behrman. 2009. "Timing and Duration of Exposure in Evaluations of Social Programs." *World Bank Research Observer* 24 (1): 55–82.

Koretz, Daniel. 2002. "Limitations in the Use of Achievement Tests as Measures of Educators' Productivity." In *Designing Incentives to Promote Human Capital*, ed. Eric Hanushek, James Heckman, and Derek Neal. Special issue of *The Journal of Human Resources* 37 (4): 752–77.

Kremer, Michael, Nazmul Chaudhury, F. Halsey Rogers, Karthik Muralidharan, and Jeffrey Hammer. 2005. "Teacher Absence in India: A Snapshot." *Journal of the European Economic Association* 3 (2–3): 658–67.

Ladd, Helen F., and Edward B. Fiske. 2003. "Does Competition Improve Teaching and Learning? Evidence from New Zealand." *Educational Evaluation and Policy Analysis* 25 (1): 97–112.

Lassibille, Gérard, Jee-Peng Tan, Cornelia Jesse, and Trang Van Nguyen. 2010. "Managing for Results in Primary Education in Madagascar: Evaluating the Impact of Selected Workflow Interventions." *World Bank Economic Review* 24 (2): 303–29.

Leung, Grace. 2005. "Textbook Count and Civil Society Participation: Effecting System Reforms in the Department of Education." Government Watch and Ateneo School of Governance Policy Report, Makati, Philippines.

Li, Tao, Li Han, Scott Rozelle, and Linxiu Zhang. 2010. "Cash Incentives, Peer Tutoring, and Parental Involvement: A Study of Three Educational Inputs in a Randomized Field Experiment in China." Unpublished manuscript, Peking University, China. http://mitsloan.mit.edu/neudc/papers/paper_223.pdf.

Loveless, Tom. 2005. "Test-Based Accountability: The Promise and the Perils." *Brookings Papers on Education Policy* (2005): 7–45.

Majumdar, Sumon, Anandi Mani, and Sharun Mukand. 2004. "Politics, Information and the Urban Bias." *Journal of Development Economics* 75 (1): 137–65.

Malena, Carmen, Reiner Forster, and Janmejay Singh. 2004. "Social Accountability: An Introduction to the Concept and Emerging Practice." Social Development Paper 76, World Bank, Washington, DC.

Mizala, Alejandra, Pilar Romaguera, and Miguel Urquiola. 2007. "Socioeconomic Status or Noise? Tradeoffs in the Generation of School Quality Information." *Journal of Development Economics* 84: 61–75.

Mizala, Alejandra, and Miguel Urquiola. 2007. "School Markets: The Impact of Information Approximating Schools' Effectiveness." National Bureau of Economic Research Working Paper 13676, NBER, Cambridge, MA.

Muralidharan, Karthik, and Venkatesh Sundararaman. 2010. "The Impact of Diagnostic Feedback to Teachers on Student Learning: Experimental Evidence from India." *The Economic Journal* 120 (546): F187–F203.

Nguyen, Trang. 2008. "Information, Role Models and Perceived Returns to Education: Experimental Evidence from Madagascar." Massachusetts Institute of Technology Working Paper, MIT, Cambridge, MA.

Ortega, Tamara. 2006. "Using Report Cards to Promote Better Education Policy in Latin America. PREAL's Experience." Paper prepared for the "Latin America and the Caribbean: Lessons from Best Practices in Promoting Education for All" joint Inter-American Development Bank and World Bank conference, Cartagena de Indias, Colombia, October 9–11.

Pandey, Priyanka, Sangeeta Goyal, and Venkatesh Sundararaman. 2009. "Community Participation in Public Schools: Impact of Information Campaigns in Three Indian States." *Education Economics* 17 (3): 355–75.

———. 2010. "Community Participation in Public Schools: Impact of Information Campaigns in Three Indian States." Draft. World Bank, Washington, DC.

Paul, Samuel. 2002. *Holding the State to Account: Citizen Monitoring in Action.* Bangalore, India: Books for Change.

Piper, Benjamin, and Medina Korda. 2010. "EGRA Plus: Liberia." Program Evaluation Report draft, RTI International, Research Triangle Park, NC.

Porta Pallais, Emilio, and Jennifer Klein. 2010. "Increasing Education Data Availability for Knowledge Generation." Background paper for the Education Sector Strategy, Human Development Network, World Bank, Washington, DC.

Raymond, Margaret E., and Eric A. Hanushek. 2003. "High-Stakes Research." *Education Next* 3 (3). http://educationnext.org/highstakes-research/.

Reinikka, Ritva, and Jakob Svensson. 2004. "Local Capture: Evidence from a Central Government Transfer Program in Uganda." *The Quarterly Journal of Economics* 119 (2): 679–705.

———. 2005. "Fighting Corruption to Improve Schooling: Evidence from a Newspaper Campaign in Uganda." *Journal of the European Economic Association* 3 (2–3): 259–67.

———. 2006. "The Power of Information: Evidence from a Newspaper Campaign to Reduce Capture of Public Funds." Unpublished manuscript, Institute for International Economic Studies, Stockholm, Sweden; World Bank, Washington, DC. http://people.su.se/~jsven/information2006a.pdf.

Reinikka, Ritva, Jakob Svensson, and Carolyn Winter. 2006. "South Africa. Citizen Report Cards to Improve Service Delivery." Document prepared for the "Monitoring and Impact Evaluation Conference" by the Presidency and the World Bank, June 19–23.

Ross, Kenneth. 2006. "SACMEQ—From Project to Development Model." *International Institute for Educational Planning Newsletter* (January–March), UNESCO, Paris. http://www.unesco.org/iiep/eng/newsletter/2006/jane06.pdf.

Rouse Cecilia, Jane Hannaway, Dan Goldhaber, and David Figlio. 2007. "Feeling the Florida Heat? How Low-Performing Schools Respond to Voucher and Accountability Pressure." National Bureau of Economic Research Working Paper 13681, NBER, Cambridge, MA.

Sawada, Yasuyuki. 1999. "Community Participation, Teacher Effort, and Educational Outcome: The Case of El Salvador's EDUCO Program." Working Paper 307, William Davidson Institute, University of Michigan, Ann Arbor. http://wdi.umich.edu/files/publications/workingpapers/wp307.pdf.

Tymms, Peter, and Carol Fitz-Gibbon. 2001. "Standards, Achievements and Educational Performance: A Cause for Celebration?" In *Education, Reform and the State: Twenty-five Years of Politics, Policy and Practice*, ed. Robert Phillips and John Furlong, 156–73. London: Routledge.

United Kingdom. 2005. "14–19 Education and Skills." White Paper presented to Parliament by the Secretary of State for Education and Skills by Command of Her Majesty, February 2005. http://news.bbc.co.uk/nol/shared/bsp/hi/pdfs/23_02_05_1419whitepaper.pdf.

van der Linden, Geert. 2007. "Philippines—Textbook Count 3: Project Completion Assessment." Assessment note by the Partnership for Transparency Fund for Government Watch, Manila, Philippines. http://www.partnershipfortransparency.info/uploads/project%20assessment%20reports/Philippines%20G-Watch%20TextBkCount2PCA26jan07%20inc%20appendices.doc.

Vasconcelos, Alcyon. 2003. "Education Management by Results." Presentation to the Human Development Forum. World Bank. Washington, DC, November. http://www1.worldbank.org/publicsector/decentralization/HDForum/BdaEDC.ppt.

Waglé, Swarmin, Janmejay Singh, and Parmesh Shah. 2004. "Citizen Report Card Surveys—A Note on Concept and Methodology." Social Development Note 91, World Bank, Washington, DC. http://siteresources.worldbank.org/INTPCENG/1143380-1116506267488/20511066/reportcardnote.pdf.

West, Martin, and Paul Peterson. 2006. "The Efficacy of Choice Threats within School Accountability Systems: Results from Legislatively Induced Experiments." *The Economic Journal* 116: C46–C62.

Wiley, Cathy. 1999. "Ten Years On: How Schools View Educational Reform." Report on 1999 survey, New Zealand Council for Educational Research, Wellington, New Zealand. http://www.nzcer.org.nz/default.php?products_id=247.

Winkler, Donald. 2005. "Increasing Accountability in Education in Paraná State, Brazil." EQUIP2 Policy Brief, U.S. Agency for International Development, Washington, DC. http://www.equip123.net/docs/e2-Increasing%20Accountability%20in%20Parana_PB.pdf.

Winkler, Donald, and Jon Herstein. 2005. "Information Use and Decentralized Education." EQUIP2 Policy Brief, U.S. Agency for International Development, Washington, DC. http://www.equip123.net/docs/e2-Information%20Use_PB.pdf.

Winkler, Donald, and Maribel Sevilla. 2004. "Report Cards and Accountability in Decentralized Education Systems." EQUIP2 Policy Brief, U.S. Agency for International Development, Washington, DC. http://pdf.dec.org/pdf_docs/PNADA604.pdf.

World Bank. 2003. *World Development Report 2004: Making Services Work for Poor People.* New York: Oxford University Press.

3

School-Based Management

Good education is not only about physical inputs such as classrooms, teachers, and textbooks, but also about incentives that lead to better instruction and learning. Education systems are extremely demanding of the managerial, technical, and financial capacity of governments, and thus, as a service, education is too complex to be efficiently produced and distributed in a centralized fashion (King and Cordeiro-Guerra 2005).

Hanushek and Woessmann (2007) suggest that most of the incentives that affect learning outcomes are institutional in nature. They identify three in particular:

- *Choice and competition*. When parents who are interested in maximizing their children's learning outcomes can choose to send their children to the most productive schools they can find (in terms of academic results), this demand-side pressure will give all schools an incentive to improve their performance if they want to compete for students.
- *School autonomy*. Similarly, local decision making and fiscal decentralization can have positive effects on outcomes such as test scores or graduation rates by holding the schools accountable for the "outputs" they produce.
- *School accountability*. Quality and timely service provision can be ensured if service providers can be held accountable to their *clients* (in the case of education, students, and their parents).

The increasing decentralization in education includes trends toward increasing autonomy, devolving responsibility, and encouraging responsiveness to local needs—all with the objective of raising performance levels—across Organisation for Economic Co-operation and Development (OECD) countries (OECD 2004). Most countries whose students perform well in international student achievement tests give their local authorities and schools substantial autonomy over adapting and implementing education content and allocating and managing resources. With a few exceptions, most students in OECD countries are enrolled in schools where teachers and stakeholders play a role in deciding which courses are offered and how money is spent within the schools. Moreover, greater school autonomy is not necessarily associated with wider disparities in school performance among schools if governments provide a framework in which poorer-performing schools receive the necessary support to help them improve. In fact, Finland and Sweden—which are among those countries with the highest degree of school autonomy on many Programme for International Student Assessment (PISA) measures—have (together with Iceland) the smallest performance differences among schools (OECD 2004).

Decentralization in School-Based Management

School-based management (SBM) is a form of decentralization. There are four sources of authority: central government; provincial, state, or regional governing bodies; municipal, county, or district governments; and schools (McGinn and Welsh 1999). Decentralization can occur from central government to lower levels of government or from lower-level government to schools. There are other names for this concept, but they all refer to the decentralization of authority from the central government to the school level (Barrera-Osorio, Fasih, and Patrinos 2009; Caldwell 2005).

In SBM, responsibility for, and decision-making authority over, school operations is transferred to local agents, which can be a combination of principals, teachers, parents, sometimes students, and other school community members. An increasing number of developing countries are introducing SBM reforms aimed at empowering principals and teachers or strengthening their professional motivation, thereby enhancing their sense of ownership of the school. Many of these reforms have also strengthened parental involvement in the schools, sometimes by means of school councils.

SBM usually works through a school committee (or a school council or school management committee) that may

- monitor the school's performance in, for instance, test scores or teacher and student attendance;
- raise funds and create endowments for the school;

- appoint, suspend, dismiss, and remove teachers and ensure that teachers' salaries are paid regularly; and
- approve (albeit rarely) annual budgets, including the development budget, and examine monthly financial statements.

Several initiatives seek to strengthen parents' involvement in school management through their involvement in the school committee. Parents participate voluntarily and take on various responsibilities, ranging from the assessment of student learning to financial management. In some cases, parents are directly involved in the school's management by being custodians of the funds received and verifying the purchases and contracts made by the school. Other times, school committees are also required to develop some sort of school improvement plan.

There are many different forms of SBM in terms of who has the power to make decisions as well as the degree of decision making devolved to the school level. In general, SBM programs devolve authority over one or more activities, such as

- Budget allocations
- Hiring and firing of teachers and other school staff
- Curriculum development
- Procurement of textbooks and other education material
- Infrastructure improvement
- Monitoring and evaluation of teacher performance and student learning outcomes.

As a strategy, SBM aims to improve the financing and delivery of education services and quality. It encourages demand and ensures that schools reflect local priorities and values. By giving a voice and decision-making power to local stakeholders who know more about the local education systems than central policy makers do, SBM can improve education outcomes and increase client satisfaction. SBM emphasizes the individual school (as represented by any combination of principals, teachers, parents, students, and other members of the school community) as the primary unit for improving education and focuses on the redistribution of decision-making authority over school operations as the primary means by which this improvement can be stimulated and sustained.

The potential benefits of SBM may include the following:

- More input and resources from parents (whether in cash or in-kind)
- More effective use of resources

- A higher quality of education through more efficient and transparent use of resources
- A more open and welcoming school environment
- Increased participation of all local stakeholders in decision-making processes
- Improved student performance (lower repetition and dropout rates and higher test scores).

Toward a Theory of School-Based Management

SBM is used to increase school autonomy and accountability, which can help solve some of the most fundamental problems in schools. Accordingly, while increasing resource flows and other support to the education sector is necessary to give the poor greater access to quality education, it is by no means sufficient. It is also necessary to translate these resources into basic services that are accessible to the poor. Therefore, under SBM, schools are given some autonomy over the use of their inputs and are held accountable for using these inputs efficiently.

The theoretical literature that promotes the use of SBM recommends four tenets for improving service delivery to the poor: increasing choice and participation, giving citizens a stronger voice, making information about school performance widely available, and strengthening the rewards to schools for delivering effective services to the poor and penalizing those who fail to deliver.

Framework for Accountability

The framework for analyzing the provision of education services defines four aspects of accountability:

- *Voice*: how citizens hold politicians and policy makers accountable
- *Compact*: how public education policy is communicated
- *Management*: how to produce effective best providers within organizations
- *Client power*: how citizens as clients increase accountability of schools and systems.

Effective solutions are likely to involve a mixture of voice, choice, direct participation, and organizational command and control. Figure 3.1 presents the *World Development Report 2004* framework as a three-cornered relationship between citizens, politicians, and service providers (World Bank 2003).

Figure 3.1 The Accountability Framework in School-Based Management

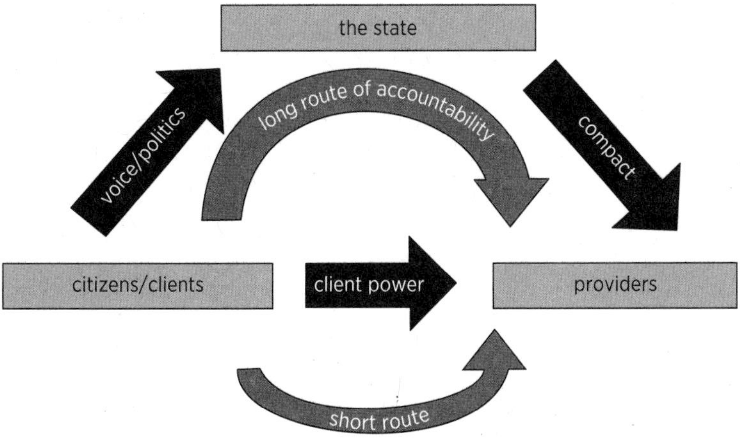

Source: World Bank 2003.

The service provision and accountability relationships among these actors are complex. Even within each group of actors, there are usually heterogeneous subgroups, and the incentives and accountability relationships that work for one group may be different from those that work for other groups.

Long and Short Routes of Accountability

Theoretically, SBM models encompass all four aspects of accountability. "Compact" refers to the *long route of accountability*, whereby the central government delegates responsibility to the line ministries, who in turn delegate it to schools to perform various tasks. In this sense, in certain models of SBM, the accountability of school principals is upward, to the ministry that holds them responsible for providing the services to the *clients*—who, in turn, have put the policy makers in power and thus have the *voice* to hold the policy makers and politicians accountable for their performance.

In most cases of SBM, the *management* mechanisms change under SBM reforms; that is, the clients themselves become part of the management along with the front-line providers. Thus, the *short route of accountability* becomes even shorter as representatives of the *clients*—either parents or community members—get the authority to make certain decisions and have a *voice* in decisions that directly affect the students who attend the school. In the framework presented in figure 3.1, the school managers (whether the principal alone or a committee of parents and teachers) act as the accountable entity.

When accountability fails, the failure can be tracked either to the long route or to the short route. Sometimes improving the long route is a long-term process and, in some situations, may not be doable. In these cases, strengthening the short route can hold service providers directly accountable to the citizens or clients. The clients can improve service delivery by (1) using their voice to ensure that services are tailored to meet their needs and (2) monitoring the providers. In cases where short-route improvements are already being tested or where society is amenable to long-route improvements, these tactics should be adopted.

Autonomy and Participation

SBM programs are far from uniform and encompass a wide variety of different approaches. As the definition of SBM reflects, it is a form of decentralization that makes the school the centerpiece of education improvement and relies on the redistribution of responsibilities as the primary way to bring about these improvements. This definition leaves plenty of room for interpretation, and the reality is that many different kinds of SBM are now being implemented. SBM reforms are shaped by the reformers' objectives and by broader national policy and social contexts. SBM approaches differ in two main dimensions: the "what" (the degree of autonomy that is devolved) and the "who" (to whom the decision-making authority is devolved).

The SBM programs lie along a continuum of the degree to which decision making is devolved to the local level—from limited autonomy, to more ambitious programs that allow schools to hire and fire teachers, to programs that give schools control over substantial resources, to programs that promote private and community management of schools, to programs that may eventually allow parents to create their own schools.

The other dimension is who gets the decision-making power when it is devolved to the school level. In a simple world, the following four models would be sufficient to define who is invested with decision-making power in any SBM reform (Leithwood and Menzies 1998):

- *Administrative control.* SBM devolves authority to the school principal. This model aims to make each school more accountable to the central district or board office. The benefits of this kind of SBM include increasing the efficiency of expenditures on personnel and curriculum and making one person at each school more accountable to the central authority.
- *Professional control.* SBM devolves the main decision-making authority to teachers. This model aims to make better use of teachers' knowledge of

what the school needs at the classroom level. Participating fully in the decision-making process can also motivate teachers to perform better and can lead to greater efficiency and effectiveness in teaching.

- *Community control.* SBM devolves the main decision-making authority to parents or the community. Under this model, teachers and principals are assumed to become more responsive to parents' needs. Another benefit is that the curriculum can reflect local needs and preferences.
- *Balanced control.* SBM balances decision-making authority between parents and teachers, who are the two main stakeholders in any school. It aims to take advantage of teachers' detailed knowledge of the school to improve school management and to make schools more accountable to parents.

Existing models of SBM around the world are generally a blend of these four models. In most cases, power is devolved to a formal legal entity in the form of a school council committee, which consists of teachers and the principal. The administrative control model can never exist in its pure form because principals can never operate on their own in practice. Principals need other people to work for them and to help them to make decisions for the school.

In nearly all versions of SBM, community representatives also serve on the committee. As a result, school personnel can get to know the local people to whom they are ultimately accountable and are thus more likely to take local needs and wishes into account when making decisions, in the knowledge that local residents can monitor what the school professionals are doing. Although community involvement can improve program planning and implementation in these ways, occasionally school personnel involve community members only superficially in a way that does not complicate the lives of principals and teachers (Cook 2007). Parents and community members have roles to play in SBM, but these roles are not universally clear and not always central. In some cases, the legal entity that has the main authority to implement SBM is a parents' council, although it cannot operate successfully without the support of the teachers and the principal.

The autonomy-participation nexus defines the essence of an SBM reform. Figure 3.2 illustrates where a few of the more popular SBM reforms around the world fall within this nexus.

Adding Accountability

There is another link to the autonomy-participation chain: accountability. In a number of countries, as shown in table 3.1, the main objectives of

Figure 3.2 The Autonomy-Participation Nexus, Selected SBM Programs

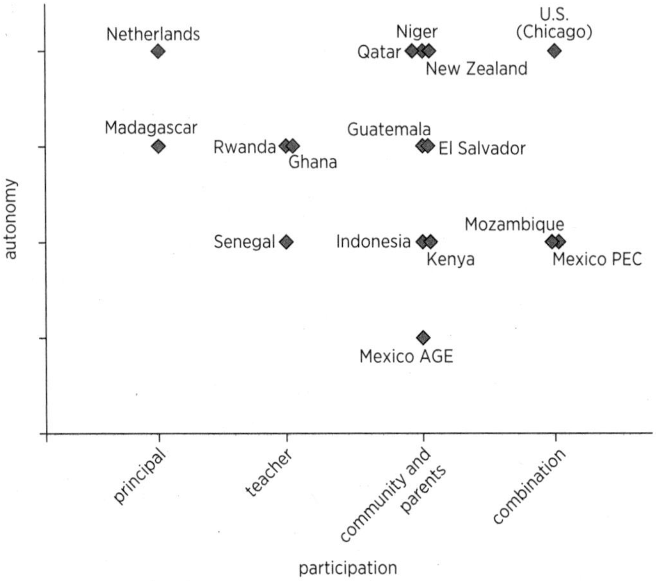

Source: Barrera-Osorio, Fasih, and Patrinos 2009.

Note: SBM = school-based management. AGE = *Apoyo a la Gestión Escolar* (Support to School Management Program). PEC = *Programa Escuelas de Calidad* (Quality Schools Program).

introducing SBM include making schools more accountable and their management more transparent.

Anderson (2005) has suggested that there are three types of accountability in SBM—that is, that those who run schools must be

- accountable for adhering to rules and accountable to the education authorities;
- accountable for adhering to standards and accountable to their peers; and
- accountable for student learning and accountable to the general public.

SBM programs both strengthen and simplify these types of accountability by empowering those at the school level to make decisions collectively, thus increasing the transparency of the process. Consequently, students' learning achievement and other outcomes can be expected to improve because stakeholders at the school level can monitor school personnel, improve student evaluations, ensure a closer match between school needs and policies, and use resources more efficiently. Thus, by its very nature,

Table 3.1 School-Based Management Reforms in Selected Countries

Country	Year first implemented	Reform objectives, motivation	SBM type[a]
Brazil	1982	Increase efficiency, participation	intermediate
Cambodia	1998	Improve education	intermediate
El Salvador	1991	Increase access, participation; improve quality of schooling	strong
Gambia, The	2008	Increase quality, awareness, coordination among stakeholders	intermediate
Guatemala	1996	Increase access; decentralize decision making, participation	strong
Honduras	1999	Increase access in rural areas; encourage participation	strong
Indonesia	2005	Increase accountability to parents; enhance role of councils	intermediate
Kenya	2003	Increase accountability through incentives and management	intermediate
Madagascar	2005	Improve education	intermediate
Mexico	1996	Increase parental participation in rural schools	weak
Mozambique	1997	Improve quality through decentralized management	weak
Nicaragua	1991	Increase participation, resources; increase efficiency	strong
Rwanda	2005	Hire contract teachers; increase involvement of PTAs	intermediate
Senegal	2008	Improve teacher training	intermediate
Thailand	1997	Improve quality of schooling; increase competitiveness	intermediate

Source: Authors' compilation; Gamage and Sooksomchitra 2004.

Note: SBM = school-based management.

a. "SBM type" is classified as strong, intermediate, or weak. "Strong": Almost full control of schools by councils, parents, and school administrators (including full choice through creation of new public schools) or high degree of autonomy given to councils over staffing and budgets. "Intermediate": Councils have authority to set curricula but limited autonomy regarding resources. "Weak": School councils established but serve mainly in an advisory role.

SBM has the potential to hold school-level decision makers accountable for their actions. However, in many countries, it may be necessary to build the capacity of community members, teachers, and principals to create or augment a culture of accountability.

SBM Results Chain

Four policy instruments can be used to link increased autonomy and standardized financing with changes in the behaviors of stakeholders and processes at the local level (intermediate outcomes) toward making decisions that eventually lead to improved quality of learning. The four policy instruments are

- *Increased understanding of the rules of the game* by which *all* stakeholders (central, local, and school-level) participate and interact in the education system
- *Incentives for high performance* at the school-level and *consequences* for schools that are noncompliant with rules and regulations
- *Strong assessment tools* for local policy makers and school principals to evaluate value added and manage learning outcomes
- *Formal channels of participation for parents and community members* (school committees) to support the processes of decision making at the school.

There are different ways in which SBM may translate into behavior and process changes among stakeholders at the school level (Barrera-Osorio, Fasih, and Patrinos 2009). Changes in the behavior of stakeholders and processes at the local and school levels are denominated as intermediate outcomes (listed in table 3.2) because they are the channels by which policies at the national level can be translated into better learning outcomes and cost-effective financial management. A way to determine whether national policies result in changes at the local level is to track the following:

- Participation of stakeholders in certain areas of decision making
- Changes in decisions made by the stakeholder to whom responsibility is devolved
- Frequency of decisions made.

The decisions regarding school management (by the responsible stakeholder) and the frequency with which these are taken can be tracked as follows:

- *Key decisions about personnel.* Which aspects of hiring, firing, rotation time, and teacher training have been devolved to the school level? Who makes

Table 3.2 Intermediate Outcomes from SBM Reforms

Outcome	Principal	Committee
Decisions about personnel (hiring, firing, rotation time, teacher training)	X	
Key decisions about spending	X	
Changes in the education process	X	
Resource mobilization	X	
Channels of direct involvement		X
Links between parental involvement and decisions at the school		X
Changes in accounting		X
Changes in school climate		X

Source: Adapted from Barrera-Osorio, Fasih, and Patrinos 2009.

Note: SBM = school-based management.

these decisions, and how frequently are they made? And how do parents influence these decisions?

- *Key decisions about spending.* Which stakeholders make decisions about expenditures in infrastructure, administration, and staff? How do parents and the community influence budget allocations? And how frequently are decisions made in this area?
- *Changes in the education process.* What changes have occurred in education methods, allocation of teacher's time in the classroom and in administrative tasks, absenteeism rates, and meetings with parents?
- *Resource mobilization.* What is the flow of private donations and grants resulting from active engagement of the school principal and parents?

How SBM policies promote active involvement of parents and communities (through school councils) in school decisions and the extent to which they influence outcomes can be tracked by following these channels and outcomes through the flow illustrated in figure 3.3:

- *Channels of direct involvement of parents and community in the school.* Determine the type of formal mechanisms that enable school councils to participate in school decisions, the frequency of the meetings, and the issues discussed.
- *Links between parental involvement and decisions at the school level.* Uncover the extent to which parental suggestions or complaints voiced through school councils are translated into actual decisions.

Figure 3.3 From School-Based Management to Measurable Results

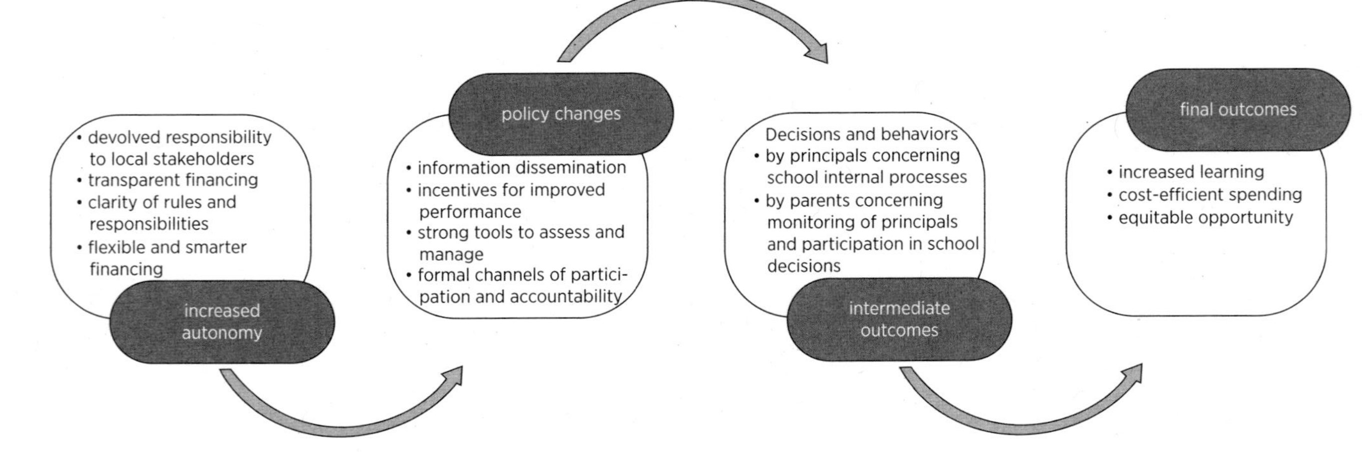

Source: World Bank 2010b.

- *Changes in accounting.* Ascertain the extent to which increased parental participation translates into more transparent and enhanced information systems that track students' academic progress and the use of financial resources.
- *Changes in school climate.* Track the extent to which increased parental involvement influences the attitudes of teachers and students positively or negatively.

Increased autonomy at the school level translates into greater efficiency based on the idea that those who work at the school level and are involved in the day-to-day operation of the school have greater knowledge and management control of the needs of the school and therefore have a better ability to make decisions that are productive in terms of academic results and efficient spending (Barrera-Osorio, Fasih, and Patrinos 2009). The idea behind involving parents and community members in decisions at the school level is that the parents of children enrolled in the school have the ability to improve their children's education and that this demand pressure is likely to drive improvements in student achievement. Also, this demand pressure ensures that the unique needs of the local community are addressed by the school—for example, by meeting the particular learning needs of minority groups.

Several instruments exist to measure change (Bauer 1997; Bauer, Bogotch, and Park 1998). However, the instruments and the scale of measurement are difficult to put into practice. For instance, several of the proposed measures are perceptions, which are subjective and difficult to compare. Some indicators by which to measure internal changes in SBM schools are described in table 3.3. When inputs inside the school (what the literature refers to as "inside the black box") change, education outcomes can change as well.

Influential Practices from High-Income Countries

Experience in high-income countries suggests that SBM programs are not a quick fix. In fact, evidence from U.S. programs implemented in various cities and states since the 1970s and 1980s, ranging from intermediate to strong types of reforms, suggest that it takes time to see results in terms of increasing student test scores.[1] In fact, it is shown that SBM needs about five years to bring about fundamental changes at the school level and about eight years to yield changes in difficult-to-modify indicators such as test scores (Borman and others 2003; Cook 2007), as box 3.1 explains.

Several high-income countries have pioneered long-term SBM approaches, beginning with Australia. In 1966, the Australian Capital Territory (ACT) established a representative committee to recommend an

Table 3.3 Inside the Black Box: How to Measure the Impact of SBM Programs

Dimension	Objective	Question type	Question or topic examples
A. Education literature			
Scope	Clarity of goals and real influence of the board	Self-diagnosis; "site team" (community, council, or school board)	Site team members agree on what kinds of decisions team may make, or site team has influence on important issues.
Decision making	Implementation practices	Self-diagnosis; "site team"	Members work to implement decisions made, or members work to correct problems that arise during implementation.
Trust	Interaction among members	Self-diagnosis; "site team"	Site team members have equal opportunity to be involved in decisions, or site team communicates openly.
B. Economic literature			
Information at local level	Changes in key decisions	Personnel (teachers and administrative)	Who makes decisions about firing, hiring, rotation time, training?
		Spending	Spending on infrastructure, training
		Changes in education process	Change in pedagogy, changes in time allocation, absenteeism of teachers
		Resource mobilizations	Amount of resources from community
Accountability and monitoring	Involvement of parents and community	Direct involvement in school	Power of board, type and number of meetings, decisions in meetings
	Better accountability and monitoring	Links between parental involvement and decisions	Do complaints or praise about teachers translate into decisions about the teacher?
		Changes in the accounting systems of the school	Implementation of EMIS, changes in account tracking system
		Changes in the climate of the school	Changes in attitude of teachers and students about the school

Sources: Bauer, Bogotch, and Park 1998; Gertler, Patrinos, and Rubio-Codina 2007.

BOX 3.1

Eight Years to See Results

In a meta-analysis of the effectiveness of SBM models in the United States—or Comprehensive School Reform (CSR)—Borman and others (2003) reviewed 232 studies with 1,111 independent observations, representing 29 CSR programs in the United States. From these observations, they computed the size of the effect that these models had on student achievement.

The researchers regressed weighted effect size on the moderator variables to obtain the residuals from the regression and added the mean weighted effect size to each observation, thus calculating effect sizes that were statistically adjusted for all of the methodological variables. They found that the number of years of CSR implementation, shown in figure B3.1, was a statistically significant predictor of the student achievement effect size.

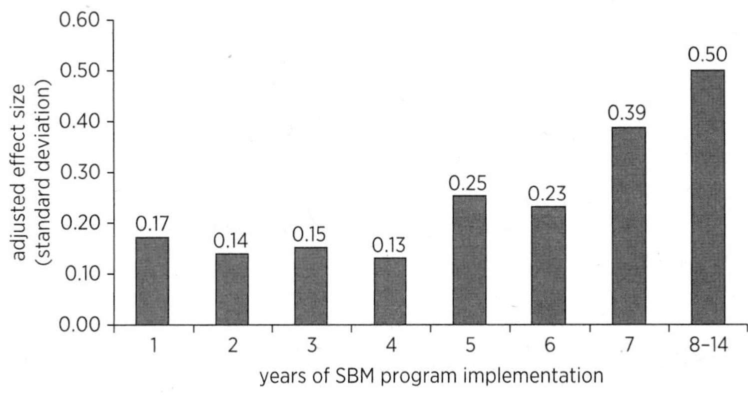

Source: Borman and others 2003.

Note: SBM = school-based management.

alternative model of school governance. The result was the Currie Report of 1967, which recommended that each school have a representative governing body consisting of teachers, parents, local community members and, in the case of secondary schools, students (Currie 1967). In 1974, the concept was implemented at ACT schools. By 1976, ACT, Victoria, and South Australia were to establish school councils or boards as mandatory, corporate governing bodies to manage their schools, with varying degrees of authority devolved to the school level. By the late 1990s, all eight Australian school systems had enacted legislation introducing reforms involving SBM.

In 1988, New Zealand introduced SBM by establishing representative boards of trustees at the school level. More than 90 percent of the cost of running each school was devolved to schools in the form of school-based budgets with authority to govern the school, including recruitment and employment of staff by the board.

In the United States, *A Nation at Risk* (Gardner 1983) led to the adoption of SBM in many schools and states—most radically in Illinois. In 1988, the School Reform Act instituted school councils as mandatory throughout the United States.

In Great Britain, the 1988 Education Reform Act empowered school communities to establish boards as mandatory, corporate bodies consisting of the head teacher and governors elected by the parents, teachers, and nominees of the local authority. Under the Act, the Thatcher government gave public secondary schools the option of leaving local education authority control and becoming autonomous, grant-maintained (GM) schools. GM schools were funded by a new agency but were owned and managed by each school's governing body, a new 10- to 15-member entity composed of the head teacher and teacher and parent representatives. Control over all staff contracts and ownership of the buildings and grounds were taken from the local school district and given to GM schools.

Between 1988 and 1997, among almost 1,000 schools holding votes on the matter, most favored conversion to GM status. An important study, using regression discontinuity design, found large achievement gains at schools in which the vote barely won, compared with schools in which it barely lost (Clark 2009). Student achievement improved by 0.25 of a standard deviation in pass rates on standardized examinations.

Assessing the Evidence

From the previous literature, there are a few well-documented cases of SBM and some documented cases of success, but the sample of carefully documented, rigorous impact evaluations is small compared with the large number of known SBM programs around the world. Some studies found that SBM policies actually changed the dynamics of the school, either because parents got more involved or because teachers' actions changed. Several studies presented evidence that SBM had a positive impact on repetition rates, failure rates, and, to a lesser degree, dropout rates. The studies that had access to SBM's impact on some variables—mainly in reducing repetition and failure and improving attendance rates—in contrast to SBM's mixed results on test scores could be due to timing.

Timing is important. As previously discussed, SBM reforms generally take a long time to produce their expected outcomes. In the first year or so of an SBM reform, there is an adjustment period during which changes in personnel occur and management changes (for example, the creation of a school council) are gradually put into operation. In the short run, these adjustments can have a negative impact on education outcomes, but once the school adjusts to the changes, positive changes can be expected. The speed of the effect depends as well on the type of outcomes being assessed. Some outcomes can be expected to change faster than others because the incentives that drive them are easier to change. For instance, attendance rates, measured by the number of days which students are present at school, are easier and faster to change than enrollment rates. So, in the short run, an SBM intervention can have a positive impact on attendance, reducing repetition, and failure rates, but outcomes such as dropout rates or test scores take longer to change.

Despite the difficulty of establishing the sizes of the outcome variables of interest due to the different metrics used in the various studies, it is nevertheless possible to list some findings about the impact of SBM based on previous rigorous analyses:

- Some studies found that SBM policies actually changed the dynamics of the school, either because parents got more involved or because teachers' actions changed (King and Özler 1998; Jimenez and Sawada 1999; Gunnarsson and others 2004).
- Several studies presented evidence that SBM had a positive impact on reducing repetition rates, failure rates, and, to a lesser degree, dropout rates (Di Gropello and Marshall 2005; Jimenez and Sawada 2003; Gertler, Patrinos, and Rubio-Codina 2006; Paes de Barros and Mendonca 1998; Skoufias and Shapiro 2006).
- The studies that had access to standardized test scores presented mixed evidence, with countries like El Salvador, Kenya, Mexico, and Nicaragua showing positive results (Jimenez and Sawada 2003; Sawada and Ragatz 2005; Lopez-Calva and Espinosa 2006; King and Özler 1998). Other reforms such as those in Brazil and Honduras appear to have had no effects on test scores. Many of the more rigorous studies are still in early stages of implementation. Therefore, few changes have been recorded thus far in terms of test scores, or the evidence presented is very preliminary.

Three studies allowed at least eight years before measuring the effects of the SBM intervention on test scores (Paes de Barros and Mendonca 1998; Lopez-Calva and Espinosa 2006; Parker 2005). Paes de Barros and Mendonca (1988) found that the reform in Brazil had produced no test score improvements after 11 years of implementation, but the other two studies showed that the reforms in Nicaragua and Mexico had positive effects on test scores after 11 and 8 years, respectively. Other studies measured SBM's impact on repetition and failure rates (intermediate indicators) closer to the initial implementation period. The authors of those studies found positive effects after only two years of implementation in the case of rural Mexico (Gertler, Patrinos, and Rubio-Codina 2006) and after only two to three years in urban Mexico (Skoufias and Shapiro 2006).

New studies of SBM reforms have validated and expanded upon the previous findings. Moreover, many of the new studies are based on randomized control trials, based on carefully designed experiments. Some of these experiments, especially in Mexico, are based on rather large samples. The presentation below of these results follows the typologies listed above—that is, beginning with strong versions of SBM (those where the school personnel can be hired and fired directly by the school councils), followed by the intermediate and weak versions of SBM.

Evidence from Strong Forms of SBM

One of the senior versions and early evaluations in the SBM literature is the EDUCO model of El Salvador. The reform began in 1991 under the name *Educación con Participación de la Comunidad* (Education with Community Participation, or EDUCO). EDUCO schools are publicly funded, and students receive free tuition, textbooks, uniforms, registration, and basic school supplies. In return, parents are expected to contribute meals, time, and in some cases, their labor to improve schools. The distinguishing feature of EDUCO schools is the Association for Community Education (ACE). Each school has an ACE, consisting of five community-elected members. ACEs receive funds directly from the Ministry of Education and are responsible for enacting and implementing ministry and community policies and for the hiring, firing, and monitoring of teachers (Sawada and Ragatz 2005).

Evaluations of the EDUCO schools found a steady increase in student enrollments, which could be directly attributed to the program (Di Gropello 2006). Student enrollments in EDUCO schools went from 8,500 students in 1991 to more than 320,000 students in 2001. This represented 50 percent of rural enrollments and 37 percent of total enrollments in the first through ninth grades (Di Gropello 2006).

In addition, Jimenez and Sawada (2003) found that, after controlling for child, household, and school characteristics, third graders in EDUCO schools were more likely than third graders in traditional schools to be studying in those same schools two years later. Jimenez and Sawada's continuation Probit coefficient for EDUCO schools was 0.36. This suggested that attending an EDUCO school raised the probability of continuing in school by 64 percent compared with attending a non-EDUCO school. These results attempted to control for selection bias, and in addition they used 1996 test scores to control for initial differences in achievement between traditional and EDUCO schools that might have affected dropout behavior. The studies also found that supply-side constraints were important in EDUCO schools; that is, most EDUCO schools do not offer the fourth through sixth grades, and this affects continuation rates. This is evident from the fact that, if the variable measuring the number of second-cycle sections in the schools is dropped from the models, the EDUCO dummy loses significance. To investigate the EDUCO effect further, the authors added a community participation variable to the estimation. The EDUCO coefficient lost magnitude and significance, and at the same time community participation emerged as a positive and statistically significant variable. The authors thus concluded that a significant portion of the EDUCO effect could be explained by community participation (Jimenez and Sawada 2003).

With respect to effects on teachers' behavior, Jimenez and Sawada (1999) found that students in EDUCO schools were less likely to miss school due to teacher absences. A more recent study by Sawada (1999) measured teachers' effort in terms of their overall attendance and the number of hours they spent on parent-teacher meetings. He found that EDUCO teachers made more effort (only when effort was defined as hours of parent-teacher meetings) than teachers in traditional schools. Instrumental variables were used to reduce the endogeneity between community participation and observed effort.

Sawada and Ragatz (2005) used propensity score matching to identify the EDUCO effect on teacher behavior, administrative processes and, ultimately, student test scores. They found that community associations managing EDUCO schools felt that they had more influence in virtually every administrative process than did the equivalent associations in traditional schools. In particular, the hiring and firing of teachers appeared to be one of the administrative processes over which the associations had the most influence. The authors also found that teachers in EDUCO schools spent more time meeting with parents and more time teaching and were absent for fewer days than teachers in traditional schools.

Last, with respect to parental involvement, parent associations in EDUCO schools visited classrooms more than once a week on average, which was almost three to four times more than parent associations in traditional schools (Jimenez and Sawada 2003). EDUCO schools also had better classroom environments (measured by smaller classroom sizes and the availability of a classroom library), leading to higher student test scores in third grade (Sawada 1999).

Impacts on learning outcomes are more limited. Jimenez and Sawada (1999) used a two-stage regression procedure to attempt to correct for selection bias. (In other words, schools that choose to become autonomous may be different in some unobservable variables that can be correlated with the outcome of interest.) They found that there were no statistically discernible effects of attending an EDUCO school on either math or language test scores among third graders. It should be noted that EDUCO schools tend to be located in poor, rural, isolated communities. Therefore, it might be reasonable to expect to see lower test scores among EDUCO students because of their disadvantaged backgrounds. Nonetheless, these results support the idea that devolving autonomy over decision making to the school level leads to a closer monitoring of teachers, which in turn results in greater teacher effort.

Similarly strong versions of SBM from other parts of Central America have been evaluated. The school autonomy reform in Nicaragua allowed councils to fire and hire school principals and become involved in maintaining school facilities and ensuring academic quality (Parker 2005; King and Özler 1998). King and Özler (1998) studied the effects of school autonomy on student test scores in mathematics and Spanish using a matched comparison design based on selecting a sample of treatment schools (autonomous schools) and a comparison group of nonautonomous public schools and private schools. The authors found that *de jure* autonomy had no statistically significant effects on student achievement. However, *de facto* autonomy had positive effects on student promotion and student achievement in math and language in primary school and in language in secondary school.

Arcia, Porta Pallais, and Laguna (2004) also found that the SBM reform in Nicaragua had a positive effect on student achievement. An attitudinal survey of school directors, teachers, and school council members in autonomous schools determined that several factors related to school management changed for the better under autonomy. The results showed a broad consensus among directors, teachers, and council members that school autonomy had brought improvements in teacher and student attendance, school discipline, and infrastructure. The director and council members agreed that they shared equal power in matters relating to the annual school plan and in the administration of the budget. Teachers seemed to agree that discipline and attendance had improved, but they felt that autonomy had not improved their salaries (Arcia, Porta Pallais, and Laguna 2004).

A subsequent analysis looked at the effects on student achievement of two more refined measures of autonomy (King, Özler, and Rawlings 1999). The first variable measured the percentage of decisions made by the school council concerning pedagogical issues (such as class size, curriculum, and textbooks). The second variable was the percentage of decisions related to teachers (hiring and firing, evaluation, supervision, training, and relations with the teachers' union). The study's findings about the influence of autonomy over pedagogical issues on student achievement were mixed. This is not surprising given that the SBM reform did not have significant effects on schools' decision making on pedagogical matters. However, it appeared that having more autonomy over teacher-related issues did have a positive and significant effect on student achievement in both primary school (both subjects) and secondary school (language only). Increasing schools' influence over teacher-related decision making was the area of the decentralization reform that appeared to have had the largest effect on student achievement (King, Özler, and Rawlings 1999). Using more recent (and nationally representative) data from 2002, Parker (2005) found that school autonomy had positive effects on third-grade mathematics test scores but negative effects on sixth-grade math scores.

In Guatemala, after controlling for student, teacher, and school factors, SBM schools outperformed traditional schools in reading (Di Gropello 2006). Teachers in autonomous schools resigned at a much higher rate (three times higher) than teachers in traditional schools, possibly because they found better salaries, working conditions, and job security in traditional schools (Di Gropello 2006.).

In Nepal, the government transferred responsibility for managing schools from the state to the community. Community schools in Nepal, working through a school management committee consisting of parents and influential local citizens, are given decision-making powers over various staffing and fiscal issues. Community-managed schools may repost regular (government) teachers back to the district headquarters, directly hire and fire community-recruited teachers, and index teacher salaries to school performance. The community-managed schools are also given more untied block grants so that the management committee has more control over discretionary spending. Since participation in the program is under the discretion of the community, an exogenous instrument was introduced in the form of an advocacy group working with randomly chosen communities to persuade them to participate in the program (Chaudhury and Parajuli 2010). Short-run (2007–09) impact estimates (derived from an empirical strategy that combined instrumental variables and difference-in-differences methods) suggested that devolving management responsibility to communities had a significant impact on certain schooling outcomes related to access and equity. There is yet no evidence of improved learning outcomes.

Das (2008) studied a reform in Pakistan where a nongovernmental organization (NGO) was hired to manage a school together with the school council. Both the managed school and the regular school received about $4,000 for school needs. The NGO was allowed to transfer teachers as well. Between 2004 and 2008, this randomized control trial (original randomization was not fully upheld, so analysis was performed using intent to treat) had yet to show any effects on student enrollment, teacher absenteeism, or the facilities index (infrastructure). It may be possible that the effects of school council management will only be evident in the long term.

Nevertheless, the proportion of council members whose children were attending the managed school significantly increased.

Evidence from Intermediate Forms of SBM

Beginning in 1982, several states in Brazil experimented with different forms of SBM. Three key innovations stand out in the Brazilian experience with SBM:

- Schools have been given financial autonomy.
- Principals are elected democratically by school officials, parents, and students; competitively appointed by local governments through examinations; or selected through a combination of election and appointment.
- Councils are established in the schools to coordinate and evaluate their pedagogical, administrative, and financial activities.

The school councils comprise the principal, representatives of teachers and other staff, and representatives of parents and students (Paes de Barros and Mendonca 1998). Only four states implemented all three reforms in a coordinated way: Minas Gerais, Rio Grande do Norte, Espirito Santo, and Mato Grosso do Sul (Paes de Barros and Mendonca 1998).

Another set of SBM reforms began in 1998 and reached more than 5,600 schools by 2001. These reforms, known as the *Plano de Desenvolvimento da Escola* (School Development Plan, or PDE), were designed to make schools more responsive to students and their communities. Under PDE, schools engage in a self-evaluation, develop a school plan focusing on two or three "efficiency factors" (one of which has to be effective teaching and learning), and design actions intended to enhance those factors. A program created by the Ministry of Education to strengthen the schools—*Fundescola* (Fund for Strengthening the School)—provides funds to support the goals and projects of PDE schools (Carnoy and others 2008).

Paes de Barros and Mendonca (1998) used census, household survey, and evaluation data from the National Basic Education System to carry out an empirical investigation into the effects of the three initial SBM innovations on student achievement. They measured the effects by assessing students' average performance in mathematics, language, and science in the first, third, fifth, and seventh grades in each school. (Test scores were averaged at the school level because not all grades were examined in these three subjects.)

For the study, the authors included such control variables as mean per capita family income, average teacher quality, and average education attainment. The unit of analysis was the state, and the time period for the study was 1981 to 1993 (some analyses used fewer years because of data restrictions). The authors' empirical strategy was to compare the performance on the states' various outcomes by using the time variation in the implementation of the innovations by each state. Their results suggested that the financial autonomy reforms did not lead to better student performance (Paes de Barros and Mendonca 1998). However, education performance tended to be better in places where principals were elected by school officials, parents, and students over 16 years old; where schools had been granted financial autonomy; or where school councils had been established. To control for unobserved heterogeneity, the authors included a series of controls to try to capture any relevant omitted variables, which reduced the magnitude and significance of the aforementioned effects. The only outcome for which the results appeared robust to the introduction of additional controls was repetition rates. The inclusion of additional controls highlighted the fact that granting financial autonomy to schools was more significant than introducing school councils or electing principals. The authors concluded that their results showed that these innovations had had a generally positive but modest impact on education performance defined broadly. As to which innovation was the most promising, the authors attached more significance to financial autonomy and much less significance to the election of principals (Paes de Barros and Mendonca 1998).

The descriptive evaluation of the PDE by Carnoy and others (2008) found that although the program did affect what went on in schools (in terms of such activities as planning, participation of parent-teacher associations, and suitable working conditions for teachers), it did not appear to have any significant effect on reading and math scores.

In Kenya, with the introduction of free primary schools in 2003, parents were no longer required to pay fees. This change resulted in large increases in student enrollment and increased pupil-teacher ratios significantly in primary schools. It also meant that school committees could no longer raise sufficient funds to pay for parent-teacher association (PTA) teachers. Community members participate in schools by serving on school committees or PTAs consisting of elected parents and representatives from the District Education Board. In general, the committee's authority is limited to suggesting (to the Ministry of Education) promotions and transfers of teachers, overseeing expenditures from capitation grants, and participating in the design and implementation of school development plans.

A recent pilot program in Kenya, called the Extra Teacher Program (ETP), provided funds to 140 schools randomly selected from a pool of 210 schools to hire an extra teacher for first-grade classes. In half of these 140 schools (nontracked ETP schools), first-grade students were randomly assigned to either the contract teacher or a civil service teacher. In the other half (tracked ETP schools), first-grade classes were divided into two classes by initial achievement, and those classes were randomly assigned to either a civil service teacher or a contract teacher. The program was funded by the World Bank and International Child Support Africa (ICS), an NGO working with schools in the region.

Among the 140 schools that received funding to hire a contract teacher from the local area, 70 schools were randomly selected to participate in an SBM intervention, in which school committees monitored the performance of these contract teachers. In the SBM schools, the school committees held a formal review meeting at the end of the first school year of the program (2005) to assess the contract teacher's performance and decide whether to renew the teacher's contract or to replace him or her. To prepare the school committees for this task, the ICS provided members with a short, focused training course on how to monitor the contract teacher's performance, including techniques for soliciting input from parents and checking teacher attendance. A subcommittee of first-grade parents was formed to evaluate the contract teacher and to deliver a performance report at the end of the first year (Duflo, Dupas, and Kremer 2007).

Eighteen months into the program, students in all treatment schools had, on average, test scores that were a 0.23 standard deviation higher than students assigned to civil service teachers. Also, the scores were a 0.3 standard deviation higher than those of students in non-ETP schools. All differences were statistically significant at conventional levels. The effect of the contract teacher appeared to be larger when the school committee was given training in how to handle the contract teachers (Duflo, Dupas, and Kremer 2007). The authors also reported evidence that the SBM initiative was helpful in raising the test scores of the students of civil service teachers, just as it was successful in decreasing the classroom absence rates of these teachers. Students with civil service teachers in ETP schools that participated in the SBM program scored a 0.18–0.24 standard deviation higher in mathematics than their counterparts in ETP schools that did not participate in the SBM program.

A more detailed look at the results suggests that, with respect to teacher absences, civil service teachers in untracked schools that did not participate in the SBM program were more likely to be absent from class than the comparison group (teacher attendance fell by 21 percentage points). The authors argued that this finding suggested that civil service teachers took advantage of the presence of the extra contract teachers to work less. However, civil service teachers in untracked SBM schools were 7.8 percentage points more likely to be found teaching in class during random spot checks by the NGO. The authors argued that it is likely that the SBM initiative emphasized the responsibility of the contract teacher with respect to the specific class to which he or she was assigned and thus made it more difficult for the principal or the civil service teachers in those schools to use the extra teacher to relieve themselves of their own duties when they actually did show up to school. Also, the contract teachers in these schools had a greater incentive to please the school committee and less of an incentive to please the other teachers and the principal (Duflo, Dupas, and Kremer 2007).

The authors also argued that the SBM initiative reinforced the role of parents (as opposed to principals, who often dominate the committees) in hiring, monitoring, and retaining the contract teachers. Although parents were instructed in how to monitor the contract teachers, the SBM initiative did not have a significant impact on the attendance records of, or the efforts made by, the contract teachers (perhaps because this was already satisfactory), but the initiative did increase the efforts of civil service teachers. Furthermore, the authors argued that the superior performance of contract teachers might have resulted from either better teacher choice by the school committees or the stronger incentives faced by contract teachers. Last, the authors noted that contract teachers might have viewed their own good performance as a stepping stone to a tenured civil service position.

The effect was larger when the school committees were trained in teacher management. Parental involvement in school management seemed to be effective; civil service teachers were more likely to be in class and teaching during random visits in schools where the school committee was empowered to monitor teachers than in schools without the monitoring (Duflo, Dupas, and Kremer 2009). Furthermore, the authors found evidence that suggested the students of civil service teachers in schools with empowered parent committees performed better (particularly in math) than their counterparts in schools without empowered committees. This finding suggests the importance of a significant reform of the education system: paying lip service to parents' participation is not sufficient if parents are not given concrete means of being effective.

In 2001, Mexico implemented the *Programa Escuelas de Calidad* (Quality Schools Program, or PEC). This program seeks to provide more autonomy to schools by giving them five-year grants of up to $15,000 to improve education quality (Skoufias and Shapiro 2006). In exchange for PEC grants, schools must prepare an education improvement plan that outlines how they intend to use the grant. Parent associations must be involved in the design, implementation, and monitoring of the plan. In the first four years, about 80 percent of the grant must be spent on school materials and facilities. In the fifth year, only part of the money must be spent on such goods, with a large proportion of the grant going to fund teacher training and development. Participation in PEC is voluntary, but the program targets disadvantaged urban schools.

PEC has been credited with preventing and limiting corrupt practices in the management of education funds (Karim, Santizo Rodall, and Mendoza 2004) because the school councils are accountable both to their central education authorities (vertical accountability) and to the school community and donors (horizontal accountability). If expanded, this program has the potential to reduce petty corruption (Transparency International 2005; Patrinos and Kagia 2007).

Skoufias and Shapiro (2006) used panel data regression analysis and propensity score matching to evaluate the impact of PEC on student dropout, failure, and repetition rates using a nationally representative panel data set covering the 2001/02 and 2003/04 school years. To establish a comparison group, they used student outcome data for the years 2000 (the year before the first schools joined PEC) and 2003. Their difference-in-differences approach assumed no differences in time trends in student outcomes. To support this assumption, the authors included several controls at the school and municipal levels taken from 2000 data, such as teacher-student ratio, school type, and participation in poverty reduction programs. They also used propensity score modeling to match treatment to comparison schools based on these same data.

The authors found that PEC participation decreased dropout rates by 0.24 points, failure rates by 0.24 points, and repetition rates by 0.31 points. To explore what brought about these results in PEC schools, the authors used qualitative data on PEC school effectiveness and parental involvement. They found that parents had increased their participation in the schools and their supervision of students' homework. Moreover, students enrolled in PEC schools and their parents expected that these students would progress to more advanced education levels (Skoufias and Shapiro 2006). Unfortunately, the authors did not have qualitative data on non-PEC schools and so were not able to investigate whether the changes that had occurred at PEC schools were unique and could reasonably be the cause of improvements in outcomes. Therefore, it cannot be concluded that these qualitative changes could be attributed solely to the participation of the schools in the PEC program.

Murnane, Willet, and Cardenas (2006) suggested that they could not. Using longitudinal data from the seven full academic years of PEC (Skoufias and Shapiro used only two years of outcome data), they found that PEC schools had a different outcome trend than non-PEC schools in the years before participating in the program. To avoid violating this key assumption, Murnane, Willet, and Cardenas used the schools that entered PEC in the program's second year of operation (the second cohort of PEC, or "PEC2," schools) as the treatment schools. Unlike the schools that entered PEC in its first year, PEC2 schools had no pre-PEC outcome trends that were significantly different from the comparison schools; the PEC2 schools, thus, represent a more credible counterfactual. The authors' results showed that participation in PEC decreased school dropout rates significantly (about 0.11 of a percentage point for each year of program participation). Given that the average dropout rate in their sample was 4.75 percent, three years of PEC would have reduced an average school's dropout rate by about 6 percent. The authors did not find that PEC had had any significant effects on repetition rates. Last, they found that PEC had its greatest impact in states with medium levels of development (according to the Human Development Index) and its lowest impact in states with low levels of development. The authors hypothesized that this was because departments of education in these low-development states had less capacity than the more-developed states to support PEC schools (Murnane, Willet, and Cardenas 2006).

In the Mexican state of Colima, the federal SBM program PEC grants were randomly assigned in 2006. After three years of implementation, preliminary analysis suggested that, in terms of the education process, the principal and the president of the parents association reported no observed changes in monthly time spent on school-related administrative tasks (Gertler and others 2010). Yet, teachers reported an increase in the time they devoted to administrative tasks. Moreover, there was a significant increase in the total amount of hours per week that teachers reported spending to support students who were lagging behind and to meet with parents to discuss student performance.

On average, there was no observed significant change in the number of meetings held by the different school agents during the academic year. However, in terms of principal and teacher absenteeism, self-reports suggested low levels of absences—at odds with the perceptions of other agents, parents, and students. Indeed, when agents were asked to rate the others' levels of absenteeism, teachers believed that principals' absenteeism was "moderate," and principals considered teachers' absences to be "high." Parents considered both principals' and teachers' absenteeism to be "high" to "very high." In treatment schools, parents reported a significantly lower level of teacher absenteeism than the parents reported in control schools. Overall, there was a high reported participation of teachers and principals in meetings over school matters. Moreover, the participation rates reported were similar regardless of the identity of the informants. There was a significant increase in principals' engagement in meetings to solve school conflicts as reported by teachers.

In terms of student achievement, the preliminary analysis suggested that test scores increased overall in Colima, in both treatment and control schools. Overall, the differences were small. But when analyzed by grade, one observes a higher achievement trend for the cohort that was exposed to the treatment the longest: students who were in third grade in the baseline year, 2005/06. The treated students scored an average of 483 points in third grade (2005/06), 518 in fourth grade (2006/07), 504 in fifth grade (2007/08), and 511 in sixth grade (2008/09), for an overall increase of

46 points, almost half a standard deviation. The control-school students went from an average of 482 points in third grade (2005/06), to 551 in fourth grade, to 505 in fifth grade, and to 512 in sixth grade (2008/09), for an overall increase of 30 points, about one-third of a standard deviation. Therefore, the difference-in-differences estimate is 16 points, or 0.16 of a standard deviation (Gertler and others 2010).

A variation of the Mexican program is the PEC-FIDE model. In 2008, the federal Secretariat of Public Education, with the state governments of Coahuila, Chihuahua, Quintana Roo, Hidalgo, Guanajuato, and the State of Mexico, implemented a pilot project derived from PEC and largely supported by the same operational structure. The pilot project, called *Programa de Fortalecimiento e Inversión Directa a las Escuelas* (Program of Strengthening and Direct Investment in Schools, or PEC-FIDE), attempts to motivate collective work in the schools to generate processes of school improvement and inclusion through a greater alignment between resources and school activities. An impact evaluation of the program using difference-in-differences and propensity score matching suggested that PEC-FIDE produced favorable effects in terms of increasing pass rates and improving test scores, especially in reading. Effects were more notable in schools that participated in PEC-FIDE for the first time and in primary schools in states that targeted the program better (Abreu and others 2010).

Evidence from Weak Forms of SBM

Another SBM reform undertaken in Mexico was *Apoyo a la Gestión Escolar* (Support to School Management Program, or AGE). AGE is part of a broader compensatory education program designed to improve the supply and quality of education in schools in highly disadvantaged communities. The larger program consists of small civil works (infrastructure improvement), provision of school equipment, materials for students (such as notebooks and pens), pedagogical training, performance-based monetary incentives for teachers, and AGE. However, not all of the subinterventions were introduced at the same time, and not all of the schools received all of the subinterventions. The overall program progressively expanded from more-disadvantaged to less-disadvantaged areas. Between 1992 and 1995, the program was introduced in the poorest municipalities of the poorest 23 states, as defined according to the index developed by the National Population Council (CONAPO). Coverage was extended to disadvantaged schools in the eight remaining Mexican states in 1998. These states have lower poverty rates and better education outcomes than the states incorporated earlier. Each state then decided which subinterventions would be allocated to each school based on the school's budgetary and logistical capacity.

AGE as a subintervention was introduced in the 1996/97 school year. AGE finances and supports the schools' parent associations. The monetary support varies from $500 to $700 per year depending on school size. The use of funds is restricted and subject to annual financial audits of a random sample of schools. Among other things, the parents are not allowed to spend money on wages and salaries for teachers. Most of the money goes to infrastructure improvements and small civil works. In return, parents must commit to greater involvement in school activities, participate in the infrastructure works, and attend training sessions delivered by state education authorities. In these sessions, parents receive instruction in the management of the funds and in participatory skills to increase their involvement in the school. Parents also receive information on the school, the role of the school's parent associations, and their children's education achievements as well as advice on how to help their children learn. While parent associations exist by law, they are rather dysfunctional and typically have little or no access to schools. AGE creates both a need and a right for parents to have access to schools to decide on the allocation of the grant, manage the funds (establish a feasible budget, record expenses, and so on), and participate in infrastructure works directly. Hence, AGE represents the first time that parents have been granted full access to the schools and certain, albeit limited, authority over school matters. In 2005, more than 45 percent of primary schools in Mexico had a parent association (Gertler, Patrinos, and Rubio-Codina 2006).

A study of the impact of the AGE program on intrayear dropouts, grade repetition, and grade failure in rural primary schools found that AGE had a significant effect in reducing grade failure and repetition (Gertler, Patrinos, and Rubio-Codina 2006). The authors found that AGE did not have any significant effects on intrayear dropout rates. Their study was conducted between 1998 and 2001 on a sample of 6,038 rural, nonindigenous primary schools, some participating in AGE and some not. They used a difference-in-differences regression approach to evaluate the intervention's impact. All outcomes were measured at the end of the school year, on the explicit assumption that AGE needs to have been in operation for some time to be effective. The authors used the phasing of schools into the AGE program to generate sufficient variation in the treatment variable to achieve identification. Schools participating in AGE before 2002 were the treatment group, while schools participating in AGE from 2002 on served as a comparison group. Gertler, Patrinos, and Rubio-Codina (2006) found that AGE reduced grade failure by 7.4 percent and grade repetition by 5.5 percent in the first through third grades.

To test the validity of the comparison group, the authors compared preintervention trends in the outcome variables controlling for school and state fixed effects and a dummy variable measuring whether the school is a potential AGE school. This analysis did not reveal significant differences in preintervention trends for schools participating in AGE in earlier and later years. Although the insignificant differences in preintervention trends should have alleviated any concerns about bias resulting from endogenous program placement, the authors used school fixed effects to address any potential bias arising from time-invariant sources. The authors also tested for biases arising from changes in the distribution of students in schools but did not find any evidence for concern (Gertler, Patrinos, and Rubio-Codina 2006).

Lopez-Calva and Espinosa (2006) yielded additional evidence to support the earlier studies. They found that participating in AGE had a positive effect on student test scores in the fourth through sixth grades (in primary school) for both Spanish and math. The authors used a propensity score matching strategy to identify their results. The results are robust to controls for such relevant socioeconomic variables as participation in Mexico's *Progresa-Oportunidades* conditional cash transfer program, teacher and school characteristics, and alternative stratification strategies.

The AGE 125 impact evaluation—a randomized control trial in four Mexican states that doubled the resources that AGE schools receive—tests whether the additional funding makes any difference (Gertler, Patrinos, and Rodríguez-Oreggia 2010). Another group of schools received the parental training but not the funding, which tests whether participation on its own is effective. Finally, a control group of schools received no treatment.

The preliminary analysis carried out thus far compared the double-funded AGE schools with the other AGE schools. After one year of implementation, the comparison of baseline and first follow-up surveys revealed that the interaction among school agents (directors, teachers, and parents) had changed. This could be observed through the participation of school agents in the design and execution of the School Improvement Plan (SIP). In the treatment schools, even though the simultaneous participation of the school directors, teachers, and parents in SIP design decreased from 2007 to 2008, the joint involvement of all three groups remained the main source of participation, followed by the participation of directors and parents. For the SIP execution, the main source of participation for both years was composed of directors, teachers, and parents (at 76 percent in 2007 and 70 percent in 2008). The interaction among directors and parents was second, increasing from 15 percent in 2007 to 21 percent in 2008. Analyzing the same information for the control schools, one observes that the participation of parents had decreased. The participation of directors, teachers, and parents in SIP design was about 68 percent in both 2007 and 2008. The second mechanism of participation, composed only of directors and parents, decreased by 7 percent from 2007 to 2008.

Analyzing both groups (treatment and control), one observes that the main expenditure item was school materials and that this expenditure increased by about 7 percent from 2007 to 2008 for both groups—rising from 45 percent to 52 percent for treatment schools and from 44 percent to 50 percent for control schools. In 2007, about one-third of AGE resources were spent on infrastructure improvements (painting supplies, classroom maintenance, furniture repair, maintenance of electricity and hydraulic lines, fans and heating, real estate, and so on). But the amount devoted to infrastructure improvement decreased by 3 percent for treatment schools and by 7 percent for control schools in the first year. In 2007, around 22 percent of the AGE grants were spent on health and hygiene materials (first-aid and hygiene products and toilet repair). In 2008, the expenditure on health and hygiene materials decreased by 4 percent for the treatment schools and increased by 1 percent for control schools.

The interest of parents in their children's school performance could be measured through their interaction with teachers—an indicator of parental involvement. The extent to which parents asked teachers about their children's performance had improved. The parents' interest increased from one year to the next among both treatment and control schools. The participation of teachers showed an improvement from 2007 to 2008 as well. Class time, preparation, and reinforcement classes increased more in the treatment schools than in the control schools. In the treatment schools, only the time for grading assignments and exams decreased, by 0.08 hours (less than 5 minutes).

To measure the improvement of the quality of education in these 250 schools for third-, fourth-, and fifth-grade students, Gertler, Patrinos, and Rodríguez-Oreggia (2010) used intermediate indicators: repetition, failure, and dropout rates. On learning outcomes, the national standardized test (ENLACE) was used for Spanish and mathematics. Unfortunately, ENLACE scores were published at the school level for 2007 and 2009 but not for 2008. Therefore, the 2009 scores were used to observe the improvements in education quality for the first follow-up.

Using a difference-in-differences approach with random and fixed effects and controlling by schools', directors', parents', and teachers' characteristics, the authors reported that the double-funded AGE program had a significant impact on the total dropout rate and on Spanish and mathematics scores of treatment schools. The estimates suggest that the AGE 125 project caused the treatment schools' dropout rate to decrease by 1.5–1.7 percentage points compared with control schools during the project's first year of implementation. At the same time, the double-funded AGE intervention had not revealed any effects on repetition or failure rates. It also seems like this project had a positive impact on Spanish and mathematics test scores, mostly for third-grade students. The results suggest that the double-funded

AGE program caused an increase of about 5.0–5.6 percent in Spanish scores and an increase of about 6.3–8.0 percent in mathematics scores for third-grade students in treatment schools (Gertler, Patrinos, and Rodríguez-Oreggia 2010).

In Cambodia, the SBM program is called the Education Quality Improvement Project (EQIP) School Grants Program. It began in Takeo Province in 1998 with a pilot group of 10 clusters and expanded to include roughly 1,000 schools in three provinces between 1998 and 2003. EQIP schools receive cash grants that are invested in priorities determined by the local cluster committee—representing six schools on average—as part of a cluster plan. The grants program is designed to improve school quality in two ways. The first is simply a resource effect, as school clusters receive money they can use to buy additional inputs such as new equipment, teacher training, and student libraries. The second involves building the schools' management capacities by giving cluster schools valuable experience in participative planning and the execution of school plans. With decentralized planning and execution, the grants program is expected to result in a more efficient use of funds than standard, top-down education interventions achieve. Qualitative reviews of the program have, so far, been positive (Geeves and others 2002). The EQIP project has delivered the money in a timely fashion, and donors are generally satisfied with how the money has been spent.

Preliminary results of EQIP program evaluations showed systematic variation in spending by school clusters associated with specific school characteristics and parental participation (Benveniste and Marshall 2004). Nonetheless, the largest variation was associated with the year and province variables, suggesting that central forces exerted considerable influence on local choices. Regarding outcomes, preliminary results suggested that participation in EQIP was associated with marginally lower dropout rates, higher pass rates, and better academic achievement. These results were robust to the inclusion of controls for school and community characteristics and province-level fixed effects. For this analysis, the authors used regression analysis with five years of data and took advantage of the phase-in strategy to decrease the potential for selection bias. The empirical strategy was to regress student test scores on student, teacher, and school characteristics, plus controls for province and year. All community, school, director, and teacher characteristics were set at their pre-EQIP levels (1998). Cost-effectiveness comparisons were also generally favorable, as EQIP money spent on specific activities such as teacher development and infrastructure improvements have been associated with higher returns than other possible interventions.

In Indonesia, a limited form of SBM is operating. Under the program, school committees were set up in 2005 to run SBM programs. All schools in Indonesia receive block grants based on a per-student formula, but school committees have control only over nonsalary operational expenditures. Over the past decade, the government of Indonesia has introduced elements of SBM into its education system by involving school personnel (principals, teachers, and other staff) and parents in the management of schools to make them more accountable and responsive to parents and students (World Bank 2008b). However, it was not until the introduction of the *Bantuan Operasional Sekolah* (School Operational Assistance Program, or BOS) in 2005 that school committees had any discretionary money to exercise their mandated role.

Based on the BOS experience, the government has taken another step toward cementing SBM and parental involvement with a regulation that enhances the role of school committees. Successful examples of community involvement in Indonesian projects—such as the National Program for Community Empowerment (PNPM), the Urban Poverty Program (UPP), and the Kecamatan Development Program (KDP)—all indicate that social pressure from an informed local community can help to reduce corruption and the misuse of funds. The design of the BOS program already closely parallels the institutional and implementation arrangements pioneered by these community-driven programs. A modified version of the program, the School Operational Assistance Knowledge Improvement for Transparency and Accountability (BOS-KITA) program, will expand and build on these lessons, enhancing the role of parents and the local community in planning (and approving) school budgets for BOS funds and monitoring BOS expenditures.

The BOS program disburses block grants to all schools throughout Indonesia based on a per-student formula. It is Indonesia's most significant policy reform in education financing in two important aspects: (1) Block grants to schools are based on a per-pupil formula, which provides incentives for principals and teachers to focus on maintaining and increasing enrollment. (2) Funds are directly channeled to the schools, which empowers school managers by allowing them to choose how best to allocate the BOS grants.

School committees are tasked with assisting in the selection of scholarship students and overseeing school spending on grants. The committees consist of representatives of parents, community leaders, education professionals, the private sector, education associations, teachers, NGOs, and village officials. Each committee must have a minimum of nine members, and the chairperson must come from outside the school. All public and private elementary and junior high schools in Indonesia are eligible to apply for BOS funding. School committees have control only over nonsalary operational expenditures. They are not allowed to hire or fire teachers or even have any control over capital expenditures. A pre-BOS comparison of data from 94 schools in 16 districts participating in the first Governance and Decentralization Survey module indicated that as much as one-third of the allocated resources may have failed to reach schools. The BOS program uses a simple, transparent formula and provides mechanisms for scrutiny both from the top (through the internal audit) and from the bottom (through community mobilization and oversight). Under the BOS program, in which schools receive operational funds directly and the funds are allocated independently, opportunities for further SBM are created.

Using data from various household surveys and the Ministry of Education's information system, a 2008 technical assessment carried out by World Bank staff identified a number of positive developments to which the BOS program contributed during its first years of operation. The BOS program has been important for promoting and facilitating SBM and parental and local community involvement. In a survey of 1,250 schools, 68 percent reported that they had implemented SBM principles. Of these schools, 95 percent claimed to have experienced positive benefits. Most schools had seen improvements in their students' grades (66 percent of schools surveyed), their attendance (29 percent of schools surveyed), and discipline (43 percent of schools surveyed). These results however, must be taken with caution as they are based neither on standardized tests (or other measures) nor on a rigorous (or even semirigorous) evaluation strategy.

Four randomized interventions—each aiming to strengthen school committees in public primary schools in Indonesia—have been evaluated (Pradhan and others 2010). Single and combined methods were experimented with, including giving the school committee a grant, training school committee members, linking school committee members with the village representative council, and democratically electing school committee members. After one year of implementation, elections in combination with the committee-council links—and, to a lesser extent, in combination with committee training—had substantial positive effects on learning. The committee-council link was the most cost-effective intervention, increasing language scores by a 0.12 standard deviation.

In the Philippines, SBM was implemented in 2003 in 23 districts. The project funded infrastructure, training, curriculum development, and textbooks. Participating schools were required to design a five-year School Improvement Plan in partnership with parents and the community, using data on student achievement, with the school principal leading the process. Khattri, Ling, and Jha (2010) evaluated the program using retrospective data, difference-in-differences, and propensity score matching. In three years, the SBM schools improved scores in math by 16 percentage points, in science by 11 percentage points, and in English by 18 percentage points; the corresponding improvements in non-SBM schools were 15, 10, and 16 percentage points. The effect sizes, however, were 0.10, 0.13, 0.09, and 0.07 of a standard deviation in overall scores, science, English, and math, respectively.

BOX 3.2

Ongoing SBM Experiments in Africa

There are various SBM reforms under way in Africa. Some are implementing initiatives similar to those that have been adopted in Central America. Mozambique, for example, was an early mover in SBM reforms and now makes small grants to schools that participate in the SBM program (World Bank 2008c). These schools are managed by a school committee that is able to spend funds on basic classroom inputs and teaching materials. As part of the reform, participating schools have to publish student achievement data and how the money is being spent.

The introduction of free primary education meant abolishing school fees that had previously been paid by parents. The expenditures that used to be covered by these fees are now funded by grants (sometimes called capitation grants) from the central government. For example, in countries such as Benin, The Gambia, Ghana, Madagascar, Niger, Rwanda, and Senegal, the government gives a direct grant to schools, the amount of which is calculated on a per-student basis. These capitation grants can be used by school councils to purchase school supplies, fund teacher training, and improve facilities. In some cases (as in Ghana and Rwanda), the grants can be used to give teachers bonus allowances (dependent on the successful completion of requirements set between teacher and principal) or support the full cost (salary and bonus) of teachers hired on a fixed-term contract (in Ghana, Niger, Rwanda, and in some forms of SBM in Madagascar).

In The Gambia, the first follow-up survey of the Whole School Development (WSD) program showed that, on an array of intermediate outcomes variables, the WSD group scored higher, and the difference observed against the control school was statistically significant in many cases. Both the WSD schools and the control schools have scored higher on many dimensions compared with the baseline a year previously. In terms of student performance (fourth and sixth grades), the level of performance was low and on a par with the outcomes of the baseline test to third- and fifth-grade students. However, substantial learning did occur from one grade to the next (World Bank 2010a).

In Senegal, the baseline report for the experiment showed the test results of children at the start of the second and fourth grades on written French and math tests and an oral test. The population served has very low levels of education, very low literacy rates (particularly for women), and low employment rates and hours of work. In terms of the experimental evaluation, the baseline data revealed that the treatment and control group were as near perfectly balanced as one could hope (Carneiro and others 2010).

Conclusions

It is important to highlight two ideas from the outset before reviewing the empirical literature on SBM. First, only a very few rigorous studies of the impact of SBM exist.[2] General descriptions of the most rigorous evaluations of SBM programs that have been conducted in recent years are presented in table 3.4.

It is also challenging to evaluate the size effect of the programs because of the heterogeneous presentation of metrics and results in the different studies. Several studies reported only the estimated coefficient of impact and, therefore, it is difficult to translate these into a size because they depend on the specific measurement of both the independent and dependent variables. Other studies presented information on the percentage changes in some outcome variables due to the intervention. Again, the metric of the output variables varies considerably among studies. Nonetheless, the size effects for those studies that have a clear interpretation of the results are reported; otherwise, only the direction and significance of the coefficient of impact is reported.

SBM Program Design

One of the noteworthy aspects of SBM programs is their diverse nature. Cook (2007) calls this their "modest entitivity." From the narrow management programs to the broad comprehensive schooling models, they vary greatly. But there are fundamentals of the narrower form of SBM. The focus on autonomous school strategic planning, multiple groups setting the goals, changes in teacher pedagogic practices, and stronger relations with parents and the surrounding community are mainstays.

In the United States, SBM practice led to the 1999 passage of the Comprehensive School Reform Act, which outlined 11 components of a more autonomous school:

1. Each school adopts a model known to be successful (or has the promise to be so).
2. Proven methods of teaching, learning, and management should be used in the school—implying that management change is not sufficient for comprehensive school reform; also needed are plans for changing teaching and learning.
3. Methods for teaching, learning, and management should be integrated in a meaningful way.
4. Staff should have continual professional development.

Table 3.4 Evaluations and Impacts: SBM Evidence from Recent Rigorous Studies

Study	Country	Program	Date of program	Date of data	Estimation or identification strategy	Limitations	Results
Randomization and regression discontinuity design							
Duflo, Dupas, and Kremer 2007	Kenya	Extra Teachers Program	2006–08	2005–08	Randomized evaluation	External validity; pilot conditions might not be able to be duplicated in noncontrolled settings	(1) Higher student test scores (2) Lower teacher absenteeism (3) Small change in student dropout rate
Chaudhury and Parajuli 2010	Nepal	Nepal Community Support Project	2007–09	2005–09	Quasi-experimental randomization approach (IV and DD); through exogenous instrument in form of advocacy group; advocacy campaign randomly assigned; intent to treat	Small-scale pilot; not pure randomization	(1) Reduced number of out-of-school children (2) Reduced repetition (3) Increased progression (4) Increased equity (disadvantaged castes performed better)
Das 2008	Pakistan	NGO hired to manage school together with school council; funds ($4,000) per school given for	2004–08		RCT in principle, though original randomization not fully upheld; analysis performed using intent to treat	Sample size not clearly defined for each part of intervention; randomization altered due to field conditions (district-level	(1) No effects on student enrollment, teacher absenteeism, or facilities index (infrastructure)

(continued next page)

Table 3.4 Evaluations and Impacts: SBM Evidence from Recent Rigorous Studies *(continued)*

Study	Country	Program	Date of program	Date of data	Estimation or identification strategy	Limitations	Results
		school needs; NGO in initial experiment allowed to transfer teachers as well (2004)				officials did not uphold original randomization as they wanted to target funds to schools that needed them most; unclear to what extent randomization altered)	(2) In treatment schools, significantly increased percentage of council members whose children were students
Pradhan and others 2010	Indonesia	school-based management	2007–08	2007–08	RCT	Pathways not identified	(1) Improved learning outcomes (2) Strongest impact from elections in combination with link (3) Increased language scores by a 0.51 standard deviation, increased math scores by 0.46
Gertler, Patrinos, and Rodríguez-Oreggia 2010	Mexico	AGE 125; doubling of grant	2007–10	2006–10	RCT	4 states, might not be replicable; required private funding to double	(1) Increased participation in first year (2) Reduced dropout rate (3) Improved reading scores for third grade only in year 2

Propensity score matching; instrumental variables; Heckman correction models							
Di Gropello and Marshall 2005	Honduras	PROHECO	1999	2003	Heckman correction model; exclusion restriction: presence of potable water and community services	Not a solid exclusion restriction	(1) Small changes in dropout rates (2) No effects on test scores
Gunnarsson and others 2004[a]	several countries	several programs	several years	1997	IV: principal's attributes and legal structure	Not a solid instrument	(1) No effects on test scores (2) Increased participation
Jimenez and Sawada 1999	El Salvador	EDUCO	1991	1996	Heckman correction model; exclusion restriction: government prioritizing targeting formula	Not a solid exclusion restriction	(1) Increased reading scores (2) Decreased absenteeism
Jimenez and Sawada 2003	El Salvador	EDUCO	1991	panel: 1996 and 2003	Heckman correction model; exclusion restriction: government prioritizing targeting formula	Not a solid exclusion restriction	(1) Increased probability of students staying in school
Gertler, Patrinos, and Rubio-Codina 2006	Mexico	AGE	1996	school panel: 1998–2002	DD fixed effects; preintervention trends	Did not control for time-variant unobservable effects	(1) Reduced failure and repetition rates (2) No effects on dropout rate

(continued next page)

Table 3.4 Evaluations and Impacts: SBM Evidence from Recent Rigorous Studies *(continued)*

Study	Country	Program	Date of program	Date of data	Estimation or identification strategy	Limitations	Results
King and Özler 1998	Nicaragua	ASP	1991, 1993	pseudo-panel: 1995, 1997	Matching, panel data	No pretrend validation	(1) *De jure* autonomy: no impact (2) Real autonomy (hire/fire teachers): increased test scores
Lopez-Calva and Espinosa 2006	Mexico	AGE	1996	2003–04	Matching, cross-section	No baseline data	Increased test scores
Murnane, Willet, and Cardenas 2006	Mexico	PEC	2001	several sources: 2000–04	DD: more systematic check of equal trends between treatment and control groups	Not controlled for time-variant unobservable effects	(1) Reduced dropout rates (2) No effect on repetition
Abreu and others 2010	Mexico	PEC-FIDE	2008–09	2008–09	DD, propensity score matching		(1) Increased promotion rates (2) Increased test scores
Gertler and others 2010	Mexico	PEC (Colima only)	2006–09	2005–09	RCT	Not strictly observed	

Paes de Barros and Mendonca 1998	Brazil	decentralization	1982	panel, state level: 1981–1993	DD; no preintervention trends	Aggregation of data; no pretrend validation	(1) Reduced repetition and dropout rates (2) No impact on test scores
Parker 2005	Nicaragua	ASP	1991–93	2002	Matching, panel data	No pretrend validation	Increased test scores
Sawada and Ragatz 2005	El Salvador	EDUCO	1991	1996	Matching, cross-section	No baseline data	Increased test scores
Skoufias and Shapiro 2006	Mexico	PEC	2001	2000–03	Matching estimation with DD; one-year preintervention trend	No pretrend validation	Reduced dropout, failure, and repetition rates
Khattri, Ling, and Jha 2010	Philippines	school-based management	2003–	2003–	DD; propensity score matching	No pretrend validation	Significant but small effects on test scores
Benveniste and Marshall 2004	Cambodia	EQIP	1998–2004	1999–2003	Program randomly implemented by district in province; fixed effects regression, DD, matching	Cannot test participation per se	(1) Increased pass rates (2) Reduced dropout rates (3) Improved achievement

Source: Authors' compilation.

Note: IV = instrumental variables. DD = difference-in-differences. RCT = randomized control trial. NGO = nongovernmental organization.

a. School self-reported levels of autonomy.

5. Staff should support the initiative.
6. Formal and informal leadership should be distributed widely within the school.
7. Parents and the local community are involved in the school.
8. There will be external technical support for whatever change the school is making.
9. Use measurable benchmarks on a short-term basis.
10. Conduct annual evaluations.
11. Mechanisms are needed for identifying and gathering needed resources from external sources.

While not all 11 components need be in place for a school to be labeled an SBM school (nor are a minimum or core number of attributes needed), it is nonetheless obvious that the more of these components an SBM plan includes, the more integral is the change being promoted. In most developing countries, there is no inventory of what works—yet. So basing the model on positive cases proves difficult; thus, programs are invented or borrowed from other countries. Many of the programs in developing countries, even those designed to improve quality, are more participatory than management-centered. That is, there are hopes for high levels of participation but little empowerment of the actors to affect core education functions such as teaching and learning. Professional development or training—of staff (teachers or directors), in a few cases, and of parents in others—is becoming a usual function. The level of staff support seems to vary. In some cases, the programs empower the principals but do not really affect the teachers. Often the leadership model is not well distributed widely throughout the school.

Programs in developing countries are heavy on parental or community participation—even if that is only a stated objective. The level of external technical support varies. Some programs build it in effectively, while others take a more informal approach.

The use of measurable benchmarks—performance metrics or information in general—is a relatively recent phenomenon. The programs described here have been subject to rigorous evaluation. But there are some 53 such programs known around the world, and few of those were evaluated because few had any performance benchmarks in the design. It seems obvious, in a report on accountability, to discuss performance measures, but the fact is that many SBM programs were designed without appropriate attention to results. Thus, there are few evaluations (at least from the old generation) of any level of rigor.

Despite the limited evidence base, one can offer a few specific ideas about the design of SBM projects based on the large number of programs that exist around the world. There are clearly a few key issues that should be settled before embarking on an SBM initiative:

- *Specify what is meant by SBM.* The autonomy and accountability definitions must be explicit. The functions to be transferred must be delineated, and the entities to which they are to be transferred should be described. A clear account of the resources that will be available, how they will be used, and the model to be developed (administrative, professional, community, balanced, or a combination) should be given.
- *Take account of capacity issues.* In all models and types of SBM, capacity considerations are crucial. Thus, SBM projects should include a component to build the managerial capacity of parents, teachers, and other key players.
- *Clearly state what is to be achieved, how, and in what time frame.* A good rule of thumb is that SBM reforms need about five years before any fundamental changes occur at the school level, and only after eight years of implementation can changes be seen in indicators such as student test scores. This has been the experience in the United States. Therefore, it is important to ensure that the time frame is understood by all involved so that their expectations are realistic.
- *Establish goals, including short-term process goals, intermediate output goals, and longer-term outcome goals.* Most important, the relevant indicators need to be measured before, during, and after the experimental stage of the reform to make it possible to evaluate the impact of the reform. The high standards that usually apply to SBM programs in developed countries will be difficult to meet in developing countries. However, even in developed countries, SBM reforms tend to take several years to have any substantial impact, depending on the country's institutional context.
- *Spell out what will have to happen at different stages for the reform to reach its goals.* There are many ways in which the components (autonomy-participation and accountability) of SBM can be combined and implemented—that is, who gets what powers to do what—that make each SBM reform unique. Therefore, it is important to be clear and precise about the goals of each SBM program from the outset. The most common goals of SBM programs so far have been (1) to increase the participation of parents and communities in schools; (2) to empower principals and teachers; (3) to improve student achievement levels (as in most OECD countries); (4) to make school management more accountable; and (5) to increase the transparency of education decision making

(in most cases). These different goals have significant implications for how each program is designed.

- *Base interventions on whatever evidence is available, and include a strong impact evaluation component that is appropriate for the program, its duration, and its time frame.* There are three evaluation approaches: (1) evaluations that randomly select treatment schools (those that will implement an SBM project) and control schools; (2) evaluations that randomize the order in which schools enter into the program; and (3) evaluations that encourage schools to participate in the program.

  The ideal evaluation will involve some form of randomization. However, if randomization is not an option, there are two alternative ways of estimating the impact of an SBM reform. First, a regression discontinuity design procedure can be used when the SBM program is targeted, using some continuous variable as the entry criterion. The estimation yields the true effect of the intervention without the need for randomization in the design of the program. The second nonrandomized way to evaluate impact uses a nonrandom phase-in strategy. For this evaluation method to be technically sound, it is critical to show that the group of schools that is treated later is the right counterfactual for the group of schools that initially enters the program; in other words, they need to have similar pretreatment observable characteristics. This method highlights the need for both good preintervention data and good postintervention data to be able to compare the values of the outcome variables both before and after the program to measure its effects.

SBM models have many positive benefits, many of which can be characterized as improved school quality. However, learning outcomes, as measured by standardized test scores and examination results, are medium- to long-term benefits. That is, SBM, though not a costly investment and one that can even produce savings, is not a quick fix. In fact, it is shown that in the United States, in a meta-analysis of 232 studies with over 1,000 observations of 29 programs, SBM needs five years to bring about fundamental changes at the school level and about eight years to yield significant changes in test scores.

Summary

Education systems are extremely demanding of the managerial, technical, and financial capacity of governments and, thus, as a service, education is too complex to be efficiently produced and distributed in a centralized fashion. Most of the incentives that affect learning outcomes are institutional in nature. Local decision making and fiscal decentralization can have positive effects on outcomes such as test scores or graduation rates by holding the schools accountable for the outputs they produce. High-quality, timely service provision can be ensured if service providers can be held accountable to their clients—who, in the case of education, are students and their parents.

There is a trend toward increasing autonomy, devolving responsibility, and encouraging responsiveness to local needs, all with the objective of raising performance levels. Most countries whose students perform well on international student achievement tests give their local authorities and schools substantial autonomy over adapting and implementing education content or allocating and managing resources. Moreover, greater school autonomy is not necessarily associated with wider disparities in school performance if governments provide a framework in which poorer-performing schools receive the necessary support to help them improve.

The argument in favor of decentralized decision making in schools is that it fosters demand at the local level and ensures that schools provide the kind of education that reflects local priorities and values. By giving voice and power to local stakeholders, decentralization increases client satisfaction and improves education outcomes. School autonomy and accountability can help to solve some of the fundamental problems in education. If schools are given some autonomy over the use of their inputs, they can be held accountable for using them in an efficient manner. Decentralizing power to the school level can also improve service delivery to the poor by giving poor families a say in how local schools operate and by giving schools an incentive to ensure that they deliver effective services to the poor and by penalizing those who fail to do so.

Past studies found that SBM policies actually changed the dynamics of the schools, either because parents got more involved or because teachers' actions changed (King and Özler 1998; Jimenez and Sawada 1999). Several studies showed that SBM led to reduction in repetition rates, failure rates, and, to a lesser degree, dropout rates (Di Gropello and Marshall 2005; Jimenez and Sawada 2003; Gertler, Patrinos, and Rubio-Codina 2006; Paes de Barros and Mendonca 1998; Skoufias and Shapiro 2006). The studies that had access to standardized test scores presented mixed evidence, with countries such as El Salvador, Mexico, and Nicaragua showing positive results (Jimenez and Sawada 2003; King and Özler 1998; Sawada and Ragatz 2005; Lopez-Calva and Espinosa 2006). Other reforms such as those in Brazil and Honduras appear to have had no effects on test scores.

The new evaluations, mostly randomized control trials—and, in almost all cases, preliminary results only—substantiate earlier studies, strengthen and expand the knowledge base, and provide new information on impacts that are substantially different from past studies in some respects.

SBM forms with weak autonomy or accountability produce small effects. Evidence from two new evaluations in Mexico showed small positive impacts on outcomes, mostly in the early grades of primary school. However, they also showed changes in school climate, parental perceptions and participation, and engagement between actors. The implications are that a larger dose of autonomy, especially in terms of labor control, would garner larger gains in terms of student learning. The AGE 125 project had a positive impact on test scores in reading and math, mostly for third-grade students. But even those significant gains did not bring the students in AGE schools—largely disadvantaged, rural, indigenous populations—close to the national average in test scores.

Strong SBM forms—meaning those affecting teacher hiring and firing decisions—have shown positive effects in improving test scores but only when it was clear what parents were supposed to do or when the SBM was combined with other incentives such as reduced class size, as in Kenya. On the other hand, a strong SBM form in Nepal has yet to show an impact two years into implementation. However, devolving management responsibility to communities has had a significant impact on certain schooling outcomes related to access and equity.

On balance, SBM has been shown to be a useful reform for a number of reasons. Yet it is better when integrated with other interventions.

Still, there are unanswered questions. For instance, do administrative-control SBMs work better than, say, more participatory models—and, if so, under what situations? Put another way, does vesting decision-making powers in the principal serve the same purposes? Or is parental participation or oversight required to instill a level of accountability? Does more autonomy need to be devolved to the school level to improve intermediate and long-term outcomes? In other words, do weak-form SBMs need to become stronger forms to have sustained impacts on learning over time?

Also, more cost-benefit analysis is needed. Clearly, SBM is an inexpensive initiative since it constitutes a change in the locus of decision making and not necessarily in the amount of resources in the system. If the few positive impact evaluations dominate, then SBM can be regarded as a cost-effective initiative. For example, in Mexico, the rural SBM program is estimated to cost about $6.50 per student (which, in unit cost terms, is only about 8 percent of primary education unit expenditures, estimated at over $800 in 2006). Moreover, the $6.50 figure includes the allocation of resources to the parent associations and the training imparted to the parents. It also compares favorably to other common interventions, such as computers ($500 per student, 10 computers per class), teacher salary increases ($240 per student), or annual school building costs ($160 per student); only student assessments have a similar unit cost, at $6 (Patrinos 2009).

Other elements that will need more analysis as the study of SBM reforms evolves are political economy issues, such as the roles played by teachers' unions and political elites. These issues could explain why we are getting ambiguous results in some cases. SBM, like any other kind of reform, requires some level of political support from the government. Political support may be more important than technical merit in the success or failure of a strong SBM reform. Teachers and their unions may want to resist SBM reforms that give parents and community members more power. How they will react to the reform is a crucial factor in its eventual success or failure. Typically, bureaucrats and teachers' unions favor increased budgets and spending on teacher-related inputs rather than on non-teacher-related investments. Thus, unions and perhaps also bureaucrats may try to limit the extent of school autonomy, especially those models that empower school councils or even just school principals to hire and fire teachers. If this is the case, then one could expect only mild forms of SBM (such as the participatory models in rural Mexico, around since the mid-1990s) to survive, challenging the existence of strong versions such as EDUCO in El Salvador. Also, the impact of such programs will be limited by design, wherein true decision making is muted in strong models and the participatory models never confront the true causes of education disadvantage.

Elite capture is another potential problem. If the programs are dominated by certain groups, they may not be working to improve outcomes for all, especially for the least able. Even local authorities can react negatively to what they perceive to be the capture of governance at the various levels by elite groups, particularly if these groups use SBM reforms as a means to further their political agendas. When local democracy and political accountability are weak, as is the case in many developing countries, especially in rural areas, then decentralization reforms can lead to elite capture (Bardhan 2002; Bardhan and Mookherjee 2000, 2005). In more traditional and rural areas, the poor or ethnic minorities, such as the indigenous peoples of rural Mexico, feel the need for a strong central authority to ensure that they are able to access services as well as more powerful local citizens. This centralization would tend to limit the amount of local decision making and reduce the overall impact of the programs. A related issue may be the lack of a culture of accountability within communities, meaning that no one would think to question any actions taken by the group running the school (De Grauwe 2005), something that was detected in focus group interviews in rural Mexico (Patrinos 2006).

Finally, there are often challenges involved in implementing SBM reforms that can undermine their potential. These challenges include the need for all the relevant actors to accept and support the reform, the fact that more time and work demands are put on teachers and parents, and the need for more local district support. The participatory models may suffer especially from the latter because they demand from parents a great investment of time, which is costly to them. In addition, if parents need to prepare for meetings or need to understand documents required for preparing school improvement plans, these requirements place the poorest and least-educated at the greatest disadvantage and limit the potential of the program to help the most deserving and neediest students.

Notes

1. Given the U.S. evidence, one might wonder whether charter schools (around since the 1990s, which one might think of as an ultimate form of SBM—that is, a public school with autonomy over personnel, budget, and pedagogical decisions) might perform any better than public schools. Indeed, the evidence is usually considered mixed, with a variety of authors showing vastly different results (Patrinos, Barrera-Osorio, and Guáqueta 2009). However, newer studies on the topic in the United States include a report by the Center for Research on Education Outcomes (CREDO) at Stanford University, which found a wide variance in the quality of charter schools, with, in the aggregate, students in charter schools not faring as well as students in traditional public schools (CREDO 2009). The study found that 17 percent of charter schools reported academic gains that were significantly better than traditional public schools, 37 percent showed gains that were worse than traditional public schools, and 46 percent demonstrated no significant difference. Hoxby (2009) claims that a statistical mistake in the CREDO study forced an underestimation of the effect of charter schools. A study of New York charter schools—where most students are admitted based on a lottery, thus representing clear evidence—found that, on average, a student who attended a charter school for all of grades kindergarten through eight would close about 86 percent of the achievement gap in math and 66 percent of the achievement gap in English (Hoxby, Murarka, and Kang 2009). A follow-up study by CREDO showed that most New York City charter school students were showing academic growth in math that was statistically larger than what non-charter school students would achieve (CREDO 2010). A recent study of Boston schools found that each year of attendance in middle-school charters raised student achievement by a 0.09–0.17 standard deviation in English and a 0.18–0.54 standard deviation in math relative to those attending traditional schools in Boston (Abdulkadiroglu and others 2009). Dobbie and Fryer (2009) studied Harlem Children's Zone, a 97-block area in central Harlem, New York, where charter schools offering a web of community services for children operate. A randomized evaluation found that students enrolled in sixth grade gained more than a full standard deviation in math and a 0.3–0.5 standard deviation in English by eighth grade—enough to reverse the black-white achievement gap. Angrist and others (2010) studied KIPP (Knowledge Is Power Program), the largest charter management organization, and found reading gains of a 0.12 standard deviation for each year and larger gains for special-education and limited-English students in the range of a 0.3–0.4 standard deviation.
2. Santibañez (2006) consists of a literature review of the 53 evaluations carried out since 1995 of the impact of SBM programs on educational outcomes.

References

Abdulkadiroglu, A., J. Angrist, S. Cohodes, S. Dynarski, J. Fullerton, T. Kane, and P. Pathak. 2009. "Informing the Debate: Comparing Boston's Charter, Pilot and Traditional Schools." Report for the Boston Foundation, Boston.

Abreu, R., M. Caudillo, L. Santibañez, and E. Serván-Mori. 2010. "Evaluación de impacto del proyecto piloto PEC-FIDE." Impact evaluation, Fundación Idea, Mexico City.

Anderson, J. A. 2005. *Accountability in Education*. Education Policy Series. Paris: International Institute for Educational Planning; Brussels: International Academy of Education.

Angrist, J. D., S. M. Dynarski, T. J. Kane, P. A. Pathak, and C. R. Walters. 2010. "Inputs and Impacts in Charter Schools: KIPP Lynn." *American Economic Review* 100 (2): 239–43.

Arcia, G., E. Porta Pallais, and J. R. Laguna. 2004. "Otro vistazo a la autonomía escolar de Nicaragua: aceptación y percepción en 2004." Study for the Ministry of Education, Culture and Sports, Managua, Nicaragua.

Bardhan, Pranab. 2002. "Decentralization of Governance and Development." *Journal of Economic Perspectives* 16 (4): 185–205.

Bardhan, Pranab, and Dilip Mookherjee. 2000. "Capture and Governance at Local and National Levels." *American Economic Review* 90 (2): 135–39.

———. 2005. "Decentralizing Antipoverty Program Delivery in Developing Countries." *Journal of Public Economics* 89 (4): 675–704.

Barrera-Osorio, F., T. Fasih, and H. A. Patrinos. 2009. *Decentralized Decision-Making in Schools: The Theory and Evidence on School-Based Management*. Directions in Development Series. Washington, DC: World Bank.

Bauer, S. 1997. "Designing Site-Based Systems, Deriving a Theory of Practice." *International Journal of Educational Reform* 7 (2): 108–21

Bauer, S. C., I. E. Bogotch, and H. S. Park. 1998. "Modeling Site-Based Decision Making: The Relationship between Inputs, Site Council Practices, and Outcomes." Paper presented at the Annual Meeting of the American Educational Research Association, San Diego, April 13–17.

Benveniste, L., and J. Marshall. 2004. "School Grants and Student Performance: Evidence from the EQIP Project in Cambodia." Unpublished manuscript, World Bank, Washington, DC.

Borman, G. D., G. M. Hewes, L. T. Overman, and S. Brown. 2003. "Comprehensive School Reform and Achievement: A Meta-Analysis." *Review of Educational Research* 73 (2): 125–230.

Caldwell, B. J. 2005. *School-based Management*. Education Policy Series. Paris: International Institute for Educational Planning; Brussels: International Academy of Education.

Carneiro, P., O. Koussihouèdé, N. Lahire, and C. Meghir. 2010. "Senegal: Evaluation of the Impact of School Grants on Educational Achievement: Baseline Report." Unpublished manuscript, World Bank, Washington, DC.

Carnoy, M., A. Gove, S. Loeb, J. Marshall, and M. Socias. 2008. "How Schools and Students Respond to School Improvement Programs: The Case of Brazil's PDE." *Economics of Education Review* 27 (1): 22–38.

Chaudhury, N., and D. Parajuli. 2010. "Giving It Back: Evaluating the Impact of Devolution of School Management to Communities in Nepal." Unpublished manuscript, World Bank, Washington, DC.

Clark, D. 2009. "The Performance and Competitive Effects of School Autonomy." *Journal of Political Economy* 117 (4): 745–83.

Cook, T. D. 2007. "School-Based Management in the United States." Background paper, World Bank, Washington, DC.

CREDO (Center for Research on Education Outcomes). 2009. "Multiple Choice: Charter School Performance in 16 States." Study report, CREDO, Stanford, CA.

———. 2010. "Charter School Performance in New York City." Study report, CREDO, Stanford, CA.

Currie, George. 1967. "An Independent Education Authority for Australian Capital Territory: Report of a Working Party (Currie Report)." Department of Adult Education, Australian National University, Canberra.

Das, J. 2008. "The Impact of Contracting Out School Management to NGOs and of Transferring Budgets to School Councils." PowerPoint presentation, World Bank, Washington, DC.

De Grauwe, A. 2005. "Improving the Quality of Education through School-Based Management: Learning from International Experiences. *International Review of Education* 51 (4): 269–87.

Di Gropello, E. 2006. "A Comparative Analysis of School-based Management in Central America." Working Paper 72, World Bank, Washington, DC.

Di Gropello, E., and J. H. Marshall. 2005. "Teacher Effort and Schooling Outcomes in Rural Honduras." In *Incentives to Improve Teaching*, ed. E. Vegas. Washington, DC: World Bank.

Dobbie, W., and R. G. Fryer Jr. 2009. "Are High-Quality Schools Enough to Close the Achievement Gap? Evidence from a Bold Social Experiment in Harlem." Unpublished manuscript, Harvard University, Cambridge, MA.

Duflo, E., P. Dupas, and M. Kremer. 2007. "Peer Effects, Pupil-Teacher Ratios, and Teacher Incentives: Evidence from a Randomization Evaluation in Kenya." Unpublished manuscript, Abdul Latif Jameel Poverty Action Lab (JPAL), Massachusetts Institute of Technology, Cambridge, MA.

———. 2009. "Additional Resources versus Organizational Changes in Education: Experimental Evidence from Kenya." Unpbulished manuscript, Abdul Latif Jameel Poverty Action Lab (JPAL), Massachusetts Institute of Technology, Cambridge, MA.

Gamage, D. T., and P. Sooksomchitra. 2004. "Decentralisation and School-Based Management in Thailand." *International Review of Education* 50: 289–305.

Gardner, D. P. 1983. "A Nation at Risk: The Imperative for Educational Reform." Report to the U.S. Department of Education, National Commission on Excellence in Education, Washington, DC.

Geeves, R., C. Vanny, K. Pharin, L. Sereyrith, S. Heng, and T. Panhcharun. 2002. *Evaluation of the Impact of the Education Quality Improvement Project (EQIP) of the Ministry of Education, Youth and Sport of the Royal Government of Cambodia*. Phnom Penh, Cambodia: World Education Cambodia.

Gertler, P., H. A. Patrinos, and E. Rodríguez-Oreggia. 2010. "Parental Empowerment in Mexico: Randomized Experiment of the *Apoyo a la Gestión Escolar*

(AGE) in Rural Primary Schools in Mexico: Preliminary Findings." Unpublished manuscript, World Bank, Washington, DC.

Gertler, P., H. A. Patrinos, and M. Rubio-Codina. 2006. "Empowering Parents to Improve Education. Evidence from Rural Mexico." Policy Research Working Paper 3935, World Bank, Washington, DC.

———. 2007. "Methodological Issues in the Evaluation of School-Based Management Reforms." Doing Impact Evaluation No. 10, World Bank, Washington, DC.

Gertler, P., H. A. Patrinos, M. Rubio-Codina, and V. Garcia-Moreno. 2010. "Impact Evaluation of a School-Based Management Program in Colima, Mexico: Preliminary Analysis." Unpublished manuscript, World Bank, Washington, DC.

Gunnarsson, V., P. F. Orazem, M. Sánchez, and A. Verdisco. 2004. "Does School Decentralization Raise Student Outcomes? Theory and Evidence on the Roles of School Autonomy and Community Participation." Working paper, Iowa State University, Ames.

Hanushek, E., and L. Woessmann. 2007. "The Role of Education Quality for Economic Growth." Policy Research Working Paper 4122, World Bank, Washington, DC.

Heckman, J. 1976. "The Common Structure of Statistical Models of Truncation, Sample Selection, and Limited Dependent Variables and a Simple Estimator for Such Models." *Annals of Economic and Social Measurement* 5 (4): 475–92.

Heckman, J., H. Ichimura, and P. Todd. 1998. "Matching as an Econometric Evaluation Estimator." *Review of Economic Studies* 65: 261–94.

Hoxby, C. M. 2009. "A Statistical Mistake in the CREDO Study of Charter Schools." Unpublished manuscript, Stanford University, Stanford, CA, and National Bureau of Economic Research, Cambridge, MA.

Hoxby, C. M., S. Murarka, and J. Kang. 2009. "How New York City's Charter Schools Affect Achievement, August 2009 Report." Second report for the New York City Charter Schools Evaluation Project, Cambridge, MA.

Jimenez, E., and Y. Sawada. 1999. "Do Community-Managed Schools Work? An Evaluation of El Salvador's EDUCO Program." *World Bank Economic Review* 13 (3): 415–41.

———. 2003. "Does Community Management Help Keep Kids in Schools? Evidence Using Panel Data from El Salvador's EDUCO Program." Discussion paper, Center for International Research on the Japanese Economy, University of Tokyo.

Karim, S., C. A. Santizo Rodall, and E. C. Mendoza. 2004. *Transparency in Education*. Paris: International Institute for Educational Planning and UNESCO; Brussels: International Academy of Education.

Khattri, N., C. Ling, and S. Jha. 2010. "The Effects of School-Based Management in the Philippines: An Initial Assessment Using Administrative Data." Policy Research Working Paper 5248, World Bank, Washington, DC.

King, E., and S. Cordeiro-Guerra. 2005. "Education Reforms in East Asia: Policy, Process, and Impact." In *East Asia Decentralizes: Making Local Government Work*, 179–207. Washington, DC: World Bank.

King, E. M., and B. Özler. 1998. "What's Decentralization Got to Do with Learning? The Case of Nicaragua's School Autonomy Reform." Unpublished manuscript, Development Research Group, World Bank, Washington, DC.

King, E. M., B. Özler, and L. B. Rawlings. 1999. "Nicaragua's School Autonomy Reform: Fact or Fiction?" Working Paper 19, Impact Evaluation of Education Reforms Series, World Bank, Washington, DC.

Leithwood, K., and T. Menzies. 1998. "Forms and Effects of School-Based Management: A Review." *Educational Policy* 12 (3): 325.

Lopez-Calva, L. F., and L. D. Espinosa. 2006. "Efectos diferenciales de los programas compensatorios del CONAFE en el aprovechamiento escolar." In *Efectos del Impulso a la Participación de los Padres de Familia en la Escuela*, ed. CONAFE. Mexico: CONAFE.

McGinn, N., and T. Welsh. 1999. "Decentralization of Education: Why, When, What and How?" Fundamentals of Educational Planning No. 64, International Institute for Educational Planning, UNESCO, Paris.

Murnane, R. J., J. B. Willet, and S. Cardenas. 2006. "Did the Participation of Schools in *Programa Escuelas de Calidad* (PEC) Influence Student Outcomes?" Working paper, Harvard University Graduate School of Education, Cambridge, MA.

OECD (Organisation for Economic Co-operation and Development). 2004. "Raising the Quality of Educational Performance at School." Policy brief, OECD, Paris. www.oecd.org/dataoecd/17/8/29472036.pdf.

Paes de Barros, R., and R. Mendonca. 1998. "The Impact of Three Institutional Innovations in Brazilian Education." In *Organization Matters: Agency Problems in Health and Education in Latin America*, ed. W. D. Savedoff. Washington, DC: Inter-American Development Bank.

Parker, C. E. 2005. "Teacher Incentives and Student Achievement in Nicaraguan Autonomous Schools." In *Incentives to Improve Teaching*, ed. E. Vegas. Washington, DC: World Bank.

Patrinos, H. A. 2006. "Mexico: AGE (*Apoyo a la Gestión Escolar*)—School Management Support: A Qualitative Assessment." Unpublished manuscript, World Bank, Washington, DC.

———. 2009. "School-Based Management." Unpublished manuscript, World Bank, Washington, DC.

Patrinos, Harry Anthony, Felipe Barrera-Osorio, and Juliana Guáqueta. 2009. *The Role and Impact of Public-Private Partnerships in Education*. Washington, DC: World Bank.

Patrinos, H., and R. Kagia. 2007. "Maximizing the Performance of Education Systems: The Case of Teacher Absenteeism." In *The Many Faces of Corruption: Tracking Vulnerabilities at the Sector Level*, ed. J. E. Campos and S. Pradhan. Washington, DC: World Bank.

Pradhan, M., D. Suryadarma, A. Beatty, and R. P. Artha. 2010. "Improving Educational Quality through Enhancing Community Participation: Results from a Randomized Field Experiment in Indonesia." Unpublished manuscript, World Bank, Washington, DC.

Santibañez, F. 2006. "School-Based Management Effects on Educational Outcomes: A Literature Review and Assessment of the Evidence Base." Working paper, World Bank, Washington, DC.

Sawada, Y. 1999. "Community Participation, Teacher Effort, and Educational Outcome: The Case of El Salvador's EDUCO Program." Working Paper 307, William Davidson Institute, University of Michigan, Ann Arbor.

Sawada, Y., and A. B. Ragatz. 2005. "Decentralization of Education, Teacher Behavior, and Outcomes." In *Incentives to Improve Teaching*, ed., E. Vegas. Washington, DC: World Bank.

Skoufias, E., and J. Shapiro. 2006. "The Pitfalls of Evaluating a School Grants Program Using Non-Experimental Data." Policy Research Working Paper 4036, World Bank, Washington, DC.

Transparency International. 2005. *Stealing the Future: Corruption in the Classroom*. Berlin: Transparency International.

Word Bank. 2003. *World Development Report 2004: Making Services Work for Poor People*. Washington, DC: World Bank.

———. 2008a. "Devolving Power to the Local Level: The Role of Information and Capacity Building in Empowering Community-based Organizations." Concept Note on Ghana, World Bank, Washington, DC.

———. 2008b. "Indonesia: BOS and BOS-KITA Project Appraisal Document." Report 45043-ID, World Bank, Washington, DC.

———. 2008c. "Mozambique DSSP." Case study for the Africa School-Based Management Report, Human Development Network, World Bank, Washington, DC.

———. 2008d. "Rwanda Impact Evaluation Incentives and Performance for Teachers on Fixed Contracts." Concept Note, World Bank, Washington, DC.

———. 2008e. "Senegal: Evaluation of the Impact of School Grants on Education Achievement." Concept Note, World Bank, Washington, DC.

———. 2010a. "Education Impact Evaluation in The Gambia: The Whole School Development: An Interim Progress Report." Unpublished manuscript, World Bank, Washington, DC.

———. 2010b. "A Review of the Bulgaria School Autonomy Reforms. Europe and Central Asia Region." Report 54890-BG, Human Development Department, World Bank, Washington, DC.

4

Making Teachers Accountable

Making schools and teachers more accountable for results, especially student learning outcomes, has become a central challenge for education policy makers in both developed and developing countries. The quantity and variety of policy innovations in this area has increased significantly over the past decade, with an especially striking increase in the developing world. This chapter reviews both the theory and the evidence base around two key types of reform focused on teacher accountability: contract tenure reforms and pay-for-performance reforms.

The first section summarizes the theoretical and empirical rationales for teacher accountability reforms. The second section reviews recent global experience with these reforms. The third and fourth sections put forth a typology of contract tenure and pay-for-performance approaches being adopted in developing countries and review the evaluation evidence around each type of reform. The fifth section compares the empirical evidence with the theoretical literature on performance incentives to identify key design issues. The final section draws cautious conclusions from existing evidence on how to design effective incentives for better teaching.

Throughout the chapter, the developing country experience and research literature are surveyed broadly, but emphasis is placed on recent evidence from well-evaluated reforms in the developing world.

Teacher Accountability Reforms: Why?

Growing interest in teacher accountability reforms stems from a confluence of factors. First, an increasing number of countries are convinced that student learning outcomes are the core barometer of education system performance. In developing countries, the use of nationally standardized tests has increased substantially over the past 10 years, as has the number of developing countries participating in internationally benchmarked assessments such as the Organisation for Economic Co-operation and Development's (OECD's) Programme for International Student Assessment (PISA). The latest wave of education research on long-term correlations between (internationally benchmarked) student learning levels and gross domestic product (GDP) growth supports this focus. Studies conclude that education investments contribute to faster GDP growth only if schooling is effective in raising student learning—and the higher the learning levels, the faster the growth (Hanushek and Woessmann 2007). In short, an increase in the quantity and quality of student learning data in developing countries has created a capacity that did not exist earlier to monitor and potentially reward school-level learning improvements.

Second, there is increasing evidence that teachers' ability to generate student learning is highly variable. Recent careful studies of the "value added" of individual teachers working in the same grade in the same school have begun to document that while students with a weak teacher may master 50 percent or less of the curriculum for that grade over a single school year, students with a good teacher can get an average gain of one year, and students with great teachers may advance 1.5 grade levels or more (Hanushek and Rivkin 2010; Farr 2010). A series of great or bad teachers over several years compounds these effects and can lead to unbridgeable gaps in student learning levels. The most rigorous research to date in this area is from the United States, and it may not proxy the variance in teacher effectiveness in other settings. But new research in Brazil, discussed later in this chapter, suggests that teachers' classroom performance and effectiveness spans a large spectrum in at least some developing country settings as well.

Third, education policy makers wishing to recruit or groom "great teachers" to raise overall learning results confront the empirical reality of recruitment and compensation systems with weak links, if any, between rewards and performance. The vast majority of education systems are characterized by fixed salary schedules, lifetime job tenure, and flat labor hierarchies, which create rigid labor environments where extra effort, innovation, and good results are not rewarded. Nor is it possible to sanction poor performance; the percentage of tenured teachers ever dismissed for poor performance is exceedingly small (Weisberg and others 2009).

Almost universally, teacher recruitment and promotion are based on the number of years of preservice training, formal certificates, and years in service. Yet an extensive body of research has documented the lack of correlation between these "observable" factors and teachers' actual effectiveness in the classroom, measured by their ability to produce learning improvement in their students (Hanushek and others 2005). The record on in-service professional development leading to measurable improvements in teacher performance is also strikingly poor (Borko 2004; Garet and others 2001; Cohen and Hill 2001). The clear implication of available research is that most school systems are recruiting and rewarding teachers for the wrong things, failing to encourage the capacities and behaviors that contribute most directly to student learning results, and unable to sanction ineffective performance.

A disconnect between the incentives teachers face and the results school systems seek is manifest in many developing countries by egregious performance failures. A study of teacher absenteeism across six different developing countries in 2004 found that, on average, 20 percent of the teaching force was absent on any given day, suggesting low accountability for attendance and performance (Chaudhury and others 2005). Classroom observations in representative samples of schools in Latin America in 2009 found more than 30 percent of instructional time lost because teachers arrived late, left early, or otherwise failed to engage in teaching (Bruns, Evans, and Luque 2010). PISA 2006 data show that teacher applicants in most developing countries are drawn from the weakest students in secondary and higher education, even as the cognitive content of basic education becomes more demanding. Above all, average learning outcomes in developing countries are low and, in most countries, have failed to improve.

Developing countries today spend an average of 5 percent of GDP on education, and many countries are on track to increase this. The impact of this investment on their subsequent economic growth hangs largely on how effectively they use the 4 percent of GDP (80 percent of total education spending) that goes to pay teachers. In a growing number of countries, the drive to improve student learning outcomes is translating into creative and sometimes radical policy reforms aimed at changing the incentives for teachers. While the share of reforms being rigorously evaluated remains small, the evidence base to guide the design of new efforts is becoming more robust. This chapter aims to distill that evidence and its implications for policy.

Recent Global Experience with Teacher Accountability Reforms

As Vegas (2005) and others have pointed out, individuals are attracted into the teaching profession and gain satisfaction from their work for a wide range of reasons. All of these factors, shown in figure 4.1, constitute part of the *incentives* for teaching. Correspondingly, school systems have numerous

Figure 4.1 Teacher Performance Incentives

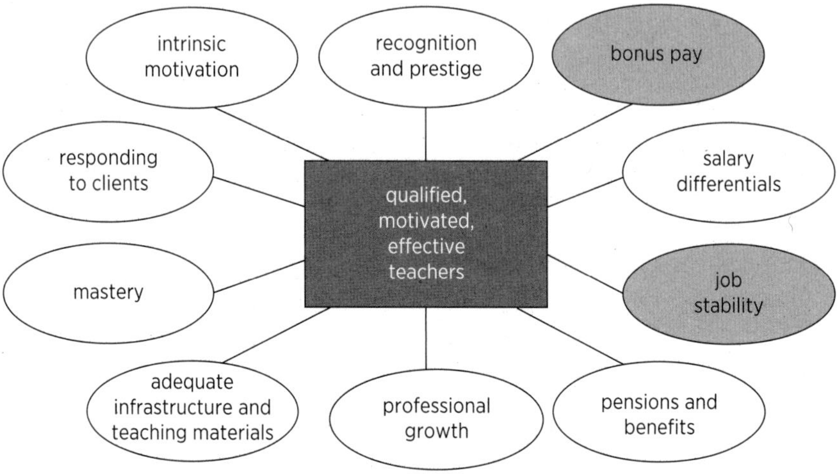

Source: Adapted from Vegas 2005.

monetary and nonmonetary levers to use in attracting and rewarding effective teachers.

Beyond the policies that touch teachers directly, broader education policies that shape the school environment also affect whether high-capacity teachers are attracted into a school system and motivated to perform. It is relatively common for private schools and charter schools to recruit teachers with qualifications equivalent to those of public school teachers while paying lower salaries or offering less job security. Teacher surveys report that attractive features of the school environment—including the quality of infrastructure, class size, availability of teaching materials, quality of principals, engagement of parents, time for collective work with other teachers, and opportunities for professional growth—influence employment decisions and can offset lower wage and benefit compensation.

This chapter zeroes in on two of the incentives pictured in figure 4.1: *job stability* (that is, teacher contract tenure) and *bonus pay* or *pay-for-performance* programs.

We differentiate bonus pay from other policies affecting salary differentials in that bonus programs generally leave base salaries and the salary scale intact but create incentives at the margin, with the offer of an annual (or monthly) bonus based on some measure of teacher performance. The performance measure may be an *input* measure, such as teacher attendance; an *outcome* measure, such as school or student results;

or a combination of the two. The distinguishing feature of pay for performance is that it rewards teachers for what they *do* or *achieve* during a specified period (typically the prior school year). In this way, pay for performance is conceptually distinct from the factors that generally determine other teacher salary differentials, such as teachers' qualifications, geographic posting, type of service (that is, hardship pay for teaching in certain schools or disciplines), or even tests of skills and capacity—all of which reward teachers for *what they are capable of doing*.

In contrast to most of the other incentives for teachers, both contracts without guaranteed tenure and pay-for-performance programs establish direct links between teachers' performance and their rewards or sanctions. Thus, contract tenure and pay-for-performance reforms are potentially two of the strongest instruments at the disposal of education policy makers to increase teachers' accountability for results. These reforms are also of special policy interest for several other reasons:

- *They are important.* While there is evidence that intrinsic motivation plays a stronger role in the teaching profession than in many other occupations, there is also evidence that compensation and contract status are key determinants of who goes into teaching, how long they remain, and how they perform (Chapman, Snyder, and Burchfield 1993; Guarino, Santibañez, and Daley 2006; Rivkin, Hanushek, and Kain 2005; Murnane and others 1991).
- *They are expensive.* Teacher contracting and pay policies are important drivers of the overall teacher wage bill, which is by far the largest component of education spending. As such, these policies have ripple effects on the resources available for all other education investments. In most developing countries, the teacher wage bill is also a large enough share of public spending to have implications for overall fiscal policy.
- *They present major challenges for policy makers in most countries.* Historically rigid policies tying teacher recruitment, tenure, and compensation to formal certification processes and seniority typically leave education officials with limited room to maneuver to either "de-select" teachers who are not effective or reward high performers. While there may be a long-term need in many countries to adjust the base wage and salary scale for teachers relative to other categories of public or private sector employment, policy makers struggle with the recognition that the impact of across-the-board increases is fiscally prohibitive and may still fail to create stronger incentives for performance.

These factors are inspiring increased experimentation in developing countries with reforms that use the levers of contract tenure and bonus pay to try to make teachers more accountable for performance. Of the two, pay for performance has the largest number of experiences under way that are being subjected to rigorous impact evaluation, in both developing and developed countries. However, both strategies are increasingly being used in both low- and middle-income developing countries. The next two sections review the leading developing-country experiences and emerging evidence base for each type of reform.

Contract Tenure Reforms

Alternative contracting, in its broadest form, means recruiting teachers on contracts that do not grant the civil service status and tenure protection offered to regular teachers. Contract tenure reforms thus can overcome the rigidity of existing teacher policies by establishing a parallel teacher corps or career stream with different rules of the game alongside the existing teacher stream.

Although fairly uncommon in most European countries, alternative contracting is used in Australia, the United Kingdom, the United States, some other OECD countries, and most developing countries. Alternative contracts are typically for one year and renewable based on performance. Alternative contracting in developing-country settings is often—but not always—associated with entry standards and pay levels that are lower than for regular civil service teachers. In OECD contexts, such contracting is often used to bring highly qualified mid-career professionals from other fields into teaching at comparable salaries.

The rationale for alternative contracting in the developing world is usually either a shortage of teachers who meet the civil service entry standards or a shortage of public sector funding for the more expensive civil service contracts. Tightening teacher accountability for performance is rarely the explicit rationale. However, being on a short-term, renewable contract can clearly generate stronger incentives for an individual teacher to meet the performance goals of the contracting unit. The share of civil service teachers dismissed on performance grounds is extremely low in most systems, and these dismissals are almost always for egregious abuses, not simply for poor effectiveness in producing student learning outcomes. Good data on turnover of contract teachers unfortunately do not exist, but in the most carefully studied environments turnover has been substantially higher—in the range of 20–40 percent annually. However, there are no data on the share of contract teacher exits strictly related to performance, and many other factors are also typically at play.

The core policy innovation is the creation of a parallel teacher cadre hired on short-term contracts, typically covering a single school year and renewable based on performance. In a large share of cases, the hiring of contract teachers is also devolved to a lower level of the education system—the school or village level—than the hiring of civil service teachers, who are typically hired at the national level. This creates potential for more effective monitoring of teacher performance by the contracting unit.

Despite this potentially tight link between contract renewal and teacher performance, goals or targets in such contracts are rarely precise or explicit. There are few developing-country cases of explicit links between contract teachers' renewal and student learning improvements. If specific metrics are mentioned at all, they are more commonly teacher attendance or community satisfaction measurements, defined fairly broadly and somewhat subjectively. Student learning progress, however, may be an implicit factor in school managers' or community satisfaction with a contract teacher's performance. Table 4.1 summarizes the evidence base from rigorously evaluated cases in the developing world.

Confounding analysis of the pure accountability effects of less-secure contract terms and possibly closer performance monitoring is the fact that both the background characteristics (level of education and socioeconomic status) and pay levels of contract teachers can be different and sometimes lower than those of civil service teachers. While economic theory predicts that contracts renewable annually based on performance and monitored locally will *increase* teachers' motivation to perform in line with performance measures established by the hiring unit, both teacher effort and results may be *decreased* by the lower compensation embodied in many of these contracts or by lower teacher capacity (at least in terms of formal preparation). How these competing tendencies play out in practice, and how they affect learning outcomes for students, has been a subject of much debate. Only recently has enough robust evidence from diverse settings begun to offer some answers.

Impact Evaluation Evidence

India: Balsakhi contract teacher program

The *Balsakhi* ("child's friend") program, implemented in two cities in India (Mumbai and Vadodara), paid locally recruited young women with a tenth-grade (secondary school) education roughly 10 percent of a regular civil service teacher's salary to teach basic literacy and numeracy skills to third- and fourth-grade children who needed remedial support. The targeted children left the classroom in the afternoon and received tutoring for two hours per day. The program was highly effective in boosting the learning of these children, to the extent that *average* math and reading test scores in the treatment schools increased by a 0.14 standard deviation in the first year and a 0.28 standard deviation after two years over the averages in the comparison schools (Banerjee and others 2007). Most of the gains were attributable

Table 4.1 Summary of Evaluated Contract Tenure Reforms

Country (evaluation date)	Design, coverage	Performance measure	Contract teacher relative wage
India: Balsakhi teacher program (Banerjee and others 2007)	pilot program, two cities	student test scores; teacher absence	10% of civil service wage; lower educational level
Kenya: contract teachers (Duflo, Dupas, and Kremer 2009)	pilot program, 140 schools in rural Kenya	student test scores; teacher attendance and time spent actively teaching; student attendance	30% of civil service wage; same educational level
India: Andhra Pradesh (Muralidharan and Sundararaman 2010a)	pilot program, 100 schools in rural Andhra Pradesh	student test scores; teacher attendance and time spent actively teaching	20% of civil service wage; lower educational level
Mali, Niger, and Togo (Bourdon, Frölich, and Michaelowa, 2007)	national programs	student test scores	—
Peru (Alcazar and others 2006)	provincial program	teacher absence	—

Locus of contracting	Contract term	Period observed	Evaluation method	Results
local NGO	annual, renewable	3 yrs.	RCT	(1) Test scores for schools with Balsakhi program 0.14 SD higher in first year, 0.28 SD higher in second year, and 0.1 SD higher one year after program end. (2) Largest gains by children at bottom of initial test score distribution and by children receiving remedial teaching.
school councils	annual, renewable	3 yrs. (2 of intervention, 1 of follow up)	RCT	(1) Test scores for students of contract teachers were 0.21 SD higher than students of civil service teachers within the same school. (2) Contract teachers 30 percentage points more likely to be found in class teaching than were civil service teachers. (3) 11% drop in absence rates for students of contract teachers. (4) Long-term impacts persisted only where school councils had received management training.
school committees	annual, renewable	2 yrs.	RCT and matching	(1) Test scores 0.15–0.13 SD higher in math and language, respectively, for students in schools with an extra contract teacher. (2) Contract teachers absent 16% vs. 27% of time for regular teachers. (3) Contract teachers found teaching 49% of time vs. 43% for regular teachers during spot visits. (4) Nonexperimental estimation finds contract teachers as effective in producing learning gains, at one-fifth the cost of regular teachers.
school councils	annual, renewable	—	matching	Contract teachers had positive effect on low-ability students in low grades and negative effect on high-ability students in high grades.
—	—	—	matching	Contract teachers 12–13% more likely to be absent.

(continued next page)

Table 4.1 Summary of Evaluated Contract Tenure Reforms *Continued*

Country (evaluation date)	Design, coverage	Performance measure	Contract teacher relative wage
India: Madhya Pradesh (Goyal and Pandey 2009a)	statewide program, 200 schools	student test scores; teacher attendance and activity	20–25% of civil service wage; higher educational level
India: Uttar Pradesh (Goyal and Pandey 2009a)	statewide program, 200 schools	teacher attendance and activity	20–25% of civil service wage; higher educational level

Source: Authors' compilation.

Note: RCT= Randomized control trial. NGO = nongovernmental organization. — = not available. SD = standard deviation(s).

Locus of contracting	Contract term	Period observed	Evaluation method	Results
district office	3 yrs., renewable	2 yrs.	matching	(1) Contract teachers absent 27% of time vs. 37% for regular teachers. (2) Contract teachers found teaching 37% of time vs. 25% for regular teachers during spot visits. (3) Student test scores positively associated with teacher effort. (4) Contract teachers' absence and activity rates worsen in second contract year but still better than regular teachers.
village education committee	10 mos., renewable	2 yrs.	matching	(1) Contract teachers absent 26% of time vs. 39% for regular teachers. (2) Contract teachers found teaching 36% of time vs. 19% of time for regular teachers during spot visits. (3) Student test scores positively associated with teacher effort. (4) Contract teachers' absence and activity rates worsen in second contract year to similar levels as regular teachers.

to increases in learning by the children who had received remedial tutoring. Even one year after the program ended, the average student in the Balsakhi schools had test scores that were 0.1 of a standard deviation higher than the average student in comparison schools.

Although the program was clearly effective as a targeted, complementary instruction strategy using low-cost community-based tutors, it was not designed as a "head-to-head" trial of the cost-effectiveness of contract teachers as opposed to civil service teachers. In addition to their different contract status and pay levels, the Balsakhi teachers had different curriculum goals, teaching hours, and class sizes from those of the regular schools. Due to the design of the study, intermediate variables of teacher effort, such as absence rates and use of instructional time, were not monitored. However, the large learning gains produced by teachers contracted at 10 percent of the prevailing civil service teacher salary provides evidence that, at least in some contexts, contract teachers' lower average qualifications, lower pay, and lack of long-term contract security do not impede effective performance.

Kenya: Extra Teacher Program

The Extra Teacher Program (ETP) in western Kenya provided funding to a randomly selected set of schools to allow their school committees to hire a local contract teacher. Given an excess supply of graduates from Kenyan teacher training schools, contract teachers in Kenya, unlike India, have the same academic qualifications as civil service teachers (Duflo, Dupas, and Kremer 2009). However, the contract teachers were paid less than one-third of the civil service pay and could be fired by the school committee after each annual performance review.

The evaluation found that contract teachers were 15 percentage points more likely to be in class and teaching during unannounced visits than were civil service teachers in the comparison schools. The attendance record of contract teachers was even more impressive—30 percentage points higher—when compared with that of civil service teachers in their own schools, whose absence rates increased when the contract teachers began working. However, training programs for the school committees in how to monitor teacher attendance and performance mitigated the "shirking" behavior of civil service teachers over time.

The overall ETP program involved a number of different school-level interventions, including cutting class size in half (through the hiring of contract teachers) and assigning students to smaller classes, either randomly or tracked by ability. Overall, the program produced significantly higher student test scores. Among the program's results was clear evidence that students randomly assigned to contract teachers scored a 0.21 standard deviation higher on reading and math tests than their schoolmates assigned to civil service teachers. Students assigned to contract teachers also attended school more regularly (88 percent of the time versus 86 percent, corresponding to an 11 percent drop in absence rates). The stronger learning outcomes produced by contract teachers provides evidence of higher—or at least more effective—teaching effort than that of civil service teachers, despite the contract teachers' lower salaries. However, the fact that contract teachers were assigned to a single class of students and stayed with those students for two successive years (unlike the typical pattern of a new teacher each year) may have played a role as well.

The evaluation evidence was less clear on *why* students of Kenyan contract teachers performed better. The contract teachers were absent less and their students' attendance was slightly better, but relatively few school committees exercised the option not to renew a teacher's contract on performance grounds. Nonetheless, provision of school-based management (SBM) training to school committees (on how to manage the hiring, performance monitoring, and renewal decisions for contract teachers) was correlated with positive long-term impacts of the program. At the three-year follow-up, only students of contract teachers in schools whose committees had been trained performed significantly better than students in control schools. The SBM schools were also more likely to use funding from the community to retain the contract teacher once program funding ended; 43 percent of them did so, compared with 34 percent of non-SBM schools.

As in other country cases, the authors noted questions around the long-term sustainability of the contract teacher advantage. The superior performance of these teachers could have been the result of better choice of teachers by the local school committees or the stronger incentives those teachers faced. But the contract teachers' performance could also have reflected their motivation to perform well as a stepping stone toward higher-paid civil service teaching positions. While the ETP program did not provide a formal pathway to civil service status, it did allow teachers to acquire valuable experience; by the end of the program, 32 percent of the contract teachers did, in fact, acquire civil service teaching positions. Duflo, Dupas, and Kremer (2009) cautioned against assuming that average teacher performance, in Kenya or elsewhere, would match the performance of contract teachers in their study if all teachers were placed on alternative tenure contracts. In every setting where they were used, contract teachers worked alongside civil service teachers with higher pay and job security; the possibility of parlaying contract teaching experience into eventual civil service positions was a part of the incentive structure that contract teachers faced.

Andhra Pradesh, India: Contract teacher program

As part of a broader study of teacher incentives, contract teachers were hired in 2005 for a randomly selected set of schools across the state of Andhra Pradesh, India. As in the Balsakhi program, the contract teachers had lower average education than the civil service teachers in these schools and also tended to be younger, female, and more likely to live in the local villages. Whereas 84 percent of civil service teachers had a college degree and 99 percent had a formal teaching certificate, only 47 percent of contract teachers had completed college and only 12 percent had a teaching certificate. Eighty-one percent of the contract teachers lived in the local village, compared with 9 percent of the civil service teachers. Seventy-two percent of the contract teachers were female, with an average age of 24, while only 34 percent of the civil service teachers were female, with an average age of 39. The contract teachers' pay was also dramatically lower: less than one-fifth of the civil service wage.

Over the two years of the program, the contract teachers were absent significantly less—16 percent of the time, compared with 27 percent for civil service teachers in the same school, with the performance differential higher in the second year than in the first (Muralidharan and Sundararaman 2010a). In both years, the contract teachers were also more likely to be found teaching during spot visits by observers. Among contract teachers, those with lower absence rates and higher rates of observed teaching activity in the first year of their contract had higher rates of contract renewal for the second year.

Higher effort from the contract teachers (measured by absence rates and observed teaching activity) plus the reduction in average class size that their recruitment permitted had positive effects on student learning. After two years, students in schools assigned a contract teacher scored a 0.15 standard deviation higher in math and a 0.13 standard deviation higher in language than their counterparts in the same grade in schools without contract teachers (Muralidharan and Sundararaman 2010a). In short, less-educated teachers who were paid a small fraction of the civil service wage in Andhra Pradesh appeared to be more accountable for performance than their civil service counterparts—in terms of both attendance and teaching activity—and helped boost overall school outcomes.

Although the study was a randomized trial, the recruitment of a contract teacher also had a major effect on class size in these small schools, so it is difficult to disentangle how much student learning outcomes were driven by the smaller classes rather than the differential effort or effectiveness of contract as opposed to regular teachers. Muralidharan and Sundararaman conducted a number of persuasive nonexperimental tests and concluded that the contract teachers were as effective as the regular teachers in improving their students' learning. Given the contract teachers' dramatically lower wages, they were five times more cost-effective in producing educational results.

Other contract teacher studies

No other randomized evaluations have directly compared the performance of contract teachers and civil service teachers, but several other developing country studies have used matching methods to explore these issues. Contract teachers are widely used in West Africa, and Bourdon, Frölich, and Michaelowa (2007) compared the experience in Mali, Niger, and Togo, updating an earlier study of Togo by Vegas and De Laat (2003). They found that the presence of a contract teacher was positively correlated with the learning performance of low-ability students in the early grades but negatively correlated with the results of high-ability students in the upper grades.

A study in a rural province in Peru was the only study to date to document *higher* absence rates for contract teachers than for civil service teachers, by 12–13 percentage points (Alcazar and others 2006). The authors speculated that the lower salaries of contract teachers, in a context of weak local supervision, were a major reason for those teachers' apparently lower effort. Unfortunately, the study did not include any data on the student learning performance of contract and civil service teachers.

In two additional states in India that made extensive use of contract teachers—Madhya Pradesh and Uttar Pradesh—Goyal and Pandey (2009a) carried out a nonexperimental analysis of the relative performance of contract and civil service teachers. In these states, unlike Andhra Pradesh, contract teachers typically were *more* educated than regular teachers, although they were much younger, had much less teaching experience, and were more likely to come from the local community. Consistent with the results of experimental studies in India, the contract teachers working in Madhya Pradesh and Uttar Pradesh public schools consistently demonstrated higher effort than regular teachers, whether measured as daily attendance or as the likelihood of being actively engaged in teaching during an unannounced visit. This higher effort was also correlated with significantly better learning outcomes for their students on language and math tests after controlling for other school, teacher, and student characteristics.

Goyal and Pandey followed the performance of the contract teachers over two years and noted that effort levels (attendance rates and likelihood of being found teaching) declined for teachers in their second contract period in both states and, in the case of Uttar Pradesh, became indistinguishable from regular teachers. They speculated that weak de facto oversight by school-level committees significantly reduced contract teachers' incentives to perform. In both states, less than 6 percent of school committee members were even aware that selection and oversight of contract teachers was one of their core responsibilities. In practice, most contract teachers were rehired after their first year, and a number of contract teachers in Madhya Pradesh were able to move into the regular teacher stream (although at a reduced salary).

Weak de facto performance oversight, high likelihood of contract renewal, and opportunities for transfer into the regular civil service stream (or of successful union mobilization to equalize contract and regular teachers' employment terms) all reduced the differential in performance incentives between contract teachers and regular teachers and thus weakened the potential power of alternative contracting to strengthen teacher accountability for results. While there is uncertainty in the Indian context, as elsewhere, about the long-term sustainability of contract teacher policies, the evidence on their cost-effectiveness as a strategy for improving education accountability and outcomes is strong.

Contract Teacher Programs: The Balance of Evidence

The most rigorous of the available studies found contract teachers to be more cost-effective than regular civil service teachers—in India, dramatically so. In both Kenya and India, randomized trials have found learning outcomes for students of contract teachers to be better than those of civil service teachers, despite contract teachers' much lower salaries. Nonexperimental studies in India have found similar results. Earlier evidence on community-hired teachers in Central America (not included here but summarized thoroughly in Vegas 2005) was less robust, but that evidence also suggested that contract teachers achieved similar or better student grade progression and learning outcomes (controlling for student background) at lower cost.

Although contract teachers almost always work for lower salaries than their civil service counterparts, the cost-effectiveness of a contract teacher policy is likely to depend on country characteristics and the level of education involved. For example, all of the recent cases cited involved contract teachers at the primary level (where the supply of potential teachers with adequate capacity is not as likely to be constrained as at the secondary level or for specialty subjects such as sciences and math). It cannot be assumed that in all contexts it will be possible to recruit adequately qualified teachers at lower salaries.

In addition, there are major questions about the sustainability of this policy over time. Most of the evaluated cases suggested that contract teachers may have accepted the lower salaries and insecure tenure because they were queuing for civil service positions. Teachers' unions have also aided contract teachers in some African countries and in Central America to press successfully not only for tenure but also for equivalent wages—undermining the rationale for alternative contracting. In many of the cases evaluated, a large share of contract teachers do end up entering the civil service.

Nonetheless, the new wave of evidence on the short-term impacts of contract teacher reforms is fairly consistent: the use of contract teachers can strengthen the scope for local monitoring of teacher performance by parents and school councils, which results in higher teacher effort, which results in better student learning outcomes. In contexts where the supply of adequately trained teachers is not constrained, these positive outcomes can also be achieved at lower costs per student.

The evidence supports a theory of action in which the positive impacts of contract teacher reforms hinge on the de facto effectiveness of local monitoring. In evaluated cases where decisions about the hiring and retention of contract teachers were made higher up the administrative chain and not at the school level, or where local school committees were not equipped or empowered to put "teeth" into contract renewal decisions, impacts have been lower or have broken down relatively quickly. Alternative contracting can stimulate higher teacher effort and resulting improvements in student learning, but only if the hiring authority actually exercises the scope for holding teachers more accountable for performance.

Pay-for-Performance Reforms

Salary scales for teachers, unlike salary scales in most other sectors of the economy, are typically highly compressed, and movement across salary bands is rarely linked to individual results. These facts are all the more striking given the research evidence that individual teachers' ability to produce educational results varies widely. There is less consistent evidence across countries (and over time) on whether the *average level* of teacher salaries is sufficiently competitive with those of comparable occupations to attract high-capacity individuals to teaching. But there is remarkable concurrence in the literature that the widespread pattern of relatively flat salary progression over teachers' careers plus promotion policies rigidly linked to seniority combine to create weak incentives for teachers to perform to the best of their abilities and for high performers to remain in teaching. Indeed, in analyzing the large-scale migration of high-ability women out of the teaching profession in the United States between 1960 and 2010, Hoxby and Leigh (2004) argued that the "push" of compressed pay scales played a stronger role than the "pull" of more lucrative jobs in other sectors (Ballou and Podgursky 2002; Delannoy and Sedlacek 2001; Odden and Kelley 1997, cited in Umansky 2005).

To address these issues, school systems—and, indeed, other sectors and employers trying to stimulate higher worker productivity and efficiency—have resorted to bonus or "merit pay" schemes that establish a direct financial reward for the desired performance. In the United States alone, there have been hundreds of merit pay programs in education over the past century (Murnane and Cohen 1986). These programs typically share the objective of introducing some degree of variable annual compensation for teachers based on a measure of relative performance. The rewards can be based on *input* measures of performance (such as teacher attendance) or *outcome* or *results* measures (such as student learning progress). They can be targeted to either individual teachers or groups of teachers, typically at the school level.

Most of the cases reviewed in this chapter award bonus pay based on *outcomes*. The increased availability of student assessment data appears to be leading more school systems to try to link teacher pay directly to the performance measure they value most: student learning progress. Bonus pay is an attractive format because it does not increase the base salary bill and maintains the annual carrot of an incentive. Group bonuses, which reward all staff in a school for the school's average results, are more common than individual teacher bonuses. One reason for this is sheer practicality; individual (classroom-level) teacher bonuses require the ability to measure learning gains for every subject and grade, which is costly administratively.

An interesting new model being used in Brazil is a combined approach. The core bonus is a group reward (for all school personnel, including administrative staff), calculated based on average school learning results, but downward adjustments are made in the amounts paid to individual teachers and staff based on their individual absence rates.

Impact Evaluation Evidence

There is tremendous policy innovation and interest in education pay for performance currently, in the OECD as well as the developing world, and a complete review is beyond the scope of this chapter. We focus on (1) developing-country experiences that have been rigorously evaluated and (2) important or innovative developing-country cases that are currently being rigorously evaluated, even if final results are not yet available.

To organize the diverse experiences, we use a typology based on two dimensions: *what* is rewarded, and whether the rewards are *individual-* or *group-based*. Table 4.2 presents a summary of data from the following reviewed cases:

- *Bonuses based on student learning outcomes*
  - — Individual bonus (Andhra Pradesh, India 2009; Israel 2009)
  - — Group bonus (Andhra Pradesh, India 2009; Kenya 2010)

- *Bonuses based on student learning plus other student outcomes*
  - Group bonus (Pernambuco, Rio de Janeiro, Sao Paulo, and Minas Gerais, Brazil forthcoming; Israel 2002)
- *Bonuses based on student outcomes and teacher input measures*
  - Group bonus (Chile 2009)
- *Bonuses based on teacher input measures only*
  - Individual bonus (Rajasthan, India 2010; Kenya 2001)

Bonuses Based on Student Learning Outcomes

India: Andhra Pradesh

An ongoing randomized study in the Indian state of Andhra Pradesh offers the most persuasive evidence to date of the potential for individual and group bonuses for teachers to motivate more effective teacher performance in a developing-country setting. In a statewide representative sample of 500 schools, Muralidharan and Sundararaman (2009) carefully measured the impact of four alternative treatments applied in 100 schools each:

- An individual teacher bonus
- A group teacher bonus
- Provision of one extra contract teacher (input strategy)
- A block grant to the school (input strategy)

One hundred schools, not eligible to receive either incentives or inputs, served as the comparison group. To minimize Hawthorne effects, all schools (including the comparison schools) received the same amount of monitoring and measurement, differing only in the treatment received. Beginning and end-of-year tests were administered to all students and used to estimate value-added (gain) scores.

All interventions were designed to cost the same: Rs 10,000 per school (around $200), roughly equivalent to a teacher's monthly salary (including benefits).[1] Even though the four interventions were calibrated to cost the same, in practice the group incentive treatment ended up costing less—about Rs 6,000 ($125) per school.[2]

The teacher incentive bonus was structured as a fixed performance standard, meaning that awards were distributed to any teacher or school that raised test scores by 5 percentage points or more over their baseline test scores. Below this threshold, the bonus was zero. Above this threshold, the bonus was calculated as the percentage additional gain in average test scores, multiplied by a slope of Rs 500 ($10). The average bonus was calibrated to be around 35 percent of a typical teacher's monthly salary. Individual bonus payments were based on the average improvement in test scores for that teacher's particular class. In group-incentive schools, teachers received the same bonus, based on the average school-level

Table 4.2 Summary of Evaluated Pay-for-Performance (Bonus Pay) Reforms

Country (evaluation date)	Bonus type	Design, coverage	Performance measure	Award process	Predictability
Bonus based on student learning outcomes—Individual					
India: Andhra Pradesh (Muralidharan and Sundararaman 2009)	indiv.	pilot, 100 schools	gain in student TS (end-of-yr. vs. start-of-yr. TS for each classroom)	piecewise formula: bonus a function of % gain in TS, above a threshold of 5% gain	60% of teachers in first yr. got some bonus
Israel (Lavy 2009)	indiv.	pilot, 629 teachers in 49 high schools	avg. student scores on matriculation exams and avg. pass rate relative to predicted scores (adjusted for student SES)	rank order of teachers	302 of 629 (48%) teachers got some award
Bonus based on student learning outcomes—Group					
India: Andhra Pradesh (Muralidharan and Sundararaman 2009)	group	pilot, 100 schools	avg. gain in student test scores at school level relative to baseline scores	piecewise formula (see above)	(most teachers got some award)
Kenya (Glewwe, Ilias, and Kremer 2010)	group	pilot, 50 schools	avg. gain in student test scores at school level relative to baseline scores	rank order of "top-scoring" and "most-improved" (schools can win in only one category)	24 of 50 schools got award
Bonus based on student learning plus other student outcomes—Group					
Brazil: Pernambuco (Ferraz and Bruns, forthcoming)	group	statewide, 950 schools	school-level targets for improvement in IDEPE (state TS and student grade progression); individuals' bonuses discounted based on absence rates	piecewise formula: above threshold of 50% of target attained, up to limit of 100% of target	479 of 929 schools (52%) in 2009; 758 of 954 schools (79%) in 2010 received bonus
Brazil: Sao Paulo (Ferraz and Bruns, forthcoming)	group	statewide, 5,500 schools	school-level targets for improvement in IDESP (state TS and student grade progression); individuals' bonuses discounted based on absence rates	piecewise formula: from 1% of target attained, up to limit of 120% of school target	2009: 100% of schools, 87% of personnel got some bonus (13% of personnel received none for excess absence); 2010: 73% of schools, 77% of personnel got some bonus
Brazil: Minas Gerais (Ferraz and Bruns, forthcoming)	group	statewide, 3,972 schools	school-level targets for improvement in IDEMG (state TS and student grade progression); individuals' bonuses discounted based on absence rates; school targets negotiated annually with regional admin.	piecewise formula: above threshold of 60% of target attained on first phase of institutional evaluation, capped at 100% of target	33% of schools in 2009

Monitoring and support	Bonus size, distribution	Bonus frequency	Cost	Evaluation method	Results
substantial: feedback on test results, interviews, classroom monitoring	35% of MW	annual during 2-yr. experiment	Rs 1.9 million ($42,200)	RCT	0.27 SD improvement in learning outcomes compared with control schools by second yr.
limited: some interviews conducted	$1,750–$7,500 per teacher per subject (70–300% of MW)	annual, 1-yr. experiment	— (est. $1.5 million)	quasi-randomized trial, RDD	(1) 14% higher math pass rate and 10% higher scores (2) 5% higher English pass rate and 4% higher scores
substantial (see above)	$125/school distributed equally across teachers (about 35% of MW)	annual during 2-yr. experiment	Rs 1.8 million ($40,000)	RCT	0.16 SD higher test scores compared with control schools by second yr.
limited: one round of interviews conducted	21–43% of MW	one-time	K Sh 1.8 million ($30,700)	RCT	(1) 0.14 SD higher test scores compared with control schools in first yr. (2) Gains not sustained one yr. after (3) No decrease in teacher absence (4) Increase in exam prep sessions
school director surveys and classroom observations in sample of 220–300 schools	all school personnel eligible, teaching or nonteaching avg. bonuses: 180% of MW (2009), 140% of MW (2010)	annual	2009: R$28.8 million ($15.3 million) 2010: R$40 million ($21.3 million)	RDD	Schools with more ambitious targets improved 0.15–0.31 SD more than comparable schools with lower targets
school director and teacher surveys	all school personnel eligible, teaching or nonteaching avg. bonuses: 150% of MW (2009), 150% of MW (2010)	annual	2009: R$600 million ($319 million) 2010: R$655 million ($350 million)	DD	—
school director and teacher surveys; classroom observations in sample of 600 schools	all school personnel eligible, teaching or nonteaching	annual	2009: R$311 million ($173 million) 2010: R$371 million ($206 million)	DD	—

(continued next page)

Table 4.2 Summary of Evaluated Pay-for-Performance (Bonus Pay) Reforms *Continued*

Country (evaluation date)	Bonus type	Design, coverage	Performance measure	Award process	Predictability
Brazil: Rio de Janeiro City (Ferraz and Bruns, forthcoming)	group	municipality-wide, 922 schools	school-level targets for improvement in IDERio (municipal TS and student grade progression); individuals' bonuses discounted based on absence rates	threshold of 100% of target for early grades, at least 50% of target for upper grades, and ceiling of 110% of targets; no bonus for personnel with more than 5 days' total absences (excused or unexcused)	—
Israel (Lavy 2002)	group	pilot, 62 high schools	avg. credits taken, percentage of students receiving matriculation certificates, school dropout rates, school scores relative to predicted scores adjusted for student SES	rank order of schools	top 33% earned award
Bonus based on student learning outcomes and teacher or school input measures—Group					
Chile: SNED (Rau and Contreras 2009)	group	national (all public and publicly subsidized basic education schools)	avg. student TS on national exam (SIMCE) (37%), SIMCE gains (28%), other school factors (35%)	rank order tournament for schools stratified by region, urbanicity, grade level, and SES	top 25–35% of schools get awards
Bonus based on teacher input measures only—Individual					
India: Rajasthan (Duflo, Hanna, and Ryan 2010)	indiv.	pilot, 113 rural NGO schools	teacher daily attendance monitored with a date-stamped camera	piecewise formula: bonus of 50 rupees per day for additional days worked over 10-day-per-month threshold	bonus attainment automatic upon attendance
Kenya: preschools (Kremer and others 2001)	indiv.	pilot; 50 preschools	school headmasters given resources to award teachers bonuses for good attendance	piecewise formula: deduction from maximum potential bonus based on days of absence; remaining funds went to school general account	headmasters granted full bonuses to all teachers, regardless of their actual attendance

Source: Authors' compilation.

Note: RCT = randomized control trial. RDD = regression discontinuity design. DD = difference-in-differences. PSM = propensity score matching. SD = standard deviation(s). SES = socioeconomic status. TS = test scores. MW = monthly wage. — = not available. IDEPE = Index of Basic Education Development, Pernambuco (Brazil). IDESP = Index of Basic Education Development, Sao Paulo (Brazil). IDEMG = Index of Basic Education Development, Minas Gerais (Brazil). IDERio = Index of Basic Education Development, Rio de Janeiro (Brazil). SNED = National System for Performance Evaluation of Subsidized Educational Establishments (Sistema Nacional de Evaluación del Desempeño de los Establecimientos Educativos Subvencionados). SIMCE = National System for Measuring the Quality of Education (Sistema Nacional de Medición de la Calidad de la Educación). NGO = nongovernmental organization.

Monitoring and support	Bonus size, distribution	Bonus frequency	Cost	Evaluation method	Results
school director and teacher surveys and classroom observations in sample of 200 schools	all school personnel eligible, teaching or nonteaching individual bonuses heavily discounted for absence	annual	2010: R$14.6 million ($8 million)	RDD, DD	—
limited	$13,250–$105,000 per school; teachers got $250–$1,000 (10–40% of MW)	one-time	$1.44 million	RDD	(1) 0.13 SD improvement in learning outcomes (2) Modest increases in credits earned and % of students taking matriculation exam
Chile has numerous teacher evaluation, observation, and school support programs not directly related to SNED	Initially 40% of MW, currently 70–80% of MW; 90% of award to teachers, 10% to school	annual for 2 yrs., then new tournament starts	—	DD with PSM, RDD	(1) 0.07–0.12 SD increase in average learning outcomes associated with introduction of SNED (2) No evidence that winning bonus stimulated subsequent improvement
teacher surveys and spot visits, classroom observation	up to 25% of MW each month	monthly	—	RCT	(1) Teacher absence in "camera" schools fell from 42% to 23% (2) Student TS increased by 0.17 SD (3) Grade completion increased
spot school monitoring visits; teacher interviews	up to 300% of MW	per term (3 terms in each school yr.)	K Sh 4.6 million ($61,700)	RCT	(1) No decline in teacher absence rate (29%) (2) No change in pupil attendance or TS

improvement in test scores. Teachers in all incentive schools were told that bonuses would be paid at the beginning of the next school year, conditional on average improvements during the current school year (first year of the experiment). Inputs (a block grant or an extra teacher) were provided unconditionally to selected schools at the beginning of the school year.

At the end of two years of the program, both the individual and group teacher incentives were effective in improving student test scores. Students in incentive treatment schools had considerably higher test scores than those attending comparison schools, by 0.28 and 0.16 of a standard deviation in math and language, respectively. The qualitative analysis suggested that the main mechanism for the incentive effects was not increased teacher attendance but greater, and more effective, teaching effort conditional on being present. In particular, teachers in incentive schools were significantly more likely to have assigned homework and class work, conducted extra classes beyond regular school hours, given practice tests, and paid special attention to weaker children. These results were obtained from self-reports—that is, answers to unprompted interview questions with treatment-school and control-school teachers. These behaviors, however, were not independently verified or observed in the classroom.[3]

At the end of the two years of the study, there were significant (at the 10 percent level) differences between individual and group incentives, and between incentive schools and input schools. Individual incentives produced an average increase in student test scores of a 0.27 standard deviation, compared with a 0.16 standard deviation in group incentive schools. The input strategies also yielded positive effects when compared to control schools, but their magnitude (a 0.08 standard deviation) was substantially lower than incentive schools. In terms of cost-effectiveness, both the group and individual bonus programs were more cost-effective than the input programs, and they were roughly equal to each other in cost-effectiveness. Although the group bonus had a weaker impact on student learning results, this was offset by its lower costs.

To analyze the possibility that bonus payments induced negative impacts on student learning in other subjects, the researchers also studied learning outcomes in science and social studies, which did not enter into the calculation of the bonus. Test scores in these subjects in the incentive schools were also higher (0.11 and 0.18 of a standard deviation in science and social studies, respectively) at the end of two years of the program. Contrary to concerns that bonus pay can lead teachers to "teach to the test" at the expense of nontested subjects, at least in some contexts there may actually have been positive externalities from bonus programs. In contexts of low average literacy and numeracy skills, the researchers hypothesized that teacher efforts to increase test scores in math and language can have positive spillover effects on students' mastery of other subjects (Muralidharan and Sundararaman 2009).

In a related experiment in the same setting, the researchers analyzed whether providing teachers with more detailed feedback on their students' performance could increase the power of bonus incentives to improve test scores. The NGO running the project provided individual teachers with written diagnostic feedback on the performance of their class of students, in both absolute and relative terms, at the beginning of the school year. The reports also included specific suggestions on how to improve learning levels in specific areas of weakness.[4] The program was implemented in 100 rural primary schools that were randomly selected from the previous treatment schools across the state of Andhra Pradesh.

The authors found that, by itself, the feedback treatment did not appear to have any significant effects. However, feedback combined with teacher incentives had a significant effect on student test scores.[5] Based on indicators of teacher activity, the researchers concluded that while teachers in all of the feedback schools *could* have used the reports effectively if they had wanted to, only teachers in the incentive schools seemed to have done so. This suggests positive interactions between incentives and inputs and the possibility for incentives to also raise the effectiveness of other school inputs such as teacher capacity building (Muralidharan and Sundararaman 2010b).

No other research to date provides a direct comparison of the impact of individual and group-based teacher bonuses in the same context. But there is additional experimental evidence on individual teacher bonuses based on student learning results from Israel and a group-based bonus program in Kenya.

Israel: Individual teacher incentive experiment

Lavy (2009) evaluated a tournament-type bonus program in Israel that ranked teachers on the basis of value-added contributions to their students' test scores on high school matriculation exams, above and beyond the predicted scores for those students based on their socioeconomic characteristics, their level of study in the relevant subject, grade level, and a fixed school-level effect. Thus, teachers competed against each other in a fair way to produce learning gains in their classes.

The program covered 629 teachers, of whom 207 competed in English and 237 in math.[6] Relative to other incentive programs, the bonuses for this program were large and could amount to $7,500 per class (one teacher won two first-place awards totaling $15,000—equal to six months of salary). Due to a measurement error in the way schools were assigned into the program, it was possible to approximate a randomized trial of the incentive offer. Lavy found that the program had significant positive effects on student achievement by increasing the test-taking rate among high school seniors as well as the average pass rates and average test scores in both math and English.

Postprogram interviews with participating teachers generated interesting insights into how they responded to the incentives. Compared with teachers in schools not eligible for the program, teachers offered the incentive modified their teaching methods in several ways. They were significantly more likely to add after-school classes, to track students by ability within the classroom, and to tailor instruction to the needs of individual students, with special focus on students of weaker ability. These actions resulted in a higher share of students taking the matriculation exams than otherwise would have and higher pass rates and average scores across all test takers.

Lavy also found that teachers' effectiveness (measured by their success in achieving the bonus) was not highly correlated with "observable" teacher characteristics such as age, education level, teaching certification, or years of experience. However, teacher performance *was* correlated with the caliber of university attended; teachers who had graduated from top-ranked Israeli universities were significantly more effective than those who had attended less-prestigious universities or teachers' colleges. Unfortunately, although the program was initially designed to run for three years, a change of government caused its cancellation after a single school year.

Kenya: ICS teacher incentive program

A program in Kenya provided a group-based incentive to teachers, based on improvements in average student performance (Glewwe, Ilias, and Kremer 2010). Fifty rural schools were randomly selected (out of 100) for the incentive program, which was implemented over two years with one additional year of follow-up to observe long-term effects. Each year the program provided in-kind prizes, such as bicycles, valued at up to 43 percent of a typical fourth- to eighth-grade teacher's monthly salary. The prizes were awarded based on the performance of the school as a whole on the Kenyan government's districtwide exams. Performance was measured relative to baseline test scores at the beginning of the school year.[7] Awards were offered to "top-scoring" or "most-improved" schools (schools could win in only one of the two categories). In each category, prizes were awarded for first place (three prizes), second place (three prizes), third place (three prizes), and fourth place (three prizes). Overall, 24 of the 50 selected schools received a prize of some kind, and teachers in most schools felt they had a reasonable chance of winning a prize (Glewwe, Ilias, and Kremer 2010).

The program was careful to track the students initially enrolled in each school to ensure that new (potentially talented) students could not be recruited to take the exam and that poor-performing students were not held back from taking the exam. During the two years the program operated, a higher share of students in treatment schools than in comparison schools took the exam, which did generate gains in test scores. By the second year, students in the bonus schools scored, on average, a 0.14 standard deviation higher on the exams than did students in comparison schools, with the strongest improvements seen in geography, history, and religion (around a 0.34 standard deviation during the first and second years versus the baseline ["year 0"] on the district exam, and a 0.20 standard deviation versus the comparison schools in the second year on the district exam). The next-largest effects were in science and math (0.20 and 0.15, respectively, of a standard deviation on the district exam versus the baseline year), with no significant effects in other subjects.

However, these gains proved short-lived. One year after the program ended, there were no significant differences in test performance across the schools. Glewwe, Ilias, and Kremer (2010) speculated that teachers' strategies for achieving the bonus focused on short-run efforts to boost performance on the government tests, such as after-school tutoring in test-taking techniques, rather than changes in their core pedagogy or effort levels that might have had a higher chance of promoting long-term learning. For example, teacher absence rates did not decline from the baseline level of 20 percent of school days missed. Classroom observations did not detect any changes in homework assigned or use of learning materials. But by the second year of the program, bonus-eligible schools were 7.4 percentage points more likely than comparison schools to conduct exam preparation sessions. The benefits of this strategy were narrow, however. When researchers applied tests using a format different from those of the government exams, they found no difference in student performance between treatment and comparison schools.

Bonuses Based on Learning Improvement Plus Other Outcomes (Group-Based)

We know of no evaluated pay-for-performance programs based on multiple student outcomes that reward *individual* teachers, but the evidence on group-based bonuses of this type is increasing, thanks to a wave of innovation in this area in Brazil. Part of the reform stimulus is a conviction among Brazilian policy makers that low teacher quality is the binding constraint to education improvement and that restructuring the incentives for teachers must be part of the solution.

Another factor appears to be the federal government's establishment of the IDEB (Index of Basic Education Development) in 2007 (discussed further in box 4.1), which has provided states and municipalities with a convenient, transparent, and universally accepted metric for setting and monitoring annual school-level targets for improvement. Between 2008

BOX 4.1

Targets that Avoid Perverse Incentives: Brazil's Index of Basic Education Development

The Brazilian Ministry of Education in 2007 introduced an innovative tool for systematic annual monitoring of basic education progress in every school, municipality, state, and region of the country: the *Índice de Desenvolvimento da Educação Básica* (Index of Basic Education Development, or IDEB). The innovation lies in IDEB's combined measure of student learning results and student flows (grade progression, repetition, and graduation rates). Because the index is the product of both test scores and pass rates, it discourages automatic promotion of children who are not learning. However, it also discourages schools from holding children back to boost learning scores. Avoiding incentives for grade retention is important in Brazil, where the average repetition rate in primary school is approximately 20 percent, the highest in Latin America.

IDEB builds on the progress Brazil has made in scaling up its national student assessment system to a technically well-regarded learning assessment of math and language—called the *Prova Brasil* (Brazil Test)—that is applied every two years to every fifth-, ninth-, and twelfth-grade student. The IDEB measure combines Prova Brasil test results with administrative data on school enrollments, repetition, and grade promotion. The raw scale of the exams varies from 0 to 500, and the standardized scale ranges from 0 to 10. Pass rates are calculated based on the information reported by each school to the National School Census, applied yearly by the Ministry of Education.

The IDEB for each grade-subject is calculated as the product of the standardized Prova Brasil score and the average pass rate for the cycle evaluated (π):

$$IDEB_{asj} = ProvaBrasil_{asj} * \pi_{asj} \quad (4.1)$$

where a is the subject evaluated (Portuguese or mathematics),
s is the cycle evaluated,
j is the school.

The average pass rate in the cycle varies between 0 and 1 (1 if the pass rate equals 100 percent). The standardized IDEB measure thus varies between 0 and 10.

The index has become rapidly accepted in Brazil as the leading metric for gauging the relative performance of individual schools as well as municipal, state, and private school systems. Biannual IDEB results are

(continued next page)

BOX 4.1 *continued*

widely reported in the media, and the federal government has established targets for IDEB improvement for all of Brazil's 26 state and 5,564 municipal school systems.

IDEB has also facilitated the implementation of teacher bonus programs at both the state and municipal levels over the past three years. Although the different state and municipal programs in operation have a number of alternative design features, all are based on the IDEB metrics (states typically apply state-level tests that are equated with the Prova Brasil in the off years to generate a corresponding annual measure of performance). From the standpoint of federal education policy, IDEB has created a powerful platform for comparative analysis of state and municipal innovations in basic education.

Source: Fernandes 2007.

and 2010, six states and one large municipality in Brazil adopted annual teacher bonus programs based on IDEB results.

Because each of the Brazilian programs is being implemented systemwide, it is not possible to evaluate rigorously the fundamental question of whether introducing a bonus program *causes* the education system to improve. In these systems, there are no schools operating outside of the bonus regime and thus no perfectly valid comparison group. However, researchers plan to track the evolution of results in the "bonus" and neighboring nonbonus states and municipalities over time, using difference-in-differences analysis. And rigorous evidence on how different design features of the bonus programs affect school performance is being generated, exploiting discontinuities in the ways that school-level targets have been set. The "rules of the game" for the bonus programs in Pernambuco state and Rio de Janeiro municipality are most conducive to this approach. Although both evaluations are in an early stage, some first-round results from Pernambuco are discussed here.

Pernambuco, Brazil: Group-based teacher bonus program
In 2008, Pernambuco became the third state in Brazil to introduce a pay-for-performance system that rewards school personnel for the attainment of annual school improvement targets. All schools that achieve at least 50 percent of their targets receive a proportional bonus, up to a cap of 100 percent. Because the state budgets one month's education payroll for the program annually, the average bonus will exceed one month's

salary if less than 100 percent of schools achieve it. In the first year of the program, 52 percent of schools achieved over 50 percent of their targets, and the awards averaged 1.8 months of salary for most recipients. In the second year, 79 percent of schools received the bonus, and the average award was 1.4 months of salary.

This is a relatively large incentive compared with other programs internationally. Pernambuco's rule that schools achieving less than 50 percent of their targets receive nothing also creates a strong incentive. In some other Brazilian states, the rules of the game allow every school to receive some degree of bonus proportional to results, no matter how slight. Although the bonus is group-based (in that it rewards the whole school for its results), school directors have no discretion in how the funds are distributed. Each member of the school staff (teaching and nonteaching) receives the equivalent percentage bonus applied to the staff member's monthly salary.

The "strength" of the incentives embedded in the Pernambuco program's design make it an important case to analyze. The rules used to set the initial targets in Pernambuco—based on whether schools fell in the bottom 25 percent, 26–50 percent, 51–75 percent, or 76–100 percent of the performance distribution in 2007—created discontinuities in the targets that permit rigorous evaluation of their effects. Similarly performing schools had more or less ambitious targets depending on which side of these cutoffs they happened to fall. These discontinuities permit research on a number of important questions: How, in the short run, do schools respond to targets for improvement that are more or less ambitious? Do "stretch" targets motivate higher effort, or do they cause schools to give up?

Pernambuco's rule restricting bonus payments to schools that achieve at least 50 percent of their targets allows analysis of how achieving or not achieving a bonus payment in a given year affects a school's effort and strategies in subsequent years—including adverse impacts such as encouraging more time on tested subjects, teaching narrowly to the test, or inducing teachers to migrate to schools that are successful in achieving the bonus. Finally, as the evolution of Pernambuco's student outcomes can be compared over time to those of other states without bonus programs (using difference-in-differences analysis), the comparison will shed some light on the ultimate question: how does introducing a system of pay for performance affect student learning, pass rates, and teaching practices?

Results reported here are preliminary (Ferraz and Bruns, forthcoming). The first bonus was awarded in June 2009, based on schools' performance relative to their targets for the end-2008 school year (measured on standardized tests and administrative data collected by the federal government in December 2008). Fifty-two percent of Pernambuco's 929 schools achieved the bonus. A new set of targets was established for each school for the 2009 school year, and in mid-2010 the second round of bonus payments was made. This time, 79 percent of schools (and 81 percent of Pernambuco's 41,337 school-level personnel) received the bonus. The key findings thus far from the Pernambuco study are summarized below.

Acceptance of the program was relatively high. Sixty-four percent of school directors surveyed believed that the policy is an appropriate one, and 66 percent believed the program was having a positive impact on their school—whether or not they received the first-year bonus.

Schools with more ambitious targets achieved more progress (other things being equal). In almost every performance category (fourth-, eighth-, or twelfth-grade math or Portuguese), schools falling on the "higher target" side of the performance cutoffs made larger test score gains than the comparison schools just below the cutoffs. The differential learning gains were sharpest for schools just above the 25th percentile of performance. For the eighth grade in 2008, for example, schools on the "higher target" side of the cutoff improved average Portuguese scores by a 0.31 standard deviation more than the schools just below the cutoff (with less-ambitious targets). In math, the differential gain was a 0.15 standard deviation. At the second cutoff, just above and below the 50th percentile in the performance distribution, improvements were also higher for the schools with more ambitious targets, but they were also of smaller magnitude. For the other tested grades (fourth and eleventh), impacts were in similar ranges but varied across subjects and, in a few cases, by cutoff point. Overall, however, the evidence was consistent—at least over the very short term—that higher targets in the presence of an attractive incentive in Pernambuco induced higher learning results by schools.[8]

Learning levels across the state improved significantly. By the end of 2009, the second year of the bonus program, Pernambuco's state schools as a whole registered significant average improvements in learning, especially in Portuguese. Average Portuguese scores in the eighth and eleventh grades increased by 0.44 and 0.57 of a standard deviation, respectively. Math scores in the eighth and eleventh grades rose by 0.27 and 0.31 of a standard deviation, respectively. These learning gains are large relative to observed results from other teacher incentive programs. However, since this was a universally applied program within the state, these are raw gains, not gains relative to a comparison group. Difference-in-differences analysis will be needed to bound these gains. As Pernambuco ranked last among Brazil's 26 states on the 2007 IDEB rankings for primary schools (through eighth grade) and 19th for secondary schools, a significant part of these gains likely reflects reversion to the mean.

Schools that just missed receiving the bonus in 2008 improved more in the following year than schools that barely achieved the bonus. A key research question is whether schools that received the bonus in 2008 would be more motivated in 2009, or would they exert less effort and coast. To examine this, the performance of schools that fell just short of 50 percent of their 2008 targets (and did not receive the bonus) was compared with the performance of schools that achieved just over 50 percent of their targets and did get the bonus. Controlling for schools' 2008 test results and other school characteristics, schools that barely missed the bonus in 2008 improved more than schools that barely achieved it. It appears that—at least for schools that came fairly close in 2008—not getting the bonus had a positive effect on schools' motivation and performance.

Schools whose teachers spent more time on instruction were much more likely to achieve the bonus. In contrast to studies that have found no clear evidence of changes in teacher classroom practice to explain student learning improvements caused by the bonus, researchers in Brazil found significant correlations. A novel feature of the research is use of the Stallings "classroom snapshot" instrument (Abadzi 2009; Bruns, Evans, and Luque 2010) to generate detailed data on the pathways through which teacher incentive programs such as Pernambuco's bonus affect teacher practice in the classroom. In theory, if an incentive *causes* an improvement in student outcomes, it should operate through changes in teacher behavior that are induced by the incentive, such as increased or more-effective teaching effort.

Periodic observations are tracking comprehensive indicators of classroom dynamics (teachers' use of instructional time, materials, interaction with students, and student engagement) in a large sample of Pernambuco's 950 schools (1,800 classrooms in close to 300 schools, with oversampling of schools just above and below the original target discontinuities). Both tested and nontested subjects are being observed to try to capture adverse effects, such as diversion of school time from nontested subjects.

The first of several unannounced observations was carried out one month before the end-of-year tests that entered into the second-year bonus calculation. The data, shown in table 4.3, uncovered two main findings.

First, average teacher practice diverges widely from norms observed in the United States, where the Stallings instrument has been most extensively used. Against a U.S. good-practice benchmark of 85 percent of total class time effectively applied to instruction, the average observed in Pernambuco schools was 61 percent. Against a good-practice benchmark of 15 percent of time spent on routine classroom processes (such as taking attendance, passing out papers, or cleaning the blackboard), schools in Pernambuco averaged 28 percent.

A second finding, however, was that significant disparities existed across schools, and these were highly correlated with schools' likelihood of achieving the 2009 bonus (paid in 2010 based on year-end performance in 2009). While teachers were off-task a very high 12 percent of the time across the whole sample—either out of the classroom due to late arrival or

Table 4.3 Classroom Dynamics in 220 Pernambuco Schools, November 2009

Teacher use of classroom time	U.S. good-practice benchmarks (percent)	Overall PE sample (percent)	Achieved 2009 bonus (percent)	Didn't Achieve 2009 bonus (percent)	Difference, bonus Vs. nonbonus schools
Learning activities	85	61	62	53	0.09 (0.04)**
Classroom management	15	28	27	30	-0.03 (0.03)
Teacher off-task	0	12	10	17	-0.04 (0.02)***
Teacher out of classroom	0	8	8	12	-0.04 (0.02)***

Source: Bruns, Evans, and Luque 2010.

Note: PE = Pernambuco.

Standard errors in parentheses: ** significant at the 5% level; ***significant at the 1% level.

early departure or engaged in social interaction with students or colleagues—such time loss was much more significant in the schools that did not subsequently achieve the bonus (17 percent of total class time) than in those that did (10 percent of time lost).

Teachers in both successful (bonus-achiever) and less-successful schools spent a high share of total class time on routine management processes by U.S. standards. However, teachers in the bonus schools registered significantly less time off-task and were able to devote this time to instruction: learning activities absorbed 62 percent of total class time in schools that did go on to achieve their targets, compared with only 53 percent of time in schools that did not. There is also evidence of more intensive use of learning materials and higher rates of student engagement. The research as yet cannot determine whether these teacher behaviors *caused* students to improve more or whether the behaviors simply reflected the fact that better students are easier to manage and teach. But the sample of bonus achievers included schools from all parts of the performance distribution, including a large number of low-income and low-performing schools, because the targets measured improvement from a school's own baseline. The second year of observations will measure whether and how teachers' practice and classroom dynamics evolve after schools process the "information shocks" and incentives of either achieving or not achieving the bonus.

The evaluation of Pernambuco's pay-for-performance program is expected to continue for several more years, permitting deeper analysis of how annual targets and past rewards affect schools' improvement strategies, teacher behaviors, and overall system progress. Pernambuco's results will also be directly comparable with the new program in the municipality of Rio de Janeiro, which also sets targets for improvements in IDEB outcomes as the basis for the bonus and which also has established performance bands that generate discontinuities in school targets around several different thresholds. As in Pernambuco, a large sample of schools is being followed in a panel study that includes systematic classroom observation, using the Stallings instrument. The Rio program design is additionally interesting because it embodies strong sanctions against teacher absence: only employees with five or fewer absences for the entire school year (whether excused or not) receive the bonus. In 2010, 290 of Rio's 1,044 municipal schools qualified for the bonus based on their schools' 2009 IDEB improvements, but more than one-fourth of these schools' 11,000 employees did not meet the bar for individual attendance. Rio's program is currently the strongest effort to attack absenteeism; it will be important to measure how the bonus incentives affect these rates over time.

These and the other new Brazilian experiences offer a promising opportunity to generate comparative evidence on some key issues in the design of teacher pay-for-performance programs. Before the new wave of programs in Brazil, however, the main evidence on group-based bonus incentives for improvements in student outcomes was a small-scale program implemented in the 1990s in Israel.

Israel: Ministry of education school performance program

Lavy (2002) examined a tournament-type program implemented in 1995 that provided a group incentive to teachers in 62 nonrandomly selected secondary schools.[9] The objective of the program was to reduce dropout rates and improve academic achievement. The program used three performance measures: average number of credit units per student, proportion of students receiving a matriculation certificate,[10] and the school dropout rate. Participating schools competed for a total of $1.44 million in awards.

School performance was measured in two stages. First, school average outcomes (the three performance measures used in the program) were normalized relative to an expected score, estimated using regressions that controlled for socioeconomic background of the students. Second, schools were ranked according to improvement in average outcomes. The top third of schools won awards. In 1996, the highest-scoring of these schools won $105,000, and the lowest-scoring won $13,250. Seventy-five percent of the award was distributed among teachers in the school, and the remaining 25 percent could be used for schoolwide improvements (for example, teacher common rooms). Teachers' individual share of the school-level bonuses ranged from $250 to $1,000 (10–40 percent of the average monthly wage) depending on the size of the school's award.[11] All teachers in a school received the same award, regardless of individual contribution to the school's average results.

Lavy used a regression discontinuity approach to compare student outcomes in the 62 treatment secondary schools with 119 similar schools that just missed the program's eligibility rules. Lavy's results suggested that the monetary incentives had some effect in the first year of implementation (mainly in religious schools) and by the second year caused significant gains in student outcomes in all schools. The program led to improvements in the number of credit units taken by students and average test scores in matriculation exams. Average exam scores across treated schools in the second year of the program increased 2.4 points more than in the comparison group. From Lavy's descriptive statistics, this can be estimated as approximately .12 of a standard deviation. In addition, Lavy reported that more students in treatment schools gained matriculation certificates, and these schools also reduced dropout rates in the transition from middle school (grades 7–9) to high school (grades 10–12).

An interesting feature of the Lavy (2002) paper is that it compared the incentive intervention with a "resource" intervention. The resource intervention was a separate program that rewarded schools showing improvement with in-kind resources, such as teacher training, of identical monetary value to the bonus program. Twenty-two schools were selected for the resource-intervention program. A comparison group of schools not admitted into the resource program served as the basis for identification of program effects. The results of the resource program (evaluated only for secular schools) suggested that it also led to statistically significant improvements in student performance, but of much smaller magnitude. Lavy concluded that the school bonus program was more cost-effective.

Bonuses Based on Student Learning Outcomes Plus Teacher Input Measures (Individual)

Several new teacher bonus programs being implemented in Chile and at the state level in Mexico use a very different—and quite interesting—model. They provide individual rewards to teachers based on a combination of student outcomes and evaluation of teachers' individual merit (including tests of teachers' content mastery, direct observation of their classroom practice, and written assessments by principals and master teachers.)

The 2004 Chilean *Asignación Variable por Desempeño Individual* (Variable Allocation for Individual Performance, or AVDI) program is the most sophisticated example, given its use of comprehensive, high-stakes performance reviews (including videotapes of teachers' classroom practice) and a significant bonus in the form of a four-year increase in base pay for teachers who are rated highly. New programs in the state of Mexico (PROEBB and *Ser Maestro*) and the *Premio al Merito Docente* (Teaching Award of Merit) in the state of Nuevo Leon also combine evaluation of teachers' individual performance with student outcome measures. Unfortunately, none of these promising experiences is being evaluated rigorously.

Bonuses Based on Student Learning Outcomes Plus Teacher Input Measures (Group-Based)

Chile: National System for Performance Evaluation of Subsidized Educational Establishments (SNED)

One of the earliest experiences with performance pay in Latin America was Chile's *Sistema Nacional de Evaluación del Desempeño de los Establecimientos Educativos Subvencionados* (National System for Performance Evaluation of Subsidized Educational Establishments) or SNED. The program was introduced in 1996 and offers group bonuses to schools every two years based on an index that combines student learning results with other indicators of school and teacher performance.

Student learning counts for 65 percent of the total score through a combined measure of a school's results on the current year's national assessment (37 percent) plus a value-added measure of the difference in its average scores over the past two cycles (28 percent). The other indicators include schools' initiative (6 percent, based on school surveys); labor conditions (2 percent, based on presence of a complete teaching staff, replacement of absent teachers, and other indicators); equality of opportunities (22 percent, based on the school's retention and passing rates and lack of discriminatory practices, also measured through survey data); and integration of parents and guardians (5 percent, also based on survey data).

SNED is conducted as a tournament. Once the SNED index is estimated, schools are ranked within homogenous groups.[12] Schools in the top 25 percent of the ranking within each group receive the SNED award of excellence.[13] Ninety percent of the bonus is distributed to teachers, while 10 percent is distributed by the principal. The bonus for teachers typically represents an annual increase equal to approximately 40 percent of a teacher's monthly salary. About 20–30 percent of schools win the award.

The most recent evaluation of SNED estimated the impact of the incentive program by comparing its effects on privately managed, government-subsidized schools (about 30 percent of total enrollment) that are eligible for the incentive with results for privately unsubsidized schools, which are not eligible (Rau and Contreras 2009). Controlling for all other differences across these schools, the researchers found that the introduction of SNED in 1996 stimulated a statistically significant 0.12 standard deviation improvement in average student learning outcomes in the eligible schools relative to schools not covered by the program. Rau and Contreras (2009) also explored the effects of winning the SNED award on subsequent school performance. Over six rounds of SNED awards, however, they found no statistically significant evidence that schools winning the award performed better in the next period. They did, however, find that although SNED's stratified "homogenous group" performance bands are designed to help equalize schools' chances of winning the bonus, almost 40 percent of schools have not yet done so.

Bonuses Based on Teacher Input

Two rigorously evaluated programs, in India and Kenya, have explored the impact of bonus pay for teachers based on attendance.

Kenya: Pre-school teacher bonus program

Kremer and others (2001) evaluated a program that allowed school headmasters in rural Kenya to award individual teachers bonus pay for regular attendance. The size of the bonus was large—up to three months' salary for no absences. They found that the program had no impact on actual teacher attendance (measured by unannounced random visits). Absence rates remained at 29 percent. There was also no evidence of change in teachers' pedagogy, pupil attendance, or pupil test scores, although it could be argued that both pedagogy and test performance at the preschool level may be noisy measures.

Researchers also found that headmasters simply distributed the full bonus to all teachers regardless of attendance. Even though there was a financial incentive for headmasters to hold back part of the funding (any funds not allocated to teacher bonuses reverted to the schools' general fund), they chose not to do so. School headmasters clearly found it difficult to play a strict monitoring role at the school level.

Rajasthan, India: "Camera" program

An innovative program in rural India produced very different results (Duflo, Hanna, and Ryan 2010). In a randomly selected set of rural, NGO-run schools in Rajasthan, a schedule of monthly teacher bonuses and fines based on attendance was monitored in a creative way—with daily date- and time-stamped photographs. A student was asked to photograph the teacher and the children in the class at the beginning and end of each school day. Teachers' salaries were a function of the number of "valid school days," in which the school was open for at least five hours and at least eight students appeared in each picture. Unannounced visits to the "camera" and comparison schools measured actual absence rates and observed teacher activity.

The maximum bonus for a teacher with no days absent was approximately 25 percent of a month's salary. The program over three years had a dramatic effect on teacher absenteeism, which fell from 42 percent to 23 percent in the treatment schools. While there were no observed changes in teachers' classroom behavior and pedagogy (other than greater presence), student test scores rose by a 0.17 standard deviation, and graduation rates to the next level of education also rose significantly. While students' attendance rates (conditional on the school being open) did not increase, there was a significant increase in the total amount of time children in treatment schools spent in classes: on average, 2.7 more days of schooling per month.

Duflo, Hanna, and Ryan (2010) noted that the intervention was quite cost-effective. The base salary for teachers in the treatment and comparison schools (Rs 1,000 per month) was the same. All of the other costs of the program (the bonuses, the cameras, and monitoring) totaled roughly $6 per child per year. In terms of raising test scores, the per-child cost of a 0.10 standard deviation increase in test scores was only $3.58.

These contrasting experiences suggest that it is possible to stimulate higher teacher attendance with bonus pay, but the credibility of the system for monitoring performance is important. At least in the rural India setting—a context of very high teacher absence—teacher attendance also appears to be an important correlate of the desired education outcome: student learning. In other high-absenteeism settings, or settings where standardized annual student learning data is not available, bonus pay linked to teacher attendance is a reasonable approach, although it would be good to have additional evaluation evidence confirming its impact on learning.

Pay-for-Performance Programs: The Balance of Evidence

The most recent and robust developing-country evidence on pay-for-performance programs suggests that bonus pay incentives can improve learning outcomes, at least in the contexts studied most carefully to date. This evidence is in contrast to the more mixed, but less rigorous, developing-country evidence that existed just five years ago. It is also in sharp contrast to the most recent evaluation evidence from U.S. programs. In carefully conducted randomized trials of relatively generous bonuses aimed at both individual teachers (Nashville public schools) and schools (group-based bonuses in New York City public schools), researchers have failed to find any impact on student learning outcomes.

Under the aegis of the National Center on Performance Incentives, an impressive number of new U.S. education pay-for-performance programs are being evaluated experimentally. A three-year randomized trial of an individual bonus for 297 math teachers in Nashville public schools that offered large bonuses (up to $15,000 per year or 400 percent of a teacher's monthly wage) found no difference in average learning outcomes among students of the teachers who were and were not eligible for the bonuses. The first-year results from a randomized trial of a school (group-based) bonus program in 323 schools in New York City, which also offered a relatively large award (up to $3,000 per staff member), have also shown no student test-score differences between treatment and comparison schools. However, in the New York case, the tests were administered only three months after the program was announced, and the researchers note that it is logical to expect that impacts from incentives may take more time to develop.

In no study to date have long-term effects of performance-based pay been analyzed. Both theory and experience with performance-based rewards in other sectors indicate that the scope for perverse behaviors, such as gaming, cheating, or teaching to the test, can rise with time as system actors become more familiar with the rules of the game. As performance-based pay becomes increasingly—and logically—linked to student test results in many countries, the validity of those tests and the legitimacy of their application become centrally important challenges for education systems.

In a context of persistently low education outcomes and widespread evidence of "accountability failures" on the part of teachers and other education system actors, the evidence that pay-for-performance programs and the use of contract teachers can raise student outcomes in developing-country contexts is important. But the contrasting U.S. evidence suggests that it is important to note that these developing-country contexts are characterized by

- *Weak systems for performance monitoring and accountability*—evidenced by relatively high teacher absence rates, low teacher dismissal rates, and low student learning performance
- *Relatively weak teacher professionalism*—evidenced, in most cases, by low standards for entry
- *Relatively large bonus size*—for example, an annual bonus equaling 30–300 percent of a month's salary
- *Focused performance metrics*—emphasis on a small number of key, measurable results, notably student learning improvements or relatively easily measured teacher "inputs" such as monthly attendance, rather than more complex, subjective, and comprehensive performance evaluations
- *"Fair" performance metrics*—rewards to schools on a value-added basis (for progress relative to their starting point) or compared with schools with similar geographic and student socioeconomic conditions, not for absolute levels of performance
- *Rewards clearly linked to prior-period results*—annual bonuses directly linked to results for the previous school year, such as school-level learning improvement, or monthly bonuses for input measures monitored over the previous month, such as attendance.

These pay-for-performance programs in developing countries have "worked" in the sense that student learning outcomes improved in the presence of the bonus. In the most careful studies, the size of the effect—a 0.19–0.27 standard deviation increase in average student learning—is impressively large compared with the effects typically measured for other types of education programs.

The sole developing-country evaluation to date designed as a "head-to-head" comparison of individual bonus pay (rewarding each teacher for his or her own classroom's average learning progress over the course of a school year) with "group" bonus pay (rewarding schools for their average learning improvement) showed similar results in the first year but a stronger effect on learning outcomes from the individual bonus by the second year. The impact measured in that program in rural Andhra Pradesh, India—a 0.27 standard deviation increase in language scores—remains the largest reported causal impact from an education pay-for-performance program. However, the group bonus alternative proved to be more cost-effective because the average amounts awarded were smaller. In general, school systems will likely find group bonus pay more technically feasible than individual bonus pay, which requires the ability to test students in every grade, subject, and classroom and thus presents significant technical challenges and costs.

Our understanding of the mechanisms through which bonus pay improves student outcomes is still weak. In several randomized trials, at least over the short term, the bonus program did not induce any reduction in teacher absence rates, which is one of the most obvious ways teachers can increase their efforts in response to an incentive. These teachers did nonetheless produce statistically significant improvements in their students' learning outcomes relative to comparison groups of teachers who were not offered a bonus. Most did so by increasing the intensity of their work during school hours (assigning more homework and class work) and conducting test preparation sessions outside of school hours.

In Brazil, where all programs to date have been implemented system-wide, it is not possible to estimate how the introduction of a bonus *per se* affects schools' performance. At the end of the day, this is the critical question for policy makers: how cost-effective is the bonus program as a whole relative to alternative uses of education funds? But the Brazil studies can help elucidate both the pathways through which bonus incentives can change teacher behavior and the kinds of changes that are most effective in improving learning. There is intriguing evidence from Pernambuco that more-ambitious targets stimulated larger increases in student learning than less-ambitious targets did in comparable schools. This evidence suggests that, in the presence of an attractive performance award, schools focus on and are motivated to try to achieve specific targets. The Brazil research has also generated evidence of more efficient use of instructional time by teachers in the schools that subsequently earned the bonus. Teachers in bonus-earning schools lost less time due to late arrival or early departure, spent more time on instruction, made more intensive use of classroom resources such as learning materials, and kept a higher share of students engaged in learning.

Designing Teacher Accountability Reforms

What can recent experience tell us about the design of effective teacher incentives? How does the latest developing-country evidence square with issues that have long been associated with pay-for-performance programs, both in theory and in practice? In the United States alone, there is a long history of merit pay efforts in the education sector, and few have survived (Murnane and Cohen 1986). In this section, we review the theory on performance incentives and try to unpack the evidence from recent program experience to generate practical guidance for policy makers.

Principal-Agent Theory

Many of the issues in designing effective performance contracts transcend the education sector. As discussed in chapter 1, "principal-agent" (or employer-employee) relationships are a central topic of economics and industrial relations research because while employers (principals) need employees (agents) to help achieve organizational objectives, the two parties have divergent interests. Employees want to maximize compensation and minimize effort, and employers want the opposite. The two parties also have asymmetric information: the employer cannot perfectly monitor the effort and activities of the employee.

Under these circumstances, the role of the contract between the principal and the agent is to align their objectives by specifying the activities and results wanted and the compensation offered for these. An effective contract will motivate the agent to focus his or her efforts on efficiently achieving the principal's objectives. On the other hand, if the contract is structured so that agents are paid a flat rate irrespective of their level of effort or ability, or if job tenure is guaranteed irrespective of performance, it is unlikely that employees will exert additional effort or focus on doing the things that matter to the principal. It is striking how closely this textbook definition of an ineffective performance contract parallels the typical teacher contract (Prendergast 1999, cited in Courty and Marschke 2003).

Some issues in designing effective performance-based contracts in education are shared more broadly by public or nonprofit sectors. In contrast to firms that operate in a competitive environment, public sector agencies often face difficulties in specifying performance goals. Even when they have clear objectives, they can have difficulty establishing a clear hierarchy among competing objectives—something that is straightforward for firms, which seek to maximize profits or shareholder value. Baker (2002) argues that "the difficulty in defining 'good' performance measures in nonprofit organizations is one reason for the weak incentives that so often characterize organizations of this type, and for the dysfunctional consequences that often arise when these types of organizations try to use strong incentives." In addition, agents may not "know the technology" for achieving complex organizational goals. Vegas (2005), among others, has questioned whether teachers in many developing-country settings have the core content mastery and teaching skills required to produce desired learning improvements, no matter how strong their incentives to do so.

On the other hand, the assumption that agents work only for extrinsic (financial) rewards has come under scrutiny in both the psychology and economics literature in recent years. In their review of the economics and industrial relations literature on contracting, Fehr and Falk (2002) observed that "while it is certainly true that [agents'] desires to avoid risk and to achieve income through effort are important, it is equally true that there are powerful non-pecuniary motives that shape human behavior"—such as the desire to reciprocate, the desire for social approval, and the desire to work in interesting tasks.

Pink (2006) has argued that once a certain threshold level of financial remuneration is achieved in knowledge professions, the most powerful incentives are individual workers' own desires for autonomy, mastery, and a sense of contribution. It is interesting to note that all three of these incentives figure prominently in the core "industrial model" of the school: Teachers enjoy substantial autonomy within their own classrooms. The process of intellectual mastery is at the core of the work, for both teachers and their students. And abundant survey and other literature documents the attraction of the education profession for individuals seeking to make a social contribution.

These different strands of the academic literature suggest two hypotheses about performance contracts in education.

Hypothesis 1: Other things equal, it may be easier to attract individuals into teaching than into equivalently remunerated professions

The experience of Teach for America and its recent Teach for All offshoots in European and developing countries provides some support for this hypothesis. These programs have found it possible to attract high-capacity individuals to teach in disadvantaged schools (at prevailing wages) by stressing the scope for social contribution and offering strong organizational support for professional growth and mastery. However, the numbers of teachers recruited through these or parallel programs remain small relative to the system as a whole; after 20 years of experience, Teach for America placements represent only 7,000 of 3.2 million teachers in the United States.

The broader lesson for public sector school systems is the power of these levers. The "intrinsic" rewards of teaching—even if they are explicitly maximized by a well-managed school system—cannot substitute indefinitely for financial remuneration. But public education systems in developing countries likely have more scope than they are currently exploiting to incorporate appeals to the intrinsic motivation of prospective teachers into their human resources policies.

Hypothesis 2: Agents' (teachers') performance in education may be enhanced by clearer expression of performance goals and feedback

Research shows that public and nonprofit agencies in general have difficulty in specifying or prioritizing performance goals. In this context, improving the quality of performance feedback to teachers and the clarity of targets and goals, in theory, should enhance the efficiency of agents' performance. This belief is an important driver of the standards and accountability-based reforms in education seen in many OECD countries (such as Australia, New Zealand, the United Kingdom, and the United States) and some of the developing-country cases discussed in this chapter.

Measuring Performance in Education

The growing availability of nationally and internationally standardized data on student learning results over the past 20 years has reshaped the landscape on performance measurement in education systems. Despite deep controversies over the quality, credibility, and implementation of specific tests or testing in general, there is broad acknowledgment that learning outcomes are appropriate metrics for school system results. Education systems today in most countries are more advanced than other parts of the public sector in being able to track a meaningful indicator of system progress on an annual basis and, often, to be able to disaggregate results for specific subnational regions and target groups.

This advantage has clear implications for the design of effective incentive programs in education. Much of the theoretical literature on principal-agent contracts centers on the challenge of identifying an appropriate performance measure that will align the employer's goals with the employee's efforts. Not only must the measure be appropriate and meaningful, it must also be something that can be adequately measured—meaning regularly, inexpensively, and credibly. The scope for gaming (efforts by the employee to set artificially low targets), outright cheating, and other perverse behaviors must be managed. Psychologists argue that even valid and informative performance measures have a tendency to "degrade" or become dysfunctional by the mere act of being used for incentive purposes (Darley 1991, cited in Baker 2002).

None of these challenges is easy. But it is increasingly evident that, in the context of education, a core performance measure in most incentive programs will be student learning outcomes. Thus, the sheer identification of a meaningful and appropriate performance measure—which presents major problems for many public sector and nonprofit actors—is less of a challenge in education. This does not mean that learning outcomes are, or should be, the only performance measure used by school systems. There are clearly other important goals (building children's self-esteem, appreciation for culture and the arts, physical development, citizenship, and so on), and concerns are often expressed that these goals are shortchanged by excessive focus on learning outcomes. School systems must manage this tension. But what seems increasingly accepted is that a central task for every 21st-century school system is ensuring that well-designed and legitimately managed testing systems to track student learning progress are in place.

While high validity, well-administered testing programs are important for education systems irrespective of incentives, there is evidence that the stakes around test legitimacy and the scope for abuses become higher when incentives are introduced (Jacob and Levitt 2002). Rivkin (2009) recently articulated this point well:

> Over the long run, the success of [accountability and pay-for-performance] reforms hinges on a number of factors, but the validity of the teacher effectiveness (a term I use interchangeably with teacher quality) measures is one of the most important. Unless the quality estimates are accepted as informative and fair, opposition will remain strong. Moreover, inaccurate or inadequate quality measures and poorly designed pay-for-performance programs will introduce adverse incentives to teach narrowly to test content, concentrate on only a fraction of the students, forgo important non-tested outcomes, or elicit frustration and distrust in response to reward structures with systemic flaws.

Design Elements of Teacher Incentives: A Preliminary Typology

Our review of 15 different teacher incentive programs implemented in developing countries and Israel over the past decade offers an opportunity to analyze some of their design features. In doing so, we try to move beyond the basic taxonomy most commonly used in the education literature—for example, group or individual; input-based or outcome-based, and so on. In focusing on additional aspects of incentive design that theory predicts are important for effective performance-based contracts, we also hope to create a framework that can be tested as the evidence from these experiences accumulates. Because the current set of cases remains too small for any definitive conclusions, this is an exploratory exercise only.

Based on the evaluation evidence reviewed, three key dimensions may predict an incentive program's effectiveness: *controllability, predictability,* and *bonus size.* We assess these features of different programs and examine the correlations with available empirical evidence of program impact.

Transcending these features is something that might be termed the legitimacy or credibility of the incentive program as a whole. Achieving this legitimacy involves, in Rivkin's (2009) words, ensuring that the specific performance measures used are perceived as "informative" and "fair." But legitimacy also speaks to the perception that all aspects of the program are managed honestly and transparently. Further, legitimacy implies an acceptance that the rules of the game will be stable over time or that adaptations will be undertaken with due process and consultation, rather than through ad hoc adjustments. Murnane and Cohen's (1986) observation that the longest-standing pay-for-performance programs in the United States typically have been redesigned several times, with teacher input, suggests that sustaining credibility over time requires effort and processes that are perceived as legitimate.

We have argued that improved measurement of student learning outcomes in many countries has created an expanded political space for pay-for-performance programs because the technical platform—a relevant and meaningful source of data on schooling outcomes—has been established. A well-designed and cleanly administered national or subnational student assessment program could provide a ready anchor for pay-for-performance schemes. Brazil's IDEB goes one step further by establishing a high-quality national data source on both student learning outcomes and grade progression. The combined measure mitigates at least one undesired teacher behavior that may be induced by a high-stakes focus on test scores: the risk that teachers trying to boost average student learning outcomes will hold back slower students. By combining the two measures of learning outcomes and grade progression, IDEB builds in protection against this form of distortion. The degree of legitimacy that Brazil's high-quality national testing system and IDEB have achieved over the past five years appears to be a factor in the increasing adoption of pay-for-performance programs there. It is interesting to note that several earlier pay-for-performance programs in Brazil, based on individual states' testing programs, had difficulty with credibility issues and were not sustained long.

Perceived legitimacy may be the single most important factor in the impact and sustainability of teacher incentive programs, but it is difficult to assess objectively and especially difficult to assess ex ante.[14] Our typology, therefore, focuses on more specific and tractable design features. However, it bears noting that the experimental design programs reviewed here—which constitute a strong part of the current evidence base on teacher incentives in developing countries—have special characteristics that positively affect their legitimacy.[15]

Given the context for teacher incentive reforms in most developing countries—a status quo of poor education results—the potential for undesired consequences is not per se an argument against teacher incentives so much as a call for eyes-open efforts to manage known risks. Some of these risks relate to specific choices in the design of incentives in the three areas we identified: controllability, predictability, and bonus size.

Table 4.4 shows the hypotheses regarding program effects that can be derived from the principal-agent model and our typology.

Controllability in Incentive Program Design

Controllability refers to how much of the measured outcome depends on actions taken by an individual teacher (or employee). Performance measures related to a teacher's own behavior, such as attendance or training course participation, are directly dependent on the teacher's actions. Awards based on such measures create incentives with a high degree of controllability from the standpoint of the employee or, conversely, low risks. Theory predicts that riskier contracts, based on less controllable factors, either demand a larger incentive (other things being equal) or will not be as effective.

However, while school systems *could* reward many behaviors that are highly controllable from a teacher's perspective, these may not be the most important behaviors for producing the results school systems desire most. The problem for incentives design is that teacher behaviors that contribute to student learning improvement are more difficult to specify, observe, and measure directly across an entire school system. On the other hand, it is easy to see why basing incentive programs on system results, especially student learning outcomes, is often resisted by teachers; these outcomes are less controllable—that is, riskier for the agent.

The sources of risk can be unpacked into at least two dimensions that policy makers need to consider and manage: noise and locality.

The noise factor

"Noise" refers to the degree to which the specific performance measure is affected by factors outside of the agent's control. Student learning results for a particular classroom, for example, cannot be completely attributed to a teacher; they are also influenced by noise from other variables such as students' prior grade preparation, socioeconomic level, or distractions

Table 4.4 Incentive Program Design Features and Possible Effects

Feature	Description	Hypothesis
Controllability		
Noise	The degree to which factors other than the teacher's behavior (for example, student characteristics or the actions of other teachers) can affect the performance measure, therefore making it a less credible and adequate measure of a teacher's individual contribution	The less noise in the measure, the more controllable it is and the more effective the incentive will be (at least in the short term).
Locality	The degree to which an individual teacher's performance affects the result relative to other actors being incentivized. Measures based on individual performance (group size = 1) are maximally local. If group performance is being measured, as group size grows larger, the measure becomes less local.	The more local the measure, the more controllable it is and the more effective the incentive will be.
Predictability	An individual teacher's likelihood of achieving the bonus	If probability of earning the bonus is close to either zero or 100%, the incentive will not be effective. Piecewise formulations (which allow workers to earn some bonus in line with their production) will create stronger incentives than tournament-style awards (which set an ex ante cap on the share of schools or teachers that can win).
Bonus size	Bonus payment as a proportion of monthly wages	The larger the bonus, the more effective the incentive will be, all things being equal. But larger bonus size can also stimulate cheating and other undesirable behaviors and can make bonus programs fiscally unsustainable or less cost-effective.

Source: Authors' compilation.

on the day of the exam. A specific test instrument can be noisy if it is not well mapped onto curriculum goals or fails to discriminate between students who have and have not mastered the content. The noisier a performance measure, the less responsive it is to the agent's behavior and effort. Even on the same test instrument, cross-sectional student scores are noisier than longitudinal (value-added) measures that can identify learning gains for individual teachers' classrooms. Finally, test scores for small classes are inherently much noisier than for larger classes (Kane and Staiger 2001).[16]

School systems can reduce the noise involved in test scores by grouping schools into comparative strata on socioeconomic grounds (as in Chile's SNED) or using school-level targets (as in Pernambuco and other Brazilian states) that measure each school's progress relative to its own baseline. A noteworthy feature of many of the new bonus programs is sensitivity to this issue, with built-in adjustments for schools' baseline performance levels or performance comparisons for schools grouped by socioeconomic and geographic strata.

The locality factor

"Locality" refers to the scope for an individual teacher to influence the results being rewarded. If the result is produced by a group of teachers or schools, it will be less controllable from the standpoint of an individual teacher because the teacher's actions will contribute only a fraction to the result. As the group gets larger, the individual's contribution gets smaller, and he or she is less able to control the final outcome. Controllability is higher (all things being equal) in highly local measures, such as classroom-level learning outcomes or individual contract teachers' attendance records.

An important issue with group rewards (typically schoolwide rewards, in the case of education) is not only that they are less controllable from the perspective of an individual teacher but also that they can motivate free-rider behavior. Free riders are members of a group who refuse to exert effort while counting on others to produce the group result (Holmstrom 1979). In large schools, where an entire staff's achievement of a school-level bonus may depend on the results of a small handful of tested subjects and grades, free-riding can become an important issue. If teachers perceive that others are free-riding on their efforts—that is, the locality and thus controllability of the incentive is lower—the effectiveness of the incentive will be weaker.

Does this mean that education incentives should be focused on outcomes at the teacher level? More sophisticated testing data in developing countries is opening the possibility of measuring classroom-level learning gains for individual teachers, as is now possible in the United States and other OECD countries. Rewarding individual teachers can provide strong work incentives and negate free-riding. But on the other hand, individual rewards can discourage collaboration and teamwork to the detriment of overall school results. They also create incentives within a school for teachers to avoid weaker students. This can complicate the work of principals; matching the more effective teachers with more difficult students might be in the best interest of those students and the school's overall results, but it would impede those teachers' ability to earn fair rewards for their talent and effort.

The question for policy makers is whether focusing incentives at the school level creates benefits—in terms of stimulating collaborative work among school personnel—that outweigh the free-rider concerns. Hybrid approaches (which reward school-level outcomes but adjust the award received by individual employees within the school for some measure of their individual effort, such as attendance) are an interesting alternative. Most of the experimental teacher incentive programs in developing countries to date have been in settings with very small schools (three to five teachers, on average). Therefore, the new wave of research on the Brazilian programs (where urban schools can have 40 or more teachers) that is focusing research attention on the measurement of free-rider behavior may be a useful contribution.

Predictability in Incentive Program Design

For an incentive to be effective, agents must perceive realistic scope to achieve it. If the likelihood of achieving a bonus is close to zero, teachers will have little incentive to exert effort. On the other hand, teachers with near certainty of receiving a bonus will also have little incentive to increase effort. Theory predicts that if performance-based contracts result in awards distributed to a share of workers nearer the midpoint of 0 and 1, rather than at the extremes, they will elicit the most effort. Dampening or enhancing this effect, however, would be the agents' assessment of controllability or risk and the amount of payoff expected.

For incentive programs that include sanctions—such as the prospect of contract nonrenewal for poorly performing contract teachers—the strength of the incentive is proportional to the likelihood of enforcement.

Bonus Size in Incentive Program Design

Theory predicts that larger bonuses elicit stronger responses, conditional on the degree of risk inherent in the contract, the chance of earning the bonus or being sanctioned, and the cost of the effort. Even if teachers are intrinsically motivated, incentive contracts must still offer payoffs that exceed the marginal cost of effort, although this cost might be lower than it would have been for less intrinsically motivated individuals. The incentive power of a given financial bonus is, of course, relative to the base wage and price levels in a given country context. Therefore, we attempt to standardize bonus size in relation to average monthly wages. We find significant divergence across programs, with annual bonuses ranging from 35 percent of a monthly wage (Andhra Pradesh, India) to 150–200 percent (Brazil) and even to 300 percent in one of the programs in Israel.

Table 4.5 categorizes the incentive programs reviewed for which there is some impact evidence. Categorizations of this kind always involve a degree of subjectivity, and the small number of programs makes this typology preliminary and illustrative only. But this framework and the associated impact evidence may assist policy makers in thinking through the design features of new pay-for-performance programs. The impacts presented are typically for student learning outcomes, expressed as the average improvement in learning for the treated schools or classrooms compared to control groups, as a proportion of one standard deviation in the test score distribution. Our ratings of program design elements are on a standard Likert-type scale, from 1 (very low) to 5 (very high). The annex at the end of the chapter explains in further detail how the ratings for each feature were assigned.

Core Design Features

The strength of a program's core design features (controllability and predictability) is, to some extent, complementary to the financial size of the bonus. In other words, an incentive program with high controllability and predictability—such as an individual incentive that teachers have a reasonable chance of attaining and that is based on student learning progress on a well-designed test—will induce stronger performance than a program offering an equivalent financial reward with lower controllability and predictability. The implication for policy makers is that what matters is the balance of these factors. The fiscal costs of an incentive program can to some extent be reduced by attention to the complementary design features of controllability and predictability. To put it another way, for every pay-for-performance program, there is an optimal design that bundles these features to stimulate the maximum performance response from teachers and schools at minimum fiscal cost.

We explore this hypothesis in table 4.5 by averaging the ratings for a program's noise, locality, and predictability features into a separate score, labeled "core design" (in column 4)—which is a simple average of the three preceding subscores. We compare programs' scores on the strength of their core design with the size of the bonus. We then generate a combined measure that averages the scores for all of the program design features, including the size of the bonus. This overall score is the program's "predicted overall incentive strength." We compare this predicted incentive strength with the observed impacts that the different bonus programs had on desired educational outcomes.

In table 4.5, the programs are ordered by the strength of their "predicted overall incentive strength," from lowest to highest. Comparing

Table 4.5 Pay-for-Performance Programs by Core Design Features and Effect Size

Likert-scale ratings (1–5) except where otherwise specified

Program	Noise[a]	Locality[b]	Predictability[c]	Predicted Strength, Core Design	Bonus Size[d]	Average Bonus Value (% MW)	Predicted Overall Incentive Strength	Observed Effect Size (Max.)[e]
Israel (group) (Lavy 2002)	5	1	2	2.7	2	40	2.5	0.13
Chile SNED (group) (Rau and Contreras 2009)	4	3	2	3	2	40[f]	2.8	0.12
Brazil (group) (Ferraz and Bruns, forthcoming)	4	2	3	3	5	180	3.5	0.31–0.57[g]
Kenya (group) (Glewwe, Ilias, and Kremer 2010)	5	4	3	4	2	43	3.5	0.14
India (group) (Muralidharan and Sundararaman 2009)	5	4	4	4.3	2	36	3.8	0.16
India (individual) (Muralidharan and Sundararaman 2009)	5	5	4	4.7	2	36	4	0.27

(continued next page)

Table 4.5 Pay-for-Performance Programs by Core Design Features and Effect Size *(continued)*

Program	Noise[a]	Locality[b]	Predictability[c]	Predicted Strength, Core Design	Bonus Size[d]	Average Bonus Value (% MW)	Predicted Overall Incentive Strength	Observed Effect Size (Max.)[e]
India (attendance) (individual) (Duflo, Hanna, and Ryan 2010)	5	5	4	4.7	2	30	4	0.17
Israel (individual) (Lavy 2009)	5	5	3	4.3	5	300	4.5	14% higher pass rates and 10% higher test scores

Source: Authors' compilation.

Note: MW = monthly wage. SNED = National System for Performance Evaluation of Subsidized Educational Establishments (Sistema Nacional de Evaluación del Desempeño de los Establecimientos Educativos Subvencionados).

a. Some programs used multidimensional performance measures. In these cases, each measure was rated separately and then averaged out.

b. Average group sizes are as follows: Brazil: 43 teachers; Chile: 18 teachers (figures from 2004); India: 3 teachers; Israel: 80 teachers; and Kenya: 6 teachers.

c. Predictability was based on actual award rates as follows: In Brazil, 51 percent of schools got the bonus in 2009. In Chile, 20–28 percent of schools got the awards (est. 2004). In the India programs, most teachers under all programs got some award. In Israel (both programs), about 33 percent of teachers got awards. In Kenya, about 48 percent of participating schools got the award.

d. See annex for description of Likert scale used for bonus size.

e. Effect size typically represents the increase in learning caused by the program expressed in terms of standard deviation. For the Israel group incentive program, the authors converted Lavy's (2002) reported impact into standard deviations, drawing on descriptive data presented. For the Israel individual bonus, this was not possible, so the outcomes presented are not strictly comparable to the others in the table.

f. Average award during the initial years of the program, which was the period evaluated. More recently, the average award is 70–80 percent of MW.

g. Impact estimates for Pernambuco, Brazil, are not rigorously estimated and thus not directly comparable to other estimated program impacts.

the scores for "core design" features with the bonus size does suggest some complementarity. Except for the 2002 individual bonus program in Israel, in all cases where programs' core design features rated a (strong) score of 4 or higher, the size of the bonus adopted was relatively low.

However, programs with core design features rated lower than 4, such as Chile's SNED, the Brazilian bonus program, and the Israel group incentive, show no clear pattern. In all three cases, the performance measures on which the bonus is based are rated highly for being designed in a way to minimize noise; Chile's SNED pays careful attention to schools' socioeconomic contexts, and Brazil's target-based system effectively focuses each school on improvement relative to its own prior-year performance. But locality and predictability ratings are relatively low because these bonuses are school-based rewards and typical school size is relatively large. In the Israel and Chilean cases, moreover, the tournament-style programs reward a relatively small share of schools.

In the Brazil case, a relatively large bonus size (average awards more than one month's salary) compensates for the relatively weaker incentives created by these core design features. It is interesting to note that Chile's SNED program has increased the average bonus size significantly over the years as well—from an initial 40 percent to a current 80 percent of the average monthly teacher wage. The Israel group bonus program appears exceptional in this regard. It is the only program in which the bonus size does not compensate for a relatively low score on core design features; instead, the relatively small maximum bonus further lowers the predicted strength of the incentive.

Both of the Israel programs, in fact, are striking in that they are the only two programs where the bonus size does not exert a moderating effect on the strength of the "core design" but instead exacerbates it—making a rather weak incentive program weaker in the case of the group bonus and making an already strong incentive stronger in the case of the individual design. One might ask what is wrong with making a strong design stronger. In the context of our comparators, the answer appears to be that it makes a bonus program more expensive than it needs to be—an important concern from a policy standpoint.

The overarching question is whether the "predicted strength" of a bonus program based on these design features is correlated with its impact. All of these programs were associated with positive outcomes and, in many cases, causality has been rigorously established. But the small number of programs and the limited years of observation for most of them make the comparisons here illustrative only. Figure 4.2 provide a simple visual mapping of how program impacts compare with estimates of predicted incentive strength.

Figure 4.2 Comparison of Bonus-Pay Programs by Impact Size and Predicted Incentive Strength

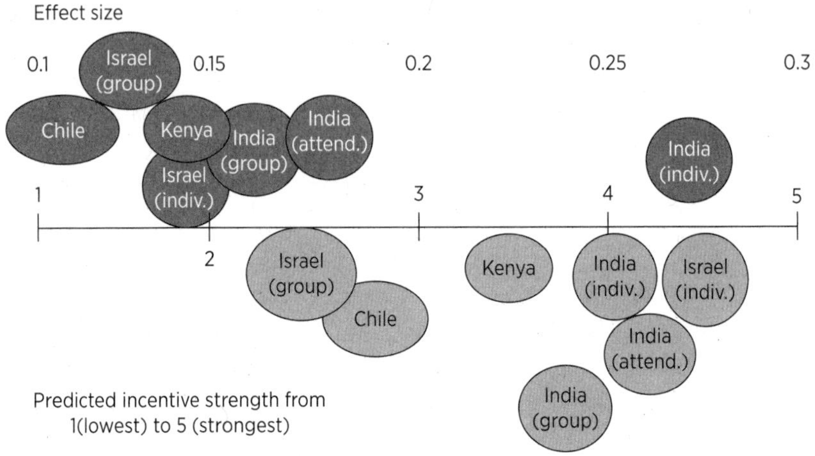

Source: Authors.

Note: "Indiv." designates individual teacher bonus. "Group" designates group bonus (or school-level). "Attend." indicates a study of programs rewarding teacher input (attendance) rather than student outcomes. Relative effect size (upper axis) ranges from a low effect on learning outcomes (less than a 0.1 SD) on the left to a high effect (almost a 0.3 SD) on the right. Relative strength (5-point scale along lower axis) indicates the overall "predicted strength" of each bonus-pay program according to the authors' framework.

Programs are presented below the axis along the scale derived from table 4.5, which predicts the overall strength of the incentives. Note that the scale is purely illustrative. Programs are presented above the axis in terms of the reported size of their effects on student outcomes. This continuum ranges from low effects (less than 0.1 of a standard deviation) to high effects (close to 0.3 of a standard deviation) relative to those usually seen in the economics of education and development literature. The Brazil program is not included here as it does not yet have equivalently rigorous impact estimates. The estimated impacts on student learning range from a 0.12 standard deviation for Chile's SNED to a 0.27 standard deviation for the Andhra Pradesh, India, individual bonus program by the second year of implementation.

A few cautious observations may be made. First, these pay-for-performance programs have had positive effects on student learning, of roughly a 0.15 standard deviation. In comparison with the evaluation evidence on other types of education interventions, it is noteworthy that these effects are statistically significant and consistently positive across different bonus program designs and very different country contexts. But the effects are not huge. The one exception is the second-year impact observed in the Andhra Pradesh, India, program, which offered schools individual teacher incentives. It stands out, having produced a very large 0.27 standard deviation increase in average math and language learning outcomes compared with randomly selected schools that were not eligible for an incentive.

Second, according to the metrics constructed for predicting the strength of a pay-for-performance incentive program, most of the programs cluster fairly closely around a rating of between 3 and 4 in our schema. The two outliers are the Israel programs. Across the entire set of programs, however, there does not appear to be any obvious correlation between the "overall incentive strength" of a program and its impact—at least in our simple ratings scheme and for this small sample of programs. In connection with our earlier observation that strength of these programs' core design features tended to be dampened or balanced by the decisions on the average bonus size, there is an intriguing suggestion that there may be some kind of threshold incentive strength for a pay-for-performance program to "work." However, beyond this point, there may not be any payoff to making programs more generous. At least in the two Israel cases, there is no evidence that the considerably stronger and more expensive individual bonus scheme produced better results than the "weaker" group bonus program.

These observations, however, are highly speculative. The number of evaluated programs is small, and most of the impact data come from two years or less of program experience. Both positive and negative features of performance-pay programs develop with experience and can exert potentially strong effects on their impact. On the positive side, agents' awareness of programs and the experience of actually seeing benefits paid out will increase the credibility of the incentive and presumably its strength. Indeed, interviews with teachers and school directors in the first year of Pernambuco's bonus program showed that schools were not universally aware of their performance targets and had quite uncertain expectations about the potential size of performance bonuses. In the second year of the program, awareness was, as expected, much higher.

On the other hand, schools' and teachers' ability to "game" the system also rises as their understanding of the rules of the game deepens with time. Evidence of gaming, cheating, scandals in test administration or the other performance measurement processes, or general perceptions of unfairness in the mechanics underlying a bonus program will undermine its credibility, in turn dampening its incentive effects.

There is much to be gained from additional, careful evaluations of new pay-for-performance programs in education—perhaps especially in developing countries, where the challenges of improving teachers' performance are most acute. The framework presented here is simple, but it is grounded in key elements of principal-agent theory. It appears to map well onto the types of pay-for-performance programs being developed in experimental pilot studies as well as systemwide education reforms. If this framework can assist policy makers in thinking through key design issues and encourage the systematic analysis of future programs, it will serve a purpose.

Summary and Conclusions

Teachers and school-level administrators are the front-line providers of education services. Their work determines the quality of services delivered and their results—above all, how well students learn. New research shows convincingly that student learning outcomes drive the overall benefits from education investments. If rising access and schooling attainment do not result in higher learning levels on globally benchmarked assessments, national investments may be largely wasted.

Recent research has also established that individual teachers vary widely in their ability to help their students learn. This evidence is leading countries to reexamine how they select, groom, and motivate teachers. It is also raising awareness of disconnects between the incentives teachers face and the results school systems want. Most school systems recruit teachers based on criteria that are not correlated with real effectiveness in the classroom, fail to reward the capacities and behaviors that *are* correlated with effectiveness, and are unable to sanction teachers who do not perform. A disconnect between teacher incentives and accountability for performance occurs in OECD countries as well as in low- and middle-income countries. But the failures are deepest in the developing world, manifested in high teacher absenteeism and persistently low learning results by international standards.

Countries are not standing still, however. Innovative, sometimes radical, reforms of teacher contracting and compensation policies are springing up in developing countries—reforms aimed at linking teacher incentives more closely to performance. An encouraging number of reforms are being rigorously evaluated. Although the number of country cases is still small and most programs are still in the initial years of implementation, evidence is beginning to accumulate about their impact.

This chapter reviewed the experience with two types of policies that can make teachers more accountable for results: contract tenure reforms and pay-for-performance reforms. Both have the advantage of overcoming the rigidity of existing teacher policies without requiring wholesale reform. Alternative contracting establishes different rules of the game for a new teacher cadre that works alongside the existing teacher stream. The new teacher cadre is hired on fixed-term (usually one-year) contracts without the job stability that regular teachers enjoy.

Pay-for-performance programs leave core salary policies intact but create an incentive at the margin with the offer of an annual bonus based on some measure of teacher performance—be it an input measure, such as teacher attendance; an outcome measure, such as school or student results; or a combination.

The most rigorous of the seven available evaluations of contract teachers all found them to be more cost-effective than regular civil service teachers, and in India dramatically so. In both Kenya and India, randomized trials have found learning outcomes for students of contract teachers to be equal to or better than those of civil service teachers, despite contract teachers' much lower salaries. Nonexperimental studies in two additional states in India have found similar results. Earlier evidence on community-hired teachers in Central America (not included here but summarized thoroughly in Vegas 2005) was less robust but also suggested that contract teachers achieve similar or better student grade progression and learning outcomes (controlling for student background) at lower cost.

Although contract teachers usually work for lower salaries than their civil service counterparts, the cost-effectiveness of a contract teacher policy is likely to depend on country characteristics and the level of education involved. All of the evaluated cases involved contract teachers at the primary level, for example, where the supply of potential teachers with adequate skills is not as likely to be constrained as at the secondary level, or for specialty subjects such as sciences and math. Second, there are nagging questions about the sustainability of this policy over time. Many of the evaluated cases suggest that contract teachers may accept the lower salaries and insecure tenure because they are queuing for civil service positions. Teachers' unions have also aided contract teachers in some African countries to press successfully for tenure and, in many cases, a large share do end up entering the civil service.

Nonetheless, the new wave of evidence on the short-term impacts of contract teacher reforms is fairly strong and consistent: the use of contract teachers can strengthen the scope for local monitoring of teacher performance, which results in higher teacher effort, which produces equal or better student learning outcomes than for regular teachers. And all of this is achieved at lower costs per student.

Teacher bonus initiatives in developing countries have proliferated over the past several years, both as small-scale experiments and as high-profile, systemwide reforms. In contrast to the situation just five years ago, and in contrast to recent U.S. evidence, a growing body of developing-country studies suggests that bonus pay incentives can work—at least in contexts characterized by

- *Weak systems for performance monitoring and accountability*—evidenced by relatively high teacher absence rates, low teacher dismissal rates, and low student learning performance
- *Relatively weak teacher professionalism*—evidenced in most cases by low standards for entry
- *Relatively large bonus size*—for example, an annual bonus of 30–300 percent of monthly salary
- *Focused performance metrics*—emphasis on a small number of key, measurable results, notably student learning improvements or relatively easily measured teacher "inputs" such as monthly attendance, rather than more complex, subjective, and comprehensive performance evaluations
- *"Fair" performance metrics*—rewards to schools on a value-added basis (for progress relative to their starting point) or compared with schools with similar geographic and student socioeconomic conditions, not for absolute levels of performance
- *Rewards clearly linked to prior period results*—annual bonuses directly linked to test or other results for the previous school year or monthly bonuses for input measures monitored over the previous month, such as teacher attendance.

These programs "work" in the sense that student learning outcomes improve in the presence of the bonus. Across the eight most carefully evaluated cases, the bonus program raised average learning outcomes in incentive schools relative to control schools by about a 0.15 standard deviation; in the highest case, learning outcomes by the second year of the program were a 0.27 standard deviation higher. Although not huge, effects on this order of magnitude are relatively rare across other types of education interventions, and the consistency of positive impacts, across a wide variety of country contexts, is noteworthy.

Our understanding of the mechanisms through which bonus pay improves student outcomes is still weak, however. In Brazil, classroom observations found evidence of more efficient use of instructional time by teachers in schools that subsequently earned the bonus. Teachers in these schools also lost less time due to late arrival or early departure, made more intensive use of learning materials, and kept a higher share of students "on task." These patterns are consistent with Lavy's observations in Israel. But in some randomized trials in Kenya and India, at least over the short term, the bonus program did not induce any reduction in teacher absence rates, which is one of the most obvious ways teachers can increase their effort in response to an incentive. These teachers did nonetheless produce statistically significant improvements in their students' learning outcomes relative to comparison groups of teachers who were not offered a bonus; the likely channel is through offering extra homework and class work and conducting out-of-school sessions for test preparation.

In Brazil, where bonuses were available statewide, there is intriguing evidence that more-ambitious targets stimulated larger increases in student learning than in comparable schools with less-ambitious targets. This evidence suggests that in the presence of an attractive performance award, schools focus on and are motivated to try to achieve specific targets. However, the fact that under this program 50 percent of all schools earned the bonus during the first year, and 70 percent in the second year, suggests that the targets, overall, were relatively accessible.

Looking across pay-for-performance programs, several features derived from principal-agent theory appear important for the design of effective incentives. These include the *controllability* of the specific performance measure(s) being incentivized, from the standpoint of individual teachers; the *predictability* of the incentive (that is, what share of those eligible will achieve it); and *bonus size.*

Controllability, in our framework, is affected by two dimensions: "noise" in the performance measure and "locality" (that is, whether the bonus is an individual or group-based incentive). For group incentives, school size appears important. If a school has a large number of teachers, yet the bonus is based on results produced by only a handful of its teachers (typically, those teaching subjects and grades that are subjected to annual testing), there is room for free-riding—in other words, some teachers coasting on the work of the others.

The experience to date lends some support to the theory that core design features such as controllability and predictability affect the strength of the incentives in a pay-for-performance program. Particularly interesting from a policy standpoint is that these features appear complementary to the financial size of the bonus. In other words, bonus programs that pay attention to the design of performance measures that are perceived to reflect teachers' work fairly (for example, student test scores for schools are adjusted for socioeconomic differences) and are reasonably predictable may (all other things being equal) achieve stronger impacts. Much longer-term and deeper analysis of experience with these and other education pay-for-performance programs is needed for any conclusive observations, but the experience to date at least suggests the usefulness of considering a set of core elements systematically in the design of new programs.

In conclusion, a growing number of school systems across the developing world are adopting two specific reforms aimed at strengthening the rewards and sanctions for teacher performance: the use of contract teachers and bonus pay linked to teacher performance. These programs have different designs, costs, and primary objectives, but both address a deep issue of weak incentives for performance in education systems across the developing world.

Our review of the best-evaluated cases to date shows that the design of effective incentives presents challenges and that the impacts vary significantly. An encouraging number of recent studies show positive impacts of incentive reforms on student learning outcomes. The number of developing-country reform experiences is still small, and most are fairly recent. But they permit a preliminary typology of examples that merit consideration by any education policy maker concerned with raising student learning as well as a framework for the generation of further research evidence on "what works" to make schools more accountable for results.

Annex: Rating the Design Features of Pay-for-Performance Programs

Controllability Ratings

We measure each of the two elements of controllability—noise and locality—on a 5-point scale, ranging from very low (1) to very high (5), as described below. In some cases, programs measure results on more than one indicator, such as test scores and matriculation rates or grade progression rates. In these cases, we constructed a simple average of the noise and locality ratings for each of the different elements.

Noise ratings

1. *(very low controllability)*: programs whose performance measures are likely to exhibit high noise (for example, programs using only cross-sectional learning data with no adjustments for schools' socioeconomic context or other factors) and programs that measure performance based on outcomes for a very small group (for example, test scores calculated over fewer than 10 students)

2–4. *(moderate controllability)*: programs with measures less likely to exhibit noise

5. *(very high controllability)*: programs with performance measures designed to be as noise-free as possible—for example, programs using longitudinal data that are rich enough to produce value-added measures of teacher performance at the classroom level; programs that include adjustments for schools' socioeconomic status and other contextual factors; programs with performance measures that are inherently controllable (such as seniority, attendance, and participation in professional development);[17] and programs that avoid measuring performance of very small groups of students (less than 30) to reduce the potential for exogenous shocks or variation.

Locality ratings

1. *(very low locality)*: programs based on group performance in very large groups of more than 50 teachers
2. *(low locality)*: programs based on group performance in groups of 25–50
3. *(moderate locality)*: programs based on group performance in groups of 10–25
4. *(high locality)*: programs based on group performance in small groups of 2–10
5. *(very high locality)*: programs based on individual performance

Predictability Ratings

Predictability refers to the degree to which the agent or teacher can expect to earn the reward. A predictability rating thus ranges from 0 percent (total certainty that the bonus will *not* be attained) to 100 percent (total certainty it *will* be obtained). Theory predicts that if an individual's chance of attaining a bonus is at either of these extremes, the motivation to perform will be weaker. In the one case, there is no point; in the other, there is no need. Not surprisingly, few bonus programs in reality operate at these extremes. Most—including all of the programs reviewed here—have rules of the game that ensure that somewhere between 20 percent and 80 percent of eligible schools or teachers achieve the bonus. One might hypothesize that, all other things being equal, programs near the mid-point of predictability (about 50 percent of participants earn the bonus) would exert the strongest incentive effects, but there is little empirical evidence on this.

The programs we reviewed use two different models of bonus assignment: "piecewise" formulations and "tournaments." In piecewise formulations, each individual school or teacher's award is determined by the value of the results they produce. In the case of Andhra Pradesh, India, teachers were rewarded for every student whose test scores increased by more than 5 percent over the school year—and the higher the scores, the higher the reward. Under the tournaments used in the Israel programs and Chile's SNED, awards are restricted to a certain percentage of schools or individuals, ranked in order of their performance. In the case of Chile's SNED, the top 25 percent of schools in each socioeconomic band are rewarded, whether average scores go up or down.

Both the average share of schools or teachers rewarded and the specific model will, in practice, enter into an agent's estimation of the "predictability" of a program—that is, his or her chance of actually earning the bonus.

Figure 4A.1 Bonus Predictability Ratings
Likert scale ratings (below axis) compared with reported shares of schools/teachers rewarded (above axis)

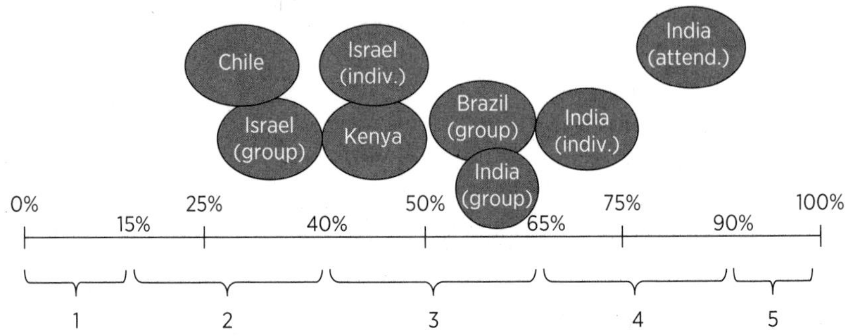

Source: Authors.

Notes: "Predictability" is the degree to which a teacher/school can expect to earn the bonus—rated from 1 (low probability) to 5 (total certainty that the award will be attained). Our ratings are divided into quartiles aligned with the reported shares of eligible teachers/schools actually receiving the awards in the programs evaluated (except for India-Attendance, for which the actual figures are not available, and thus estimated from the discussion in the text).

In other words, piecewise and tournament-style bonus programs might both result in the same numerical share of all teachers earning the bonus, but they may incentivize agents slightly differently ex ante because of differences in each individual's levels of realism and risk aversion. Also, the evolution of a piecewise program over time will enable agents to refine their perceptions of predictability as evidence about the annual share of "winners" and average award size accrues.

While the theoretical literature predicts that tournament models will induce all individuals to make the same effort, the underlying assumptions are quite strong (that all agents have symmetric information, risk neutrality, and equal abilities) (Lazear 2000). Other theoretical literature speculates that piecewise (linear) bonus contracts have the advantage of being more resistant to gaming—but again, under strong assumptions of exponential utility for the agent and normally distributed noise (Holmstron and Milgrom 1987). Again, the empirical evidence is limited.

For the purposes of this exercise, therefore, we use a limited but straightforward metric for assigning predictability ratings: the observed share of teachers or schools that accessed the bonus, on average, each year. For tournament programs, of course, this is a stable share. For the piecewise programs, the share will typically vary, but for many programs in our sample, only one year of experience was available. Figure 4A.1 indicates how

Figure 4A.2 Bonus Size Ratings

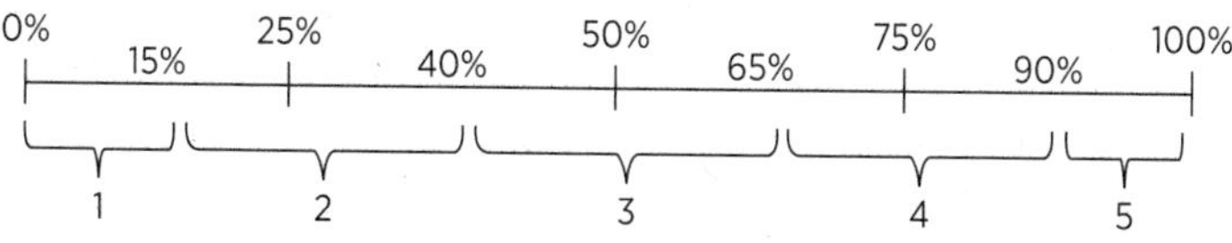

Source: Authors.

we assigned Likert-scale ratings from 1 (low predictability) to 5 (high predictability) for these programs, in line with reported data on the average share of participants (whether schools or teachers) that actually received the award. These percentages along map onto a 100-percentile scale.

Size-of-Bonus Ratings

We express the size of all bonuses in terms of their proportion of the average monthly wage. Since most programs award a range of bonuses depending on the outcome achieved, we take the maximum bonus size as the main reference point to assign ratings. In doing this, we assume that all teachers have some ex ante awareness of the maximum size of the bonus and, further, that they perceive the maximum bonus as attainable.[18] As shown in figure 4A.2, we divide the 5-point rating scale into quartiles, with a bonus of 0–25 percent of a monthly wage rated as 1 (very low) to 90 percent or more of a monthly wage rated as 5 (very high). For reference, available data on the actual maximum and average bonus size for each program are also presented.

Notes

1. When describing this experiment, all Indian rupee-to-dollar conversions use the exchange rate reported by the authors: Rs 48 per $1.
2. The bonus payment in the group-incentive schools ended up being lower than the individual incentives because the treatment effect was smaller (that is, the percentage gain in average scores was lower) and also because classes with scores below their targets brought down the average school gain, while teachers with negative gains (relative to targets) did not hurt teachers with positive gains in the individual-incentive schools (Muralidharan and Sundararaman 2009).
3. In fact, the authors argued that these kinds of behaviors would not be readily captured during classroom observations since many of these activities would be taking place after school or outside of the classroom.

4. More specifically, the material received by the "feedback" schools consisted of an independently administered baseline test at the start of the school year; a detailed written diagnostic feedback report on the performance of students on the baseline test; a note on how to read and use the performance reports and benchmarks; an announcement that students would be tested again at the end of the year to monitor progress in student performance; and low-stakes monitoring of classrooms during the school year to observe teaching processes and activity. In the feedback experiment, 100 schools received only the feedback treatment, while another set of randomly selected schools in the main experiment (those receiving incentives) also received feedback (Muralidharan and Sundararaman 2010b).
5. Because these are the results of the main experiment, the magnitude corresponds to the effects discussed above in Muralidharan and Sundararaman (2009).
6. Other subjects (Hebrew and Arabic) were tested as well, and their teachers also participated in the incentive program.
7. For the baseline, test scores in 1996 (Year 0) were used because there were no test scores for 1997. The first program year was 1998, and the second year was 1999.
8. A different model used to instrument the targets for the discontinuities also showed evidence that higher targets—all other things being equal—led to larger improvements in learning results over the short term.
9. To be eligible for the program, schools had to be comprehensive (offer grades 7–12) and be the only one of its kind in the community.
10. Students in Israel high schools must take matriculation exams in core and elective subjects for each grade of high school (grades 10–12) but have the option of taking all of the tests in their last year of high school, which most students choose to do. Matriculation exams are national exams that award credits for a particular subject. A minimum of 20 credits is required to qualify for a matriculation certificate, which is a necessary, although not sufficient, requirement for admission to a university (Lavy 2002).
11. The average annual starting teacher salary of a high school teacher in Israel is $20,000. Mean high school teacher salaries are $30,000 (Lavy 2002).
12. "Homogenous" groups are constructed based on geographical locations, educational levels, and student socioeconomic characteristics (such as parents' education levels). The result is about 100 homogenous groups composed of schools that compete against each other (Romaguera 2008).
13. Schools ranked between 25 percent and 35 percent receive 60 percent of the bonus.
14. There is significant literature documenting undesired behaviors associated with high-stakes testing and teacher incentives programs in developed countries, notably in the United States, including cheating on exams (Jacob and Levitt 2002), increasing student caloric intake on the day of the exam (Figlio and Winicki 2002), and removing low-achieving students from the classroom (Murnane and Cohen 1986). The developing-country literature on these issues is less extensive, but the Kenya and India evaluations reviewed in this chapter documented increases in test preparation tutorials offered by teachers after

school—rather than improvements in pedagogy during school hours—as one of the main teacher behaviors stimulated by pay for performance.

15. First, a significant number of these programs have been run on a pilot scale, as experiments managed closely by academic researchers. Under these conditions, the scope for poorly designed tests of student learning or abuses in test administration are minimal. Second, of the government-run initiatives being implemented at scale, several are very new. There has been little time for inconsistencies in administration to surface that may undermine the credibility and power of the incentives. Nor has there been time for system actors to develop the perverse behaviors that both theory and empirical experience predict will arise as school personnel gain better awareness of the stakes and familiarity with the rules of the game.
16. There are arguments against noise being such an important measure because it could average out in the long run. However, our rankings are based on gross differences across programs, such as having baseline exams, adjusting for student socioeconomic status and other characteristics, or having a value-added framework that, even if not perfect, is technically more sound than a simple cross-section performance measure with no baseline to use for comparison.
17. Note that rating a measure as relatively noise-free does not imply that it is not susceptible to cheating or gaming. Attendance records, for example, are notorious for their manipulability.
18. It is likely that if the experiments or programs are repeated over time, teachers can adjust their perceptions based on previous results. But most of these programs were present for only one year or two years at the most (with the exception of Chile's SNED, which is ongoing).

References

Abadzi, H. 2009. "Instructional Time Loss in Developing Countries: Concepts, Measurement, and Implications." *World Bank Research Observer* 24 (2): 267–90.

Alcazar, Lorena, F. Halsey Rogers, Nazmul Chaudhury, Jeffrey Hammer, Michael Kremer, Karthik Muralidharan. 2006. "Why Are Teachers Absent? Probing Service Delivery in Peruvian Primary Schools." *International Journal of Educational Research* 45: 117–36.

Atherton P., and G. Kingdon. 2010. "The Relative Effectiveness and Costs of Contract and Regular Teachers in India." Working Paper 2010-15, Centre for the Study of African Economies, University of Oxford, UK.

Bacolod, M., J. DiNardo, and M. Jacobson. 2009. "Beyond Incentives: Do Schools Use Accountability Rewards Productively?" National Bureau of Economic Research Working Paper 14775, NBER, Cambridge, MA.

Baker, G. 1992. "Incentive Contracts and Performance Measurement." *Journal of Political Economy* 100 (3): 598–614.

———. 2002. "Distortion and Risk in Optimal Incentive Contracts." *Journal of Human Resources* 37 (4): 728–51.

Ballou, D., and M. Podgursky. 2002. "Returns to Seniority Among Public School Teachers." *Journal of Human Resources* 37 (4): 892–912.

Banerjee, A. V., S. Cole, E. Duflo, and L. Linden. 2007. "Remedying Education: Evidence from Two Randomized Experiments in India." *The Quarterly Journal of Economics* 122 (3): 1235–64.

Basinga, P., P. J. Gertler, A. Binagwaho, A. L. Soucat, J. R. Sturdy, and C. M. Vermeersch. 2010. "Paying Primary Health Care Centers for Perfomance in Rwanda." Policy Research Working Paper 5190, World Bank, Washington, DC.

Borko, H. 2004. "Professional Development and Teacher Learning: Mapping the Terrain." *Educational Researcher* 33 (8): 3–15.

Bourdon, J., M. Frölich, and K. Michaelowa. 2007. "Teacher Shortages, Teacher Contracts and their Impact on Education in Africa." IZA Discussion Paper No. 2844, Institute for the Study of Labor, Bonn, Germany.

Bruns, B., D. Evans, and J. Luque. 2010. *Achieving World Class Education in Brazil: The Next Agenda*. Washington, DC: World Bank.

Burgess, S., and M. Ratto. 2003. "The Role of Incentives in the Public Sector: Issues and Evidence." *Oxford Review of Economic Policy* 19 (2): 285–300.

Chapman, D. W., C. W. Snyder, and S. A. Burchfield. 1993. "Teacher Incentives in the Third World." *Teaching and Teacher Education* 9 (3): 301–16.

Chaudhury, N., M. Kremer, F. H. Rogers, J. Hammer, and K. Muralidharan. 2005. "Teacher Absence in India: A Snapshot." *Journal of the European Economic Association* 3 (2–3): 658–67.

Cohen, D. K., and H. Hill. 2001. *Learning Policy: When State Education Reform Works*. New Haven: Yale University Press.

Courty, P., and G. Marschke. 2003. "Dynamics of Performance-Measurement Systems." *Oxford Review of Economic Policy* 19 (2): 268–84.

Darley, J. 1991. "Setting Standards Seeks Control, Risks Distortion." Institute of Government Studies Public Affairs Report 32 (4), University of California, Berkeley.

Deci, E. L., R. Koestner, and R. M. Ryan. 2001. "Extrinsic Rewards and Intrinsic Motivation in Education: Reconsidered Once Again." *Review of Educational Research* 71 (1): 1–27.

Delannoy, F., and G. Sedlacek. 2001. "Brazil—Teachers Development and Incentives: A Strategic Framework." Human Development Department Report 20408-BR, World Bank, Washington, DC.

Duflo, E., P. Dupas, and M. Kremer. 2008. "Peer Effects, Teacher Incentives, and the Impact of Tracking: Evidence from a Randomized Evaluation in Kenya." National Bureau of Economic Research Working Paper 14475, NBER, Cambridge, MA.

———. 2009. "Additional Resources versus Organizational Changes in Education: Experimental Evidence from Kenya." Unpublished manuscript, Abdul Latif Jameel Poverty Action Lab (JPAL), Massachusetts Institute of Technology, Cambridge, MA.

Duflo, E., R. Hanna, and S. Ryan. 2010. "Incentives Work: Getting Teachers to Come to School." Unpublished manuscript, Abdul Latif Jameel Poverty Action Lab (JPAL), Massachusetts Institute of Technology, Cambridge, MA.

Farr, S. 2010. *Teaching as Leadership: The Highly Effective Teacher's Guide to Closing the Achievement Gap*. San Francisco: Jossey-Bass.

Fehr, E., and A. Falk. 2002. "Psychological Foundations of Incentives." *European Economic Review* 46 (4–5): 687–724.

Fernandes, R. 2007. "Índice de Desenvolvimento da Educação Básica (IDEB): metas intermediárias para a sua trajetória no Brasil, estados, municípios e escolas." National Institute of Educational Studies 'Texeira' (INEP), Ministry of Education, Government of Brazil.

Ferraz, C., and B. Bruns. Forthcoming. "Incentives to Teach: The Effects of Performance Pay in Brazilian Schools." World Bank, Washington, DC.

Figlio, D. N., and J. Winicki. 2005. "Food for Thought: The Effects of School Accountability Plans on School Nutrition." *Journal of Public Economics* 89: 381–94.

Fudenberg, D., B. Holmstrom, and P. Milgrom. 1990. "Short-Term Contracts and Long-Term Agency Relationships." *Journal of Economic Theory* 51 (1): 1–31.

Gallego, F. A. 2008. "Efectos del SNED en resultados del proceso educativo." Unpublished manuscript.

Garet, M., A. Porter, L. Desimone, B. Birman, and K. S. Yoon. 2001. "What Makes Professional Development Effective? Results From a National Sample of Teachers." *American Education Research Journal* 38 (4): 915–45.

Glewwe, P., N. Ilias, and M. Kremer. 2010. "Teacher Incentives." *American Economic Journal: Applied Economics* 2 (3): 205–27.

Goldhaber, D., and Jane Hannaway. 2009. *Creating a New Teaching Profession*. Washington, DC: The Urban Institute Press.

Goyal, S., and P. Pandey. 2009a. "Contract Teachers." South Asia Human Development Sector Report 28, World Bank, Washington, DC.

———. 2009b. "How Do Government and Private Schools Differ? Findings from Two Large Indian States." South Asia Human Development Sector Report 30, World Bank, Washington, DC.

Guarino, C. A., L. Santibañez, and G. A. Daley. 2006. "Teacher Recruitment and Retention: A Review of the Recent Empirical Literature." *Review of Educational Research* 76 (2): 173–208.

Hanushek, E. A., J. F. Kain, D. M. O'Brien, and S. G. Rivkin. 2005. "The Market for Teacher Quality." National Bureau of Economic Research Working Paper 11154, NBER, Cambridge, MA.

Hanushek, E. A., and S. G. Rivkin. 2010. "Generalizations about Using Value-Added Measures of Teacher Quality." *American Economic Review* 100 (2): 267–71.

Hanushek, E. A., and L. Woessmann. 2007. "The Role of Education Quality for Economic Growth." Policy Research Working Paper 4122, World Bank, Washington, DC.

Heinrich, C. J., and G. Marschke. 2010. "Incentives and Their Dynamics in Public Sector Performance Management Systems." *Journal of Policy Analysis and Management* 29 (1): 183–208.

Holmstrom, B. 1979. "Moral Hazard and Observability." *Bell Journal of Economics* 10 (1): 74–91.

Holmstrom. B., and P. Milgrom. 1987. "Aggregation and Linearity in the Provision of Intertemporal Incentives." *Econometrica* 55: 303–28.

Hoxby, C. M., and A. Leigh. 2004. "Pulled Away or Pushed Out? Explaining the Decline of Teacher Aptitude in the United States." *American Economic Review* 94 (2): 236–46.

Jacob, B. A., and S. D. Levitt. 2002. "Rotten Apples: An Investigation of the Prevalence and Predictors of Teacher Cheating." National Bureau of Economic Research Working Paper 9413, NBER, Cambridge, MA.

Kane, Thomas J., and Douglas O. Staiger. 2001. "Improving School Accountability Measures." National Bureau of Economic Research Working Paper 8156, NBER, Cambridge, MA.

Kerr, S. 1975. "On the Folly of Rewarding A, While Hoping for B." *Academy of Management Journal* 18 (4): 769–83.

Kremer, M. E., D. Chen, P. Glewwe, and S. Moulin. 2001. "Interim Report on a Teacher Incentive Program in Kenya." Unpublished paper, Harvard University, Cambridge, MA.

Kremer, M., E. Miguel, R. Thorton, and O. Ozier. 2005. "Incentives to Learn." Policy Research Working Paper 3546, World Bank, Washington, DC.

Lavy, V. 2002. "Evaluating the Effect of Teachers' Group Performance Incentives on Pupil Achievement." *The Journal of Political Economy* 110 (6): 1286–317.

———. 2009. "Performance Pay and Teachers' Effort, Productivity, and Grading Ethics." *The American Economic Review* 99 (5): 1979–2011.

Lazear, E. P. 2000. "Performance Pay and Productivity." *The American Economic Review* 90 (5): 1346–1361.

———. 2003. "Teacher Incentives." *Swedish Economic Policy Review* 10 (2): 179–214.

Lemieux, T., W. B. Macleod, and D. Parent. 2009. "Performance Pay and Wage Inequality." *The Quarterly Journal of Economics* 124: 1–49.

Manzi, J. 2008. "Individual Incentives and Teacher Evaluation: The Chilean Case." Paper prepared for the "Quality of Education" International OECD and Mexico Joint Conference, Teacher Incentives and Stimuli Session, Mexico City.

McCaffrey, D. F., J. Lockwood, T. R. Sass, and K. Mihaly. 2009. "The Inter-temporal Variability of Teacher Effect Estimates." Unpublished paper.

McEwan, P., and L. Santibáñez. 2005. "Teacher and Principal Incentives in Mexico." In *Incentives to Improve Teaching: Lessons from Latin America*, ed. E. Vegas, 213–53. Washington, DC: World Bank.

Miller, R. T., R. J. Murnane, and J. B. Willett. 2007. "Do Teacher Absences Impact Student Achievement? Longitudinal Evidence from One Urban School District." National Bureau of Economic Research Working Paper 13356, NBER, Cambridge, MA.

Ministry of Education, Government of Chile. 2010. Programa Asignación Variable por Desempeño Individual. http://www.avdi.mineduc.cl.

Mizala, A., and P. Romaguera. 1999. "El Sistema Nacional de Evaluación del Desempeño Docente en Chile." Paper prepared for the "Los Maestros en América Latina: Nuevas Perspectivas Sobre su Desarrollo y Desempeño" conference, San José, Costa Rica.

Mizala, A., P. Romaguera, and M. Urquiola. 2007. "Socioeconomic Status or Noise? Tradeoffs in the Generation of School Quality Information." *Journal of Development Economics* 84 (1): 61–75.

Muralidharan, K., and V. Sundararaman. 2009. "Teacher Performance Pay: Experimental Evidence from India." National Bureau of Economic Research Working Paper 15323, NBER, Cambridge, MA.

———. 2010a. "Contract Teachers: Experimental Evidence from India." Unpublished paper, World Bank, Washington, DC.

———. 2010b. "The Impact of Diagnostic Feedback to Teachers on Student Learning: Experimental Evidence from India." *The Economic Journal* 120 (546): F187–F203.

———. 2010c. "Teacher Opinions on Performance Pay: Evidence from India." Unpublished paper, World Bank, Washington, DC.

Murnane, R. J., and D. K. Cohen. 1986. "Merit Pay and the Evaluation Problem: Why Most Merit Pay Plans Fail and a Few Survive." *Harvard Educational Review* 56 (1): 3–17.

Murnane, R. J., J. Singer, J. Willett, and R. Olsen. 1991. *Who Will Teach? Policies that Matter*. Cambridge, MA: Harvard University Press.

Odden, A., and C. Kelley. 1997. *Paying Teachers for What They Know and Do*. Thousand Oaks, CA: Corwin Press.

Pandey, P., S. Goyal, and V. Sundararaman. 2009. "Community Participation in Public Schools: Impact of Information Campaigns in Three Indian States." *Education Economics* 17 (3): 355–75.

Pink, D. H. 2006. *A Whole New Mind: Moving from the Information Age to the Conceptual Age*. New York: Riverhead Books.

Podgursky, M. J., and M. G. Springer. 2007. "Teacher Performance Pay: A Review." *Journal of Policy Analysis and Management* 26 (4): 909–49.

Prendergast, C. 1999. "The Provision of Incentives in Firms." *Journal of Economic Literature* 37 (1): 7–63.

Rau, T., and D. Contreras. 2009. "Tournaments, Gift Exchanges, and the Effect of Monetary Incentives for Teachers: The Case of Chile." Department of Economics Working Paper 305, University of Chile, Santiago.

Rivkin, S. G. 2009. "The Estimation of Teacher Value-Added as a Determinant of Performance Pay." In *Creating a New Teaching Profession*, ed. Don Goldhaber and Jane Hannaway. Washington, DC: The Urban Institute Press.

Rivkin, S. G., E. A. Haunshek, and J. F. Kain. 2005. "Teachers, Schools and Academic Achievement." *Econometrica* 73 (2): 417–58.

Romaguera, P. 2008. "Incentives and Stimuli for Teachers: The Case of Chile." Paper prepared for the "Quality of Education" International OECD and Mexico Joint Conference, Teacher Incentives and Stimuli Session, Mexico City.

Santibañez, L., J. F. Martínez, P. J. McEwan, C. Messan-Setodji, and R. Basurto-Dávila. 2007. *Haciendo Camino: Análisis del Sistema de Evaluación y del Impacto del Programa de Estímulos Docentes Carrera Magisterial en México*. Santa Monica, CA: RAND Education.

Solmon, L. C., and M. Podgursky. 2000. "The Pros and Cons of Performance-Based Compensation." Opinion Paper 120, Milken Family Foundation, Santa Monica, CA.

Springer, Matthew G., ed. 2009. *Performance Incentives: Their Growing Impact on American K–12 Education*. Washington, DC: Brookings Institution.

Stallings, J. 1985. "Instructional Time and Staff Development." In *Perspectives on Instructional Time,* ed. C. W. Fisher and D. C. Berliner, 283–98. New York: Longman.

Steele, J. L., R. J. Murnane, and J. B. Willett. 2009. "Do Financial Incentives Help Low-Performing Schools Attract and Keep Academically Talented Teachers? Evidence from California." National Bureau of Economic Research Working Paper 14780, NBER, Cambridge, MA.

Umansky, I. 2005. "A Literature Review of Teacher Quality and Incentives: Theory and Evidence." In *Incentives to Improve Teaching: Lessons from Latin America,* ed. E. Vegas, 21–61. Washington, DC: World Bank.

Valenzuela, J. P., A. Sevilla, C. Bellei, and D.d. Ríos. 2010. "Remuneraciones de los Docentes en Chile: Resolviendo una Aparente Paradoja." Iniciativa Científica Milenio Serie Documentos de Orientación para Políticas Públicas. Santiago, Chile.

Vegas, E., ed. 2005. *Incentives to Improve Teaching: Lessons from Latin America.* Washington, DC: World Bank.

Vegas, Emiliana, and Joost de Laat. 2003. "Do Differences in Teacher Contracts Affect Student Performance? Evidence from Togo." Working Paper No. 26955, World Bank, Washington, DC.

Vegas, E., S. Loeb, P. Romaguera, A. Paglayan, and N. Goldstein. 2010. "Teacher Policies Around the World: Objectives, Rationale, Methodological Approach, and Products." Education Department, World Bank, Washington, DC.

Weisberg, D., S. Sexton, J. Mulhern, and D. Keeling. 2009. *The Widget Effect: Our National Failure to Acknowledge and Act on Differences in Teacher Effectiveness.* Brooklyn, NY: The New Teacher Project. http://widgeteffect.org/downloads/TheWidgetEffect.pdf.

5

Making Schools Work through Accountability Reforms

Drawing on new evidence from 22 rigorous impact evaluations across 11 developing countries, this book has examined how three key strategies to strengthen accountability relationships in school systems—information for accountability, school-based management, and teacher incentives—can affect school enrollment, completion, and student learning. Overall, the evidence base has increased significantly, but broader country experience is needed, including much more experience in moving from efficacy trials (pilot programs) to systemwide reform implementation.

This chapter reviews the major conclusions and caveats that we draw from the evidence base to date in each of the three areas. It also looks across these three accountability reform strategies to consider how they may complement each other when implemented in combination. We review the technical issues posed by extrapolating from small-scale pilot evaluations to broader program design and the political economy issues of implementing or scaling up these three types of accountability reforms. We conclude with some suggested directions for future research.

Information-for-Accountability Strategies

Impact evaluations are an important tool for establishing "proof of concept"—that an intervention or type of intervention *can* have an impact on outcomes. The studies to date suggest that information for accountability can improve outcomes (see box 5.1). The three-state study in India and the studies in Liberia, Pakistan, and Uganda show that, under some configurations, information provision can stimulate actions on the part of school stakeholders, or politicians, that result in increased learning outcomes.

Such positive change can come through a variety of channels. In India, client power led to increased community oversight and increased effort on the part of teachers. In Liberia, information appeared to leverage parent engagement to make teacher capacity building effective. In Pakistan, information distributed to parents and teachers strengthened the village markets for education. In Uganda, empowering the school community with knowledge of school budgets affected both their "voice" and their "client power."

However, the evidence also suggests that information is not a panacea. The Jaunpur study in India, the Chilean example, and the Liberian "information-only" intervention all had no, or very limited, impacts. Clearly, school-based information can be used effectively for change, but its effectiveness will depend on a variety of factors—not all of which are well understood. The four new field studies, along with the two retrospective evaluations, do not provide a rich enough information base to parse out what makes information "work." Nevertheless, two questions related to intervention design appear to be important and merit serious thought in any new program:

1. *What* information should be disseminated? Simplicity seems to be an important feature. The Pakistan case, which had some of the largest impacts identified here, involved limited information—focused only on test score results. This is not to say that all school report cards should limit themselves to test scores only. But the fact that the information was narrow made it relatively easy for parents to understand and made the schools' comparative performance unambiguous.

2. *How* should information be disseminated? The two India cases documented a high degree of disengagement on the part of village-level education stakeholders. In this context, it is unlikely that a "hands-off" approach to providing information will have large impacts. Finding ways to ensure that these stakeholders absorb and understand the information, and also understand the actions they can potentially take, is likely crucial. This may need to be done creatively—and several of the interventions suggest it may need to be done repeatedly—to effect change. In some contexts, ensuring that information feeds into the political process, and finding ways to make that happen, will be the key to effecting change.

When designing information-for-accountability interventions, it is also important to keep in mind potential downsides. First, information can exacerbate, rather than reduce, inequalities in the voice and power of different socioeconomic groups. If the most highly educated or politically

BOX 5.1

New Evidence on Information for Accountability

Pakistan: Report Cards

In the context of a school management reform in the Punjab province of Pakistan, student and school "report cards" were produced and disseminated to parents and students in randomly selected villages—a setting in which a substantial number of students attended private schools (Andrabi, Das, and Khwaja 2009). The content of the cards was based on the results from a set of tests in English, mathematics, and Urdu—the local language. Parents received information about their child's individual scores and quintile rank, the school's average scores and quintile rank, and the average scores and quintile ranks of all other public and private schools in the village. Cards were delivered through discussion groups in which most of the time was spent explaining how to interpret the cards—with little advice provided as to what parents should do with the information. The evaluation ran over the course of two years.

The impact of the program rippled through local education markets. Learning achievement increased by between 0.10 and 0.3 of a standard deviation in government and lower-quality private schools, and the fees charged at higher-quality private schools fell by 21 percent. Among private schools, the results were consistent with the increased competition that information was introducing into the market: initially poorly performing schools responded by increasing the quality of teaching, and initially high-quality schools responded by reducing fees. It is less clear why learning increased in government schools. Unpacking the changes, the researchers found that schools in villages that received report cards were more likely to have textbooks by the end of the study, and they devoted around 30 more minutes per day to teaching and learning activities.

India: Jaunpur District and Three-State Studies

Two studies in India evaluated the impact of providing villagers with information about their rights and responsibilities regarding education provision and oversight. The settings were communities suffering from a substantial disconnect between the users and the providers of schooling—despite the existence of formal community oversight groups. Indeed, one of the studies found that most members of the Village Education Committees (VECs) did not even know they were members or what the role of the council was.

(continued next page)

BOX 5.1 *continued*

The first study, carried out in the Jaunpur district of Uttar Pradesh (Banerjee and others 2008), included a three-arm research design—with villages randomly assigned to each arm or to a comparison group. In the first arm, community members were informed of the structure of service provision and of the role and responsibilities of VECs. The second arm added an activity in which local volunteers were trained to administer a simple learning assessment to all children in the village and to publicize the results. The third arm added a component in which local volunteers were trained to provide reading instruction to village children. The study impacts were evaluated after a period of three to six months after the initial intervention.

The second study was carried out in selected districts in three Indian States—Uttar Pradesh, Madhya Pradesh, and Karnataka (Pandey, Goyal, and Sundararaman 2009, 2010). The intervention was similar to that of the first arm of the Jaunpur study, although the modalities for delivery of the information differed. For example, videos were shown on a mobile video screen, banners were erected in villages, and material such as calendars were distributed to parents. Impacts were evaluated over the course of two years (within which a "refresher" intervention took place).

The two evaluations came to different findings. The Jaunpur study found virtually no impact of the first two intervention arms—those that emphasized information alone. At the six-month follow-up, village members *did* know more about the role of the VEC and of the state of education in the village, although the magnitude of the increase in knowledge was small. But children in these villages performed no better on a range of tests designed to measure basic reading and math abilities.

The results from the three-state study were more pronounced. While the impacts were not consistent across all states and grades, they were measurable in several. For example, about 16 percent of third- and fourth-grade students in Uttar Pradesh had mastered one or more of the math competencies tested at baseline; the impact of the program was to raise that by about 5 percentage points more than the control group. Digging deeper into the sources of change, the study found that both knowledge and behaviors were affected by the intervention. Community members tended to know more about school oversight committee functions and other school matters, such as school accounts. Teacher effort, as measured by teacher attendance and by teaching activity conditional on attendance, also increased measurably.

(continued next page)

BOX 5.1 *continued*

Liberia: Early Grade Reading Assessment

In the context of an Early Grade Reading Assessment (EGRA) in Liberia, two strategies for improving reading outcomes were evaluated and compared with a control group (Piper and Korda 2010). Assignment to each of the treatment groups or the comparison group was random. The first evaluated approach consisted of publicizing the EGRA results to parents and communities and showing teachers how to prepare quarterly report cards for parents. The second approach added an intensive teacher-training component focused on methods for reading instruction.

After two years of the program, the "information-only" intervention had very small impacts. Only one of nine measures of children's reading skills (letter fluency) was affected by the intervention. On the other hand, the "full" intervention had large impacts on reading abilities—ranging from a 0.38 standard deviation in listening comprehension to 1.4 standard deviations for unfamiliar word decoding. Intriguingly, the study also found large and significant impacts on an assessment of math skills, even though math instruction was not a part of the teacher training. Given the study design, it is impossible to know whether the teacher training without the information would have had a similar impact. However, given the typically disappointing results from in-service teacher-training programs (World Bank 2003) and the spillover effects to math skills, it is possible that the increased accountability associated with the dissemination of scores, as well as the interaction (and supervision) associated with the "full" program, contributed to the adoption of more effective teaching methods and the resulting higher learning achievements.[a]

Uganda: Public Information Campaign

An alternative type of information intervention concerned not rights, responsibilities, or test scores but rather focused on inputs. Education funding in Uganda in the early 1990s was plagued by the fact that few of the resources allocated to schools actually reached them. A large-scale information campaign was launched to sensitize parents and communities to the exact amount of operational funding each school could expect and the date when the transfer to the school would be made. Two main information channels were used: (1) posting of school budgets in prominent locations on school grounds and (2) local newspaper listings of the amounts and dates of the school grant distributions. Importantly, these reforms were undertaken in the context of a

(continued next page)

BOX 5.1 *continued*

larger-scale political focus on the education sector, including a drive to universalize public primary education by eliminating school fees. Retrospective evaluations of the information campaign have used exposure to media as an instrumental variable (Reinikka and Svensson 2005, 2006; Björkman 2006). Assuming that exposure is exogenous (conditional on other observed characteristics), the impacts of disseminating this information through the media can be identified in this way.

The studies found large impacts from the information campaigns on several outcomes. First, as mentioned earlier, the public media campaign was associated with a sharp reduction in the leakage of school grant expenditures; by the early 2000s, more than 80 percent of funds spent on the school grants program actually reached schools. The researchers also documented that schools in districts with higher media exposure—and therefore more information conveyed—experienced greater increases in enrollments and higher test scores on the primary school exit exam than schools in districts with lower exposure.

Chile: School Rankings

A very different study exploited the long history of student testing and public dissemination of school-level results in Chile—the first country in Latin America to introduce standardized student testing. Since 1996, Chile's *Sistema Nacional de Evaluación del Desempeño de los Establecimientos Educativos Subvencionados* (National System for Performance Evaluation of Subsidized Educational Establishments, or SNED) program of school-level bonuses has also provided cash rewards to schools that show the largest improvements in student scores and other outcomes. The impact of these incentives on school performance is discussed in Chapter 4 and summarized elsewhere in this chapter, in the context of evidence on pay-for-performance reforms. But researchers Mizala and Urquiola (2007) recently analyzed the SNED experience from another angle, asking whether the program may also produce separate impacts through an information channel. SNED's identification of "outstanding" schools and rankings of school quality by administrative region, adjusted for student socioeconomic characteristics, are widely publicized in Chile. Does this information affect parents' choice of school? To analyze the extent to which this information dissemination affects school enrollments, the level of school fees, and the degree of socioeconomic heterogeneity in schools, Mizala and Urquiola (2007) exploited the fact that, within each "homogenous" group of schools, 25 are selected as winners in each round of the program. Schools "just

(continued next page)

BOX 5.1 *continued*

above" and "just below" the cutoff can be considered similar, although the former receives publicity associated with being a winner.

The researchers found that none of the outcome measures appeared to be affected by the program. A variety of robustness checks confirmed that this was not because of low literacy among parents (the result held for more-educated parents) nor because of limited student mobility across schools (the results also held for the secondary level, where students move more freely). Instead, the authors hypothesized that the program may fail to register with parents, leading to limited impact on their choices. Or other factors—such as school proximity or peer group preferences—may play a more dominant role than school performance information in school choices in Chile.

a. Li and others (2010) document how parental communication worked as a complement to tutoring in improving learning outcomes in a randomized field experiment in China.

powerful members of society are better positioned to use information for their own benefit (to the detriment of others), then information provision may foster elite capture.

Second, a number of different studies in the context of high-stakes information and testing (primarily in the United States) have documented strategic behavior on the part of schools—for example, manipulating who takes the test or outright cheating—that undermines the validity of the information intervention.

Third, the validity of test scores themselves as a fair and accurate signal of learning progress and the relative performance of schools is subject to debate. Test scores can be a noisy measure, especially in small schools which are common in much of the developing world.

Last, for information to have an impact, school-level actors must know how to improve service delivery. Some behavior changes may be straightforward—for example, improved teacher attendance—but others, such as more effective instructional techniques, are harder to achieve. Unless agents possess the tools and the scope for change, additional information may produce only frustration.

In summary, information for accountability—on its own—is a potentially useful tool for improving learning outcomes but one whose success at leveraging change is sensitive to many factors. For information provision to be effective, service providers must have the ability to change in response to the accountability pressures it can induce. If providers are circumscribed in their ability to take action, it is unsurprising if information has no impact. Information is therefore critically linked to local decision-making authority—a theme explored more extensively in the discussion of school-based management. The impact of information is also likely to be higher if it is linked to performance rewards or sanctions, which we consider in the discussion of teacher incentives.

School-Based Management Strategies

School-based management (SBM) models may have many positive benefits, all of which are associated with an improved and inclusive learning environment. At the same time, it is important to keep in mind that the institutional changes implied by SBM reforms may take time to affect test scores—both because it may take time for the new institutional arrangements to solidify and because it may take time for those changes to translate into test scores or examination results. That is, SBM is not a "quick fix." A meta-analysis of 232 studies with over 1,000 observations from 29 programs implemented in the United States showed that SBM reforms need at least five years to bring about fundamental changes at the school level and about eight years to yield significant changes in test scores, as figure 5.1 illustrates.

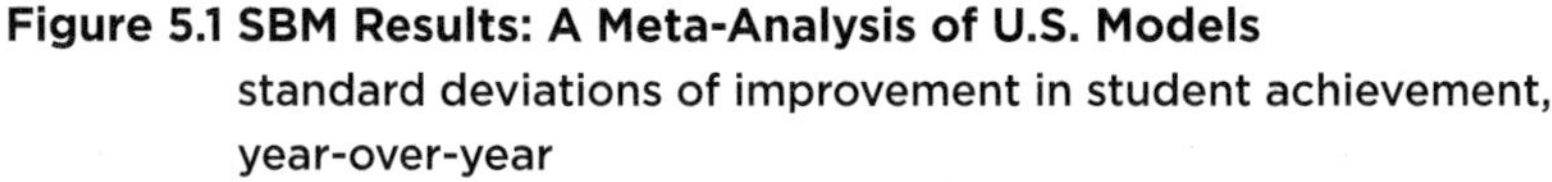

Figure 5.1 SBM Results: A Meta-Analysis of U.S. Models
standard deviations of improvement in student achievement, year-over-year

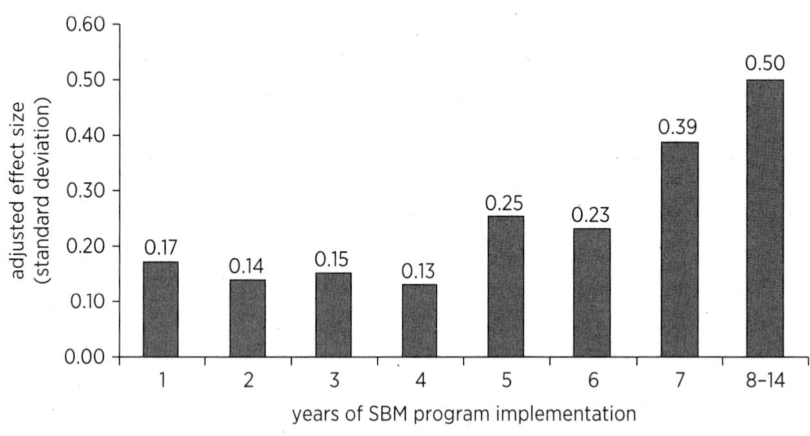

Source: Borman and others 2003.

Notes: SBM = school-based management.

Autonomy and participation, key dimensions of SBM, vary substantially in implementation. But from the variety of experiences, certain fundamentals emerge as key for effective reform. These elements include a focus on autonomous school strategic planning, involvement of multiple groups in goal setting, changes in teacher pedagogic practices, and stronger relations with parents and the surrounding community, all of which are mainstays of strong programs in the United States. Many of the programs in developing countries, including those designed to improve quality, emphasize the participatory aspects of SBM rather than the management aspects. To be effective, programs likely need to move beyond participation and involve empowerment of the actors to affect core education functions, such as teaching and learning.

The evidence to date is that SBM can improve learning outcomes, though the results are mixed (see box 5.2). It is likely that for SBM to be effective, it must entail a real transfer of authority (that is, provide school committees

BOX 5.2

New Evidence on School-Based Management

Kenya: Extra Teacher Project

In western Kenya, an innovative project was designed to investigate a variety of issues related to resource allocation and learning outcomes in primary education (Duflo, Dupas, and Kremer 2008). One aspect of the project was to explicitly test whether parental oversight of teachers leads to significant gains in test scores. Out of 210 schools in the project, 140 were randomly selected to receive funding for a locally hired contract teacher. Of these, 70 schools were randomly selected to participate in an SBM initiative designed to empower the school committees to monitor teachers' performance. In those schools, school committees held a formal review meeting at the end of the first school year of the program to assess the contract teacher's performance and to decide whether to renew the teacher's contract or to replace him or her. To assist the school committee, the project provided its members with a short, focused training on monitoring the contract teacher's performance. The school committee members were taught techniques for soliciting input from parents and checking teacher attendance. A formal subcommittee of first-grade parents was formed to evaluate the contract teacher and deliver a performance report at the end of the first year.

(continued next page)

BOX 5.2 *continued*

The evaluation found that the impact of parental oversight of teachers—that is, the SBM aspect of the intervention—was strong when combined with other reforms. The effect of reducing pupil-teacher ratios from 80 to 1 to 46 to 1, absent other interventions, led to reduced teacher effort (two teachers could share the job previously done by one teacher) and to small and insignificant increases in test scores. In contrast, combining the extra teacher with better incentives; local hiring of teachers on short-term, renewable contracts; or increasing parental oversight led to significant test score gains. Eighteen months into the program, students in treatment schools had test scores a 0.22 standard deviation higher than students in comparison schools. In schools where the school committee training was absent, however, the impact was smaller—only a 0.13 standard deviation—and statistically insignificant. The effect of the extra teacher was therefore largest when school committees were given training on how to supervise and manage teachers, and this effect was largest among the students assigned to a contract teacher instead of a civil service teacher. Overall, students assigned to a contract teacher in SBM schools scored a 0.30 standard deviation higher than students in the nonprogram schools. In this case, the SBM initiative enhanced the effect of the other interventions.

Mexico: School Quality and Management Support Programs

Two new evaluations in Mexico study the impacts of autonomy reforms that can be described as weak to intermediate. Although both SBM interventions are early in program implementation and analysis, they show small impacts on outcomes, mostly in the early grades of primary school. However, they also show changes in school climate, parental (low-income, rural, indigenous) perceptions and participation, and engagement among actors.

Quality Schools Program (PEC). In the Mexican state of Colima, the federal SBM program *Programa Escuelas de Calidad* (Quality Schools Program, or PEC) was randomly assigned in 2006. The study found a mixed set of results on intermediate indicators (Gertler, Patrinos, and Rodríguez-Oreggia 2010). Teachers reported an increase in the time they devoted to administrative tasks. There was a significant increase in the total number of hours per week that teachers reported spending on supporting students who were lagging behind and on meetings with parents to discuss student performance. There was a significant increase in principals' engagement in meetings to solve school conflicts as reported by teachers (overall, there was a very high reported

(continued next page)

BOX 5.2 *continued*

participation of teachers and principals in meetings over school matters). On the other hand, there was no observed significant change in the number of meetings held by the different school agents during the academic year.

In terms of student achievement, preliminary analysis suggests that test scores increased overall in Colima, for both treatment and control schools, although the differences were small. When disaggregated by grade, however, the cohort that was exposed to treatment the longest experienced the largest gains—students who were in third grade in the baseline year (2005/06). These students' scores increased by a 0.5 standard deviation between third and sixth grade if they were in the treated schools, while those in control schools increased by a 0.34 standard deviation—for a difference-in-differences estimated program impact of a 0.16 standard deviation.

School Management Support program (AGE 125). Another evaluation focused on the *Apoyo a la Gestión Escolar 125* (Support to School Management Program, or AGE 125) program in four Mexican states, which doubled the resources that AGE 125 schools received.[a] After just one year of implementation, a first follow-up survey revealed several impacts. First, interaction among directors, teachers, and parents changed—in particular, through the increased participation of school agents in the design and execution of school improvement plans. Second, class time, preparation, and extra classes for lagging pupils all increased more in the treatment schools than in the control schools.

After the first year of implementation, the AGE 125 project caused a dropout-rate decrease of between 1.56 and 1.73 percentage points in the treatment schools compared with the control schools. Among third-graders, the program had a positive impact on Spanish and mathematics test scores. The results suggest that the AGE 125 caused an increase of about 5.0–5.6 percent in Spanish scores and of about 6.3–8.0 percent in mathematics scores for third-grade students (Gertler, Patrinos, and Rodríguez-Oreggia 2010).

Nepal: Community-Managed Schools

The Government of Nepal notionally transferred responsibility for managing schools from the state to the community in 2001. Community schools, working through the school management committee consisting of parents and influential local citizens, were given *de jure* decision-making powers over various staffing and fiscal issues. In addition, community-managed schools were given more untied block grants so that the management committee had more control over

(continued next page)

BOX 5.2 *continued*

discretionary spending. An evaluation of SBM in this context exploited a "randomized encouragement" design in which an advocacy campaign by a nongovernmental organization (NGO) encouraged a random subset of schools and school management committees to take de facto management control (Chaudhury and Parajuli 2010).

Short-run impact estimates suggest that the devolution of management responsibilities to communities had significant impacts on certain schooling outcomes related to access and equity. The impact on school governance measures was mixed, with important regional variation in outcomes. There is no evidence yet that these changes were associated with improvements in learning outcomes.

Pakistan: NGO-Managed Schools

A reform in Pakistan involved hiring an NGO to manage schools together with the school councils (Das 2008). Each school received a grant on the order of $4,000 for school needs. In addition to assisting with managing these funds, the NGO was allowed to transfer teachers. The program ran from 2004 to 2008, but the randomized controlled evaluation has yet to show any effects on student enrollment, teacher absenteeism, or an index of facilities (infrastructure). It may be possible that the effects of school council management will only be in the long term. In addition, the results are weakened because the original randomization was not fully upheld, and the analysis uses an intent-to-treat approach. Intriguingly, the results showed that the proportion of council members whose children are students in the school significantly increased in treatment schools.

a. This randomized trial built on the retrospective evaluation conducted earlier on AGE schools (Gertler, Patrinos, and Rubio-Codina 2006).

and parents with real tasks) and the building of capacity to carry out those tasks. Importantly, the transfer of authority should be accompanied by resources. Two critical elements—information and teacher incentives—relate to the other topics touched on in this book.

For SBM to work beyond merely engendering participation, as in meetings of the parent association, information is vital. When SBM requires school councils to develop school development plans, those plans have a higher likelihood of success. When goals are related to student well-being and academic success and can be based on accurate and timely information on schooling outcomes, this helps channel efforts. This information may be test scores but can be broader than that, and all can be benchmarked against other schools—either locally or nationally.

Access to relevant information, adequate resources, clear goals and pathways, and a participatory council are some of the main ingredients of a successful SBM initiative. Weak forms of SBM that do not involve personnel decisions will likely not suffice to affect learning outcomes. The programs that can significantly improve outcomes, especially for the poorest and most-lagging schools, empower parents and councils to affect personnel decisions. A critical aspect of SBM effectiveness is management of teachers, for example, the ability to establish incentives and to fire nonperforming teachers.

SBM is, of course, not without controversy. Decentralization may not necessarily give more power to the general public because the power devolved by the reform is susceptible to being captured by elites. Local control over resource allocation or decision making may not yield the desired outcomes for three main reasons (Bardhan 2002; Bardhan and Mookherjee 2000, 2005):

- Local democracy and political accountability are often weak in developing countries and can lead to elite capture.
- In more traditional and rural areas with a history of feudalism, sometimes the poor or minorities feel the need for a strong central authority to ensure that they are able to access services as well as more powerful local citizens can. A related issue may be the lack of a culture of accountability within communities, meaning that no one would think to question any actions taken by the group running the school (De Grauwe 2005).
- Challenges often arise in the implementation of SBM reforms that can undermine their potential.

Teacher Contracting and Pay-for-Performance Strategies

Contract Teacher Policy Reforms

The newest wave of evidence on the short-term impacts of contract teacher reforms in low-income developing countries is fairly consistent: the use of contract teachers can strengthen the scope for local monitoring of teacher performance by parents and school councils, which results in higher teacher effort, with positive impacts on student learning. In contexts where the supply of adequately trained teachers is not constrained, these positive outcomes can be achieved at sometimes dramatically lower costs per student.

The evidence supports a theory of action in which the positive impacts of contract teacher reforms hinge on the de facto effectiveness of local monitoring (see box 5.3). Where decisions about the hiring and retention of contract teachers are made higher up the administrative chain and not

BOX 5.3

New Evidence on Contract Teachers

India: Contract Teachers in Andhra Pradesh

As part of a broader study of teacher incentives, contract teachers were hired in 2005 for a randomly selected set of schools across the state of Andhra Pradesh (Muralidharan and Sundararaman 2010a). In general, the contract teachers were less educated than the civil service teachers working in the same schools and also tended to be younger, female, and more likely to live in the local villages. The contract teachers' pay was less than one-fifth of the civil service wage.

Despite the lower pay, the researchers found contract teachers absent significantly less—16 percent of the time, compared with 27 percent for civil service teachers. Contract teachers were also more likely to be found teaching during spot visits by observers. As theory would predict, contract teachers with lower absence rates and higher rates of observed teaching activity in the first year of their contract also had higher rates of contract renewal for the second year.

Student test scores support the hypothesis that this higher effort by contract teachers plus the reduction in class size that their recruitment permitted had positive effects on student learning. After two years, students in schools assigned a contract teacher scored a 0.15 standard deviation higher in math and a 0.13 standard deviation higher in language than same-grade students in schools without contract teachers. In short, less-educated teachers who were paid a small fraction of the civil service wage in Andhra Pradesh appeared to be more accountable for performance than their civil service counterparts, in terms of attendance and teaching activity, and helped boost overall school outcomes. The researchers concluded that, in this context of very low accountability, contract teachers were five times more cost-effective than regular teachers in producing education results.

India: Balsakhi Contract Teachers

In two cities in India (Mumbai and Vadodara), the *Balsakhi* ("child's friend") program paid locally recruited young women with a secondary school education (grade 10) roughly 10 percent of a regular civil service teacher's salary to teach basic literacy and numeracy skills to third- and fourth-grade children who needed remedial support. The targeted children left the classroom in the afternoon and received tutoring for two hours per day. The program was highly effective in boosting the learning of these children, to the extent that average

(continued next page)

BOX 5.3 *continued*

math and reading test scores in the treatment schools increased by a 0.14 standard deviation in the first year and a 0.28 standard deviation after two years over the averages in the comparison schools (Banerjee and others 2007). Most of the gains were attributable to increases in learning by the children who had received remedial tutoring. Even one year after the program ended, the average student in the Balsakhi schools had test scores that were a 0.1 standard deviation higher than the average student in comparison schools.

The program was not designed as a "head-to-head" trial of the cost-effectiveness of contract teachers vs. civil service teachers. In addition to their different contract status and pay levels, the Balsakhi teachers had different curriculum goals, teaching hours, and class sizes from those of the regular schools. Due to the design of the study, intermediate variables of teacher effort, such as absence rates and use of instructional time, were not monitored. However, the large learning gains produced by teachers contracted at one-tenth of the prevailing civil service teacher salary provides evidence that, at least in some contexts, contract teachers' lower average qualifications, lower pay, and lack of long-term contract security do not impede effective teaching performance.

Kenya: Contract Teachers

The Extra Teacher Program (ETP) in western Kenya provided funding to a randomly selected set of schools to allow their school committees to hire a local contract teacher (Duflo, Dupas, and Kremer 2008). Unlike the India cases, these contract teachers had the same academic qualifications as civil service teachers. However, they were paid less than one-third of the civil service pay and could be fired by the school committee after each annual performance review. Researchers found contract teachers significantly more likely to be in class and teaching during unannounced visits: 74 percent of the time versus 59 percent of the time for civil service teachers in comparison schools. The attendance record of contract teachers was even more impressive when compared to civil service teachers in their own schools, whose absence rates increased when the contract teachers began working. However, training programs for school committees in how to monitor teacher attendance and performance mitigated the "shirking" behavior of civil service teachers over time.

Students randomly assigned to contract teachers under the ETP program scored a 0.21 standard deviation higher on reading and math tests than their schoolmates assigned to civil service teachers,

(continued next page)

BOX 5.3 *continued*

suggesting higher—or at least more effective—teaching effort by the contract teachers despite their lower salaries. However, the fact that contract teachers were assigned to a single class of students and stayed with those students for two successive years (unlike the typical pattern of a different teacher each year) may have played a role as well.

As discussed in the previous section on SBM, the Kenya researchers also found that training school committees on how to manage the hiring, performance monitoring, and renewal decisions for contract teachers was correlated with positive long-term impacts of the program. At the three-year follow-up, only students of contract teachers in schools whose committees had been trained ("SBM schools") performed significantly better than students in control schools. The SBM schools were also more likely to use funding from the community to retain the contract teacher once program funding ended; 43 percent of them did so, compared with 34 percent of non-SBM schools.

Other Contract Teacher Studies

Mali, Niger, and Togo. Contract teachers are widely used in West Africa. Bourdon, Frölich, and Michaelowa (2007) compared the experiences in Mali, Niger, and Togo, updating an earlier study of Togo by Vegas and De Laat (2003). They found that the presence of a contract teacher was positively correlated with the learning performance of low-ability students in the early grades but negatively correlated with the results of high-ability students in the upper grades.

Peru. A study in a rural province in Peru carried out by Alcazar and others (2006) is the only study to date to document *higher* absence rates for contract teachers than for civil service teachers, by 12–13 percentage points. The authors speculate that the lower salaries of contract teachers, in a context of weak local supervision, are a major reason for these teachers' apparently lower effort. Unfortunately, the study does not include any data on the student learning performance of contract and civil service teachers.

India: Madhya Pradesh and Uttar Pradesh. In two additional states in India that made extensive use of contract teachers—Madhya Pradesh and Uttar Pradesh—Goyal and Pandey (2009) carried out a nonexperimental analysis of the relative performance of contract and civil service teachers. In these states, unlike Andhra Pradesh, contract teachers typically were more educated than regular teachers, although they were much younger, had much less teaching experience, and were more likely to come from the local community. Consistent with the

(continued next page)

BOX 5.3 *continued*

results of the experimental studies in India cited previously, the contract teachers working in Madhya Pradesh and Uttar Pradesh public schools consistently demonstrated higher effort than regular teachers, whether measured as daily attendance or as the likelihood of being actively engaged in teaching during an unannounced visit. This higher effort was also correlated with significantly better learning outcomes for their students on language and math tests, after controlling for other school, teacher, and student characteristics.

However, the researchers followed the performance of the contract teachers over two years and noted that effort levels (attendance rates and likelihood of being found teaching) declined for teachers in their second contract period in both states—and, in Uttar Pradesh, became indistinguishable from the effort levels of regular teachers (Goyal and Pandey 2009). They speculated that very weak de facto oversight by school-level committees significantly weakened contract teachers' incentives to perform. Fewer than 6 percent of school committee members were even aware that selection and oversight of contract teachers was one of their core responsibilities.

at the school level, or where local school committees are not equipped or empowered to put "teeth" into annual renewal decisions, impacts have been lower or break down relatively quickly.

The current evidence base does not answer some key questions, however. Although contract teachers almost always work for lower salaries than their civil service counterparts do, the cost-effectiveness of a contract teacher policy is likely to depend on country characteristics and the level of education involved. All of the cases cited involved contract teachers at the primary level, where the supply of potential teachers with adequate capacity is not as likely to be constrained as at the secondary level or for specialty subjects such as sciences and math. It cannot be assumed that in all contexts it will be possible to recruit adequately qualified teachers at lower salaries.

There are also questions about the sustainability of this policy over time. Contract teachers may accept lower salaries and insecure tenure because they are queuing for regular positions. In the Kenya Extra Teacher Program (further described in box 5.3), 32 percent of the contract teachers subsequently obtained relatively highly paid civil service positions. In West African countries, where contract teachers have reached a critical mass, teachers' unions have made the extension of job stability to contract teachers a political goal. Duflo, Dupas, and Kremer (2008), among other researchers, caution against assuming that average teacher performance would match the performance of contract teachers if all teachers were placed on alternative tenure contracts. Nonetheless, in developing countries struggling to achieve universal access to primary education at sustainable fiscal costs, the evidence to date clearly supports the use of contract teachers as a cost-effective policy.

Pay-for-Performance Reforms

The most recent and robust developing-country evidence on pay-for-performance programs suggests that bonus-pay incentives can improve learning outcomes, at least in the contexts studied most carefully to date (see box 5.4). This evidence is in contrast to the more mixed, but less rigorous, developing-country evidence that existed just five years ago—and in sharp contrast to the most recent evaluation evidence from U.S. programs. In carefully conducted randomized trials of relatively generous bonuses aimed at both individual teachers (Nashville public schools) and schools (group-based bonuses in New York City public schools), researchers have failed to find any impact on student learning outcomes.

BOX 5.4

New Evidence on Pay for Performance

India: Andhra Pradesh

An ongoing randomized study in the Indian state of Andhra Pradesh offers the most persuasive evidence to date of the potential for performance-based pay to motivate more effective teacher performance in a developing-country setting. In a statewide representative sample of 500 schools, Muralidharan and Sundararaman (2009) measured the relative impacts of both individual and group (school-based) teacher bonuses compared with other equivalent-cost input strategies (such as books, materials, and infrastructure improvements) and with comparison schools that received no interventions. Bonuses were linked to improvements in student learning over the course of a school year, and the average bonus was around 35 percent of a typical teacher's monthly salary.

(continued next page)

BOX 5.4 *continued*

By the end of the first year, students in both the individual and group-bonus treatment schools performed significantly better than students in comparison schools. By the end of two years, researchers also observed differentiated results between the individual- and group-incentives schools, with the former registering an average increase in student test scores of a 0.27 standard deviation compared with a 0.16 standard deviation in group-incentive schools. The input-only strategies also yielded positive effects when compared with control schools, but their magnitude (a 0.08 standard deviation) was substantially lower than in incentive schools. Both the group and individual bonus programs were more cost-effective than the input programs and were roughly equal to each other in cost-effectiveness. Although the group bonus had a weaker impact on student learning results, this was offset by its lower costs.

Qualitative analysis suggests that the main mechanisms for the incentive effects was not increased teacher attendance but greater, and more effective, teaching effort conditional on being present. In particular, teachers in incentive schools were significantly more likely to have assigned homework and classwork, conducted extra classes beyond regular school hours, given practice tests, and paid special attention to weaker children. The researchers also found that providing teachers with more detailed feedback on their students' performance increased the power of bonus incentives to raise test scores, while the same feedback provided to teachers in comparison schools had no effect. This suggests positive interactions between incentives and input and the possibility for incentives also to raise the effectiveness of other school inputs such as feedback reports or teacher capacity building (Muralidharan and Sundararaman 2010b).

Israel: Individual Teacher Incentive Experiment

Lavy (2009) evaluated a tournament-type bonus program in Israel that ranked teachers on the basis of value-added contributions to their students' test scores on high school matriculation exams. Relative to other incentive programs, the bonuses for this program were large (up to several months of salary). The program had positive effects on student achievement by increasing the test-taking rate among high school seniors as well as the pass rate and test scores in math and English. However, the experiment was maintained for only one school year.

(continued next page)

BOX 5.4 *continued*

Kenya: ICS Teacher Incentive Program

Glewwe, Ilias, and Kremer (2010) evaluated a randomized program in Kenya that provided a group-based incentive to teachers (equivalent to about 40 percent of a month's salary) based on improvements in student learning. By the second year, students in the bonus schools scored an average of a 0.14 standard deviation higher on the exams than did students in the comparison schools. However, the gains proved short-lived. One year after the program ended, there were no significant differences in test performance across the schools. The researchers speculated that teachers' strategies for achieving the bonus focused on short-run efforts to boost performance on the government tests, such as after-school tutoring in test-taking techniques, rather than on changes in their core pedagogy or effort levels that might have a higher chance of promoting long-term learning. Other puzzling findings were that teacher absence rates did not decline from the baseline level of 20 percent of school days missed, and classroom observations did not detect any changes in homework assigned or use of learning materials.

Brazil (Pernambuco): Teacher Bonus Program

Ongoing evaluations are studying recently adopted teacher bonus programs in four different states in Brazil and in the municipality of Rio de Janeiro (Ferraz and Bruns, forthcoming). All of the programs are school-based (group) incentives, and the typical bonus size is fairly large (one to two months of salary). As the programs are implemented systemwide, the evaluations use regression discontinuity designs to compare results for similar schools that face stronger or weaker performance incentives as a result of the rules for setting individual schools' performance targets. Targets are for value-added student learning improvements in math and language and student grade progression.

In Pernambuco (the state with the most advanced results to date) in the first year, schools with more ambitious targets made significantly larger test score gains than similarly performing comparison schools that had been assigned lower targets (a 0.31 standard deviation higher in language and a 0.15 standard deviation higher in math). In the second year, researchers also found that—controlling for schools' 2008 test results and other school characteristics—schools that barely missed the threshold for achieving the bonus in 2008 (at least 50 percent

(continued next page)

BOX 5.4 *continued*

achievement of the school's target) improved more than schools that barely achieved it. It appears that both higher targets and barely missing the bonus created incentives that had a positive effect on schools' motivation and performance.

In contrast to some of the studies in India and Kenya, classroom observations in a sample of over 200 of Pernambuco's 900-plus schools found significant differences in teacher practice that were highly correlated with schools' likelihood of achieving the bonus (Bruns and others 2010). Teachers in schools that went on to earn the bonus registered significantly less time off-task and were able to devote this time to instruction; learning activities absorbed 62 percent of total class time in these schools compared with 53 percent of class time in schools that did not earn the bonus. While teachers were off-task 12 percent of the time across the whole sample (either out of the classroom due to late arrival or early departure or engaged in social interaction with students or colleagues), such time loss was much more significant in the schools that did not subsequently achieve the bonus (17 percent of total class time) than in those that did achieve the bonus (10 percent of total class time). There is also evidence of more intensive use of learning materials and higher rates of student engagement in the schools that subsequently earned the bonus.

Israel: Ministry of Education School Performance Program

Lavy (2002) examined a tournament-type program implemented in 1995 that provided a group incentive to schools for progress in reducing student dropout rates and improving academic achievement. Using a regression discontinuity approach, Lavy's results suggested that monetary incentives had some effect in the first year of implementation (mainly in religious schools) and by the second year caused significant gains in student outcomes in all schools. The program led to improvements in the number of credit units taken by students and average test scores in matriculation exams. In addition, more students gained matriculation certificates, and schools reduced dropout rates in the transition from middle school (grades 7–9) to high school (grades 10–12).

Comparing the incentive program with a "resource" intervention (such as direct provision of teacher training) of equivalent overall cost, Lavy found that the resource program produced much smaller improvements in student performance; the school bonus program was more cost-effective.

(continued next page)

BOX 5.4 *continued*

Chile: National System for Performance Evaluation of Subsidized Educational Establishments (SNED)

Chile's SNED program offers group bonuses to schools based on a combination of student learning results and other indicators of school and teacher performance. It is conducted as a tournament every two years; the bonus represents an annual increase of around 70 percent of one month's salary, and approximately 25 percent of schools in Chile typically receive the award. The most recent evaluation of SNED (Rau and Contreras, 2009) concluded that the program's introduction in 1996 stimulated an overall increase in student learning outcomes of approximately a 0.12 standard deviation. The researchers also explored the effects of winning the SNED award on subsequent school performance and found, over six rounds of SNED awards, no consistent evidence that schools gaining the award performed better in the next period.

In contrast to the above programs, which rewarded schools and teachers for improving student outcomes, two programs—in Kenya and India—rewarded teachers for attendance.

Kenya: Preschool Teacher Bonus Program

Kremer and others (2001) evaluated a program that allowed school headmasters in rural Kenya to give individual teachers bonus pay for regular attendance. The size of the bonus was relatively large: up to three months' salary for no absences. They found that the program had no impact on actual teacher attendance (measured by unannounced random visits); absence rates remained at 29 percent. There was also no evidence of change in teachers' pedagogy, pupil attendance, or pupil test scores, although it could be argued that both pedagogy and test performance at the preschool level may be noisy measures. Researchers found that headmasters simply distributed the full bonus to all teachers regardless of actual attendance. Even though there was a financial incentive for headmasters to hold back part of the funding (any funds not allocated to teacher bonuses reverted to the schools' general fund), they chose not to do so. School headmasters clearly found it difficult to play a strict monitoring role at the school level.

India: Rajasthan "Camera" Program

A program in rural India evaluated by Duflo, Hanna, and Ryan (2010) produced very different results. In randomly selected rural, NGO-run

(continued next page)

BOX 5.4 *continued*

schools, a schedule of monthly teacher bonuses and fines based on attendance was monitored in a creative way with daily date- and time-stamped photographs. A student was asked to photograph the teacher and the children in the class at the beginning and end of each school day. Teachers' pay was a function of the number of "valid school days"—in which the school was open for at least five hours and at least eight students appeared in each picture. Unannounced visits to the "camera" and comparison schools measured actual absence rates and observed teacher activity.

The maximum bonus for a teacher with no days absent was approximately 25 percent of a month's salary. The program over three years had a dramatic effect on teacher absenteeism, which fell from 42 percent to 23 percent in the treatment schools. While there were no observed changes in teachers' classroom behavior and pedagogy (other than greater presence), student test scores rose by a 0.17 standard deviation, and graduation rates to the next level of education also rose significantly. While students' attendance rates (conditional on the school being open) did not increase, there was a significant increase in the total amount of time that children in treatment schools spent in classes because schools were open, on average, 2.7 more days per month.

Duflo, Hanna, and Ryan (2010) note that the intervention was quite cost-effective. As the base salary for teachers in the treatment and comparison schools was the same, the incremental costs of the program consisted of the bonus, the cameras, and monitoring—totaling roughly $6 per child per year. In terms of raising test scores, the researchers estimate the per-child cost of a 0.10 standard deviation increase in test scores was only $3.58.

In no study to date have long-term effects of performance-based pay been analyzed. And both theory and experience with performance-based rewards in other sectors clearly indicate that the scope for perverse behaviors (such as gaming, cheating, or teaching to the test) can rise with time as system actors become more familiar with the rules of the game. As performance-based pay becomes increasingly—and logically—linked to student test results in many countries, the validity of those tests and the legitimacy of their application become centrally important challenges for education systems.

Still, in a context of persistently low education outcomes and widespread evidence of "accountability failures" on the part of teachers and other education system actors, the evidence that pay-for-performance programs and the use of contract teachers can raise student outcomes in developing-country contexts is important. But the contrasting U.S. evidence suggests that it is important to note that these developing-country contexts are characterized by

- *Weak systems for performance monitoring and accountability*—evidenced by relatively high teacher absence rates, low teacher dismissal rates, and low student learning performance
- *Relatively weak teacher professionalism*—evidenced by low standards for entry
- *Relatively large bonus size*—for example, an annual bonus equaling 30–300 percent of a month's salary
- *Focused performance metrics*—emphasis on a small number of key results, usually school-level improvements in student learning measured on annual standardized tests or relatively easily measured teacher "inputs" such as monthly attendance
- *"Fair" performance metrics*—rewards to schools on a value-added basis (for progress relative to their starting points) or compared with schools with similar geographic and student socioeconomic conditions, not for absolute levels of performance
- *Rewards clearly linked to prior period results*—annual bonuses directly based on test scores or other results for the previous school year, or monthly bonuses for input measures monitored over the prior month, such as teacher attendance

In these contexts, the most recent developing-country bonus programs appear to "work" in the sense that student learning outcomes improve in the presence of the bonus. In the most careful studies, the size of the effect—a 0.19–0.27 standard deviation increase in average student learning—is impressively large compared with the effects typically measured for other types of education programs.

The sole developing-country evaluation to date designed as a "head-to-head" comparison of individual bonus pay (that is, rewarding each teacher for his or her own classroom's average learning progress over the course of a school year) with group-based bonus pay (rewarding schools for their average learning improvement) showed similar results in the first year but a stronger effect on learning outcomes from the individual bonus by the second year. The impact measured in that program, in rural Andhra Pradesh, India—a 0.27 standard deviation increase in language scores—remains the largest reported causal impact from an education pay-for-performance program. However, the group bonus alternative proved to be more cost-effective because the average awards were smaller. In general, school systems will likely find group bonus pay more technically feasible than individual bonus pay, which requires the ability to test students in every grade, subject, and classroom. The latter presents significant technical challenges and costs.

Our understanding of the mechanisms through which bonus pay improves student outcomes is still weak. In several evaluations, at least over the short term, the bonus program did not induce any reduction in teacher absence rates, which is one of the most obvious ways teachers can increase their effort in response to an incentive. These teachers did nonetheless produce statistically significant improvements in their students' learning outcomes relative to comparison groups of teachers who were not offered a bonus, but the evidence suggests that a key channel was out-of-school tutoring, which is not a wholly desirable effect.

In Brazil, where bonus programs have been implemented systemwide, it is not possible to estimate how the introduction of a bonus *per se* affects schools' performance. But detailed classroom observations in Brazil are helping to elucidate the pathways through which bonus incentives can change teacher behavior and the kinds of changes that are most effective in raising learning. There is clear evidence of more time spent on instruction by teachers in schools that subsequently earned the bonus, with less time lost by teachers due to late arrival or early departure. There is also evidence of more intensive use of learning materials and higher rates of student engagement in the successful schools.

Looking across pay-for-performance programs, several features drawn from classical principal-agent theory appear important for the design of effective incentives. These include (1) the *controllability* of the specific performance measure(s) being incentivized, from the standpoint of individual teachers; (2) the *predictability* or "coverage" of the incentive (that is, what share of those eligible will achieve it); and (3) *bonus size*.

Controllability is, in turn, affected by two dimensions—*"noise"* in the performance measure and *"locality"* (whether the bonus is an individual or group [school]-based incentive). For group incentives, school size appears important. If a school has a large number of teachers, yet the bonus is based on results produced by only a handful of its teachers (typically, those teaching subjects and grades that are subjected to annual testing), there is room for free-riding (some teachers coasting on the work of the others).

The experience to date supports a hypothesis that core design features such as controllability and predictability affect the strength of the incentives in a pay-for-performance program. Particularly interesting from a policy standpoint is that these features appear to be complementary to the financial size of the bonus. In other words, bonus programs that pay attention to the design of performance measures so that these are perceived to reflect teachers' work fairly (for example, student test scores for schools are adjusted for socioeconomic differences) may—all other things being equal—achieve larger impacts. Much longer-term and deeper analysis of experience with these and other education pay-for-performance programs is needed for any conclusive observations, but the experience to date at least suggests the usefulness of considering these three core elements systematically in the design of new programs: controllability, predictability or coverage, and bonus size.

In conclusion, a growing number of school systems across the developing world are adopting two specific reforms aimed at strengthening the rewards and sanctions for teacher performance: the use of contract teachers and bonus pay linked to teacher performance. These programs have different designs, costs, and primary objectives, but all address a deep issue of weak incentives for performance in education systems across the developing world. The best-evaluated cases to date show that the design of effective incentives presents challenges, and their impacts can vary significantly. But an encouraging number of recent studies show consistently positive impacts of incentive reforms on student learning outcomes. The number of developing-country reform experiences is still small, and most are still very new. But they offer examples that merit consideration by any education policy maker concerned with raising student learning as well as a framework for the generation of further research evidence on "what works" to make teachers more accountable for results.

Linking Accountability Reforms

The accountability-oriented education reforms reviewed in this book produced impacts on learning achievement, as measured by test scores, ranging from 0 to about 0.3 of a standard deviation. This is consistent with other assessments of education interventions, which point to a 0.2 standard deviation as a "respectable" impact (Kremer and Holla 2009). As illustrated in chapter 1, however, developing countries are currently far from Organisation for Economic Co-operation and Development (OECD) average levels on internationally comparable assessments such as the Programme for International Student Assessment (PISA) or the Trends in International Mathematics and Science Study (TIMSS), with mean scores that are more than 1 standard deviation lower than the OECD average. Clearly, the short-run impacts measured in the individual evaluations documented here will make only a limited dent in the performance gap. Allowing reforms to solidify, and impacts to accumulate over time (as shown in figure 5.1), may help.

However, even accumulated "respectable" gains may not be enough to address the challenges that developing—and especially the lowest-income—countries are facing. Multiple challenges likely need to be addressed simultaneously in a sustained manner. The three approaches to promoting accountability described here can reinforce one another as well as reinforce other strategies to improve learning outcomes. Some of the evaluations reviewed here provide insights into those reinforcing effects. For example, information dissemination seems to have enhanced the impact of teacher training in Liberia. SBM, in the form of trained school committees, enhanced the impact of locally hired contract teachers in Kenya. Information, in the form of a new national system for monitoring student learning and grade progression, has played a critical part in the implementation of teacher incentive reforms in Brazil.

Information for Accountability

Information about schooling outcomes will likely be at the heart of any program that tries to improve school quality through accountability interventions. Information can come in many forms, and strengthening administrative data systems—particularly data on outcomes—can potentially lay the foundation for a range of reforms. Because of its public-good nature, information will tend to be underproduced relative to the optimal level, and reaching that level will require subsidies—domestically from governments and internationally from donors. Information underpins knowledge of what the situation is and where more effort is needed; it also provides the means to monitor progress. Information can be an accountability tool in and of itself, but its role is also broader.

The potential for information to strengthen accountability is sensitive to several factors. First, of course, is the content and presentation of the information: it needs to be understandable. In addition, while information can highlight problems and spur action, it is also unsurprising if its impacts are limited where the scope for decision making is heavily circumscribed. Providing information on school quality to actors who lack authority over the allocation or use of inputs will have limited impact.

School-Based Management

SBM can have an impact, but only if it is meaningful, in the sense that it goes beyond simply socializing parents—generating "participation" without authority. While participation may have intrinsic merits (creating active citizens, empowering poor and indigenous peoples, promoting democracy, instilling voice, and so on), these merits may have limited power to improve schooling outcomes. SBM initiatives, to matter, need to create effective opportunities for school management committees to improve quality—for example, by increasing their ability to shape adequately resourced school improvement plans.

Successful models consistently show that clarity in the role of participation, adequate resources, and capacity building can create positive change. One of the most critical elements, however, is likely to be the ability to oversee teachers. As the Kenya school committee evaluation showed, lower pupil-teacher ratios had little effect on learning without an appropriate incentive framework for teachers.

Contract Tenure and Pay-for-Performance Reforms

Linking teacher tenure or pay for performance has potential in developing-country contexts, where monitoring and performance incentives are generally weak. The cases presented in this book suggest that, given the right set of arrangements, teacher incentive reforms can result in increased teacher effort and improved student learning. When combined with local autonomy—allowing parents to hire teachers on renewable contracts outside the civil service system and to influence those teachers' tenure—the impacts may be reinforcing.

Complementarity of Accountability Interventions

Figure 5.2 illustrates the complementarities of these reforms. Information is a fundamental building block. It signals problems in the education system, serves as an instrument to measure subsequent progress, and can be used to set goals. On its own, however, it is likely to have limited potential when not linked to changes in how inputs are allocated. SBM, in turn, offers the potential to effect change but requires an information base. And even with information, the potential impacts of SBM are limited if it does not include oversight of teachers.

Incentives that affect teachers—the most vital and expensive schooling input—have the greatest potential to affect student learning, but they also depend on information. Student test score data allows teachers to benchmark their students' current performance and to work toward specific improvement targets. The studies in this book provide evidence that information provision can be a critical input to teacher effectiveness and that its power is also increased in the presence of incentives. For example, teachers who were offered bonus pay in Andhra Pradesh, India, made more effective use of detailed feedback on their students' performance than did teachers not offered a performance incentive. In Pernambuco, Brazil, the teachers given more-ambitious targets for student learning gains produced greater improvements than comparable teachers given

Figure 5.2 Complementarities in Accountability Reform

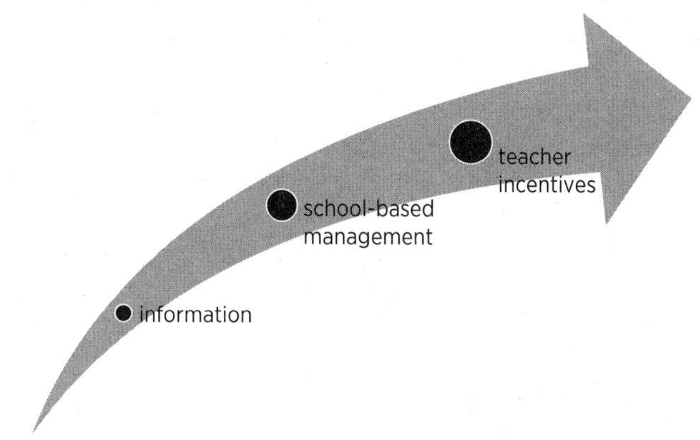

Source: Authors.

less-ambitious targets. This research base is still nascent, but it points to important interactions.

The complementarities between information for accountability, SBM, and teacher incentive reforms mirror a broader set of complementarities—those embodied in the accountability framework first described in chapter 1. Reforms that aim only at affecting citizen voice may be ineffective at improving outcomes if the compact between policy makers and front-line service providers is broken. Similarly, improvements to the compact may have perverse consequences if the priorities of citizens—or subsets of citizens such as the poor, for example—are not reflected in policy priorities.

External Validity: From Evaluated Programs to National Reforms

The Perils of Scaling Up

This synthesis has drawn from a variety of types of impact evaluations. Some were undertaken in relatively small sets of schools (sometimes less than 100) under tightly monitored conditions—for example, report cards in Pakistan, the training of school committees in Kenya, and teacher incentives in Israel. Others dealt with reforms on a systemwide scale—for example, SBM reforms in Mexico, information reforms in Chile, and teacher incentive reforms in Brazil. All impact evaluations, however, raise the issue of external validity: to what extent are the study findings relevant for other contexts or countries or for programs that are implemented at substantially larger—or smaller—scale?

The studies included in this volume all meet a fairly high bar for *internal validity:* they used evaluation methods that credibly established that measured impacts were indeed *caused* by the program. However, as we noted in chapter 1, while internal validity is necessary for external validity, it is not sufficient. Establishing external validity allows us to say that results are generalizable and replicable and to project how the size of the impacts measured in these evaluations would carry over to other samples or populations.

Any single impact evaluation raises questions of external validity. Combining theory with meta-analysis—or the systematic review of a significant body of comparable impact evaluations—is the only true strategy for establishing external validity over time. While our review takes careful stock of the current state of knowledge on these types of education accountability reforms, the number and range of cases are still too small to support conclusive meta-analysis, as we have emphasized throughout.

One concern is the limited geographic scope of the evidence to date. We have rigorous impact studies from just 11 countries, and a disproportionate share of the most compelling evidence comes from a single country: India.

Second, most of the studies reviewed (15 of 22 cases) are pilot programs implemented under careful supervision by international research teams. In a number of cases, the programs were implemented in schools run by local NGOs rather than in regular public sector schools. The reforms therefore played out within unique administrative arrangements that may not reflect the broader public sector reality in those countries, let alone in others.

Third, particularly in the case of reforms aimed at strengthening accountability, an inherently important contextual issue is the local political situation. In different countries—and even across different states in countries such as Brazil or India—the relative power of principals, teachers, and parents and community members varies. This is an especially important factor for programs that aim to *change* the power relations among these stakeholders, as in SBM programs. A program to make teachers more accountable for performance may be successful in one country because teachers' unions are relatively weak relative to other stakeholders. Where teachers are more organized and politically active, the same program might be less successful or even impossible to implement. Particularly for accountability-oriented reforms, understanding the local political context is critical.

A fourth variable that can affect external validity is the baseline quality of teachers and students—the objects of change for most programs. Even if a program improves learning outcomes by 0.20 of a standard deviation on average in one context, it does not follow that it will have the same impact if it is targeted to students from only the bottom 20 percent of performers—or the top 20 percent. The "average treatment effect" of a program may be a poor guide to the impact it will have on different categories of students, different groups of teachers, or different sets of schools. Is it easier to improve student performance for weak students? Do pay-for-performance targets motivate teachers to focus on the better students or "bubble students" (those at the threshold for incentivized performance) rather than on others? Will SBM programs have weaker impacts in poor communities than in others? There is much still to learn about how programs differentially affect different groups of system actors and beneficiaries.

Finally, taking any reform to new contexts or to scale within a given context generates questions of general versus partial equilibrium effects. From a political economy standpoint, as we discuss in the next section, experimentation on a pilot scale versus moving to statewide or national implementation pose very different challenges. But even on a technical level, since impact evaluations typically compare the difference between treatment and comparison populations in a given localized area, they are not able to pick up general equilibrium effects (Duflo, Glennerster, and Kremer 2008). These effects may be particularly important for scaling up a program. A pilot in one region of a country may work well, but it might not be possible—for technical, human capacity, or financial reasons—to replicate it on a large scale and achieve the same results. From a political economy standpoint, opponents of reform may not object to a pilot on a small scale but would mobilize against national implementation of the program if it threatened their interests.

One way to deal with these replication or generalization issues is to promote systematic experimentation with successful interventions at progressively larger scale. That is, if a small pilot works in one region of a country, then expansion would take it to the next administrative level (say, from a municipal pilot to a regional trial) before considering national expansion. Similarly, while the evaluation of national or statewide programs in Mexico or Brazil may support a judgment of their effectiveness at scale in those settings, the recommendation for other countries might still be to adapt the programs and trial them on a smaller scale first.

The generation of solid evidence on the replicability and impacts of accountability reforms and other important interventions in education would be greatly facilitated by more comprehensive and consistent cross-country data on education outcomes. One of the largest costs in any impact evaluation is the collection of outcome data—above all, on student learning. When countries have standardized national assessments in place to track student learning on a census basis every year or two years, an invaluable platform for evaluation of all types of education programs is created. Equally important, the costs of conducting good impact evaluations are radically lower. Even if national learning assessments are sample-based rather than universally applied, they are a boon to rigorous evaluation.

Global efforts to coordinate the definitions and quality of administrative data (including enrollments, completion, student-teacher ratios, and financing) and to expand developing-country participation in globally benchmarked learning assessments such as PISA, TIMSS, and the Progress in International Reading Literacy Study (PIRLS) will have payoffs for cross-country impact evaluation and our knowledge of what works under different country conditions. While the size of national test samples in most international assessments may not support evaluation of pilot programs in all areas, there are interesting examples of countries that specifically oversample certain populations to support program impact evaluations. Mexico, for example, has oversampled and stratified its sample of 15-year-old students in the OECD's PISA test to make it representative at the level of its 32 states and make it possible to evaluate state-level implementation of programs (Álvarez, García, and Patrinos 2007). Brazil has done the same. Poland has extended the application of PISA also to 16- and 17-year-olds, thus allowing researchers to evaluate the cumulative impact of some key reforms over time (Jakubowski and others 2010). In the context of its participation in TIMSS, Jordan has oversampled schools where costly information and communication technology programs are applied to measure the impact of these on learning outcomes (Patrinos and others, forthcoming).

Costs and Cost-Effectiveness

A key reason why impact evaluations are important is that they are critical inputs into cost-effectiveness analysis, or the comparison of how much alternative strategies cost to achieve the same degree of education improvement. For education policy makers and the development agencies that support them, the crucial question is not necessarily whether an intervention "works"; it is how well it works in relation to its cost and in comparison with alternative uses of those resources. Despite the centrality of this question, education economics is still far away from answers. As this book has made clear, the global evidence on programs' impact (even in areas such as SBM, which has been the subject of decades of policy experimentation across the world) is still limited by the relatively small number of rigorous studies.

A critical constraint to the cost-effectiveness analysis of alternative interventions is the lack of comparable outcome measures. While it is meaningful to compare a percentage-point increase in school enrollment or completion, an improvement of 1 standard deviation in a particular test is not necessarily equivalent to an increase of 1 standard deviation in another test.[1] Therefore, a simple comparison of "dollars per standard deviation of test score increase" across different evaluations is not necessarily meaningful. To the extent that evaluations use internationally benchmarked tests, or apply tests whose scale can be anchored to those of an internationally benchmarked test (as was done in Brazil and Mexico), this limitation can be overcome. But doing this can be logistically difficult and technically demanding. This calls for caution in comparing learning impacts across evaluations.

Even if it were possible to find a common outcome metric across evaluations, few studies track program implementation costs carefully and comprehensively enough to support the cost side of a full cost-effectiveness analysis. But even without good data, we can recognize that average implementation costs vary considerably across the three types of reforms analyzed in this book. Information interventions are likely the cheapest to implement—especially if they can draw from existing data collection systems. Those systems can be costly, but they serve multiple purposes. If information dissemination is accompanied by effective "socialization" of the results, costs also rise. Two of the studies reviewed attempted to benchmark the cost-effectiveness of the intervention internally. The Pakistan report cards study found the cost of the intervention roughly equal to the total reduction in school fees that it generated. The three-state study in India showed that the salary equivalent of the increase in teacher attendance was orders of magnitude greater than the cost of the information program.

SBM interventions are also relatively low-cost to implement—with most of the costs associated with one-time training and the dissemination of information. Costs can be higher if programs are tailored to the specific needs of dispersed rural populations, indigenous groups, illiterate parents, or other groups with special communications needs. Nevertheless, the rural SBM program in Mexico is estimated to cost about $6.50 per student—including both the training and grants allocated to parent associations. Compared with the per-student cost of schooling (estimated at over $800 in 2006), this is low (Patrinos 2009). The costs are also low compared with other potential spending on alternative classroom inputs in these schools, such as computers ($500 per student, 10 computers per class), teacher salary increases ($240 per student), or annual school building costs ($160 per student). Only the implementation of student assessments has a similar unit cost, at $6 per student (Patrinos 2009). However, because SBM involves parent participation—and therefore time—a full cost accounting would include the estimated opportunity cost of parents' time.

Contract teachers typically earn lower salaries than public sector teachers. Given clear research evidence that they can produce student learning improvements on par with regular teachers, they offer scope for net savings in public education expenditure. The political economy issues of sustained use of contract teachers must figure into such cost-effectiveness analysis, too, however—as discussed in chapter 4 and in the next section of this chapter. Political pressure to regularize contract teachers (after a net expansion of the teaching force) would raise overall education costs and wipe out efficiency gains.

Teacher bonus incentives, on the other hand, are inherently costly. Even if average awards are relatively small and relatively few schools or teachers achieve them, there is a net payroll cost that must be exceeded by the gain in desired outcomes for the program to be cost-effective. The cases reviewed in this book had annual bonuses ranging from 30 percent to 300 percent of a month's salary. At the high end of this range, programs are undeniably costly to implement on a broad scale.

However, in Brazil and many other developing counties, teachers' salaries are low in relation to other sectors of the economy, and there is evidence this is constraining the education system's ability to attract adequate talent. In such contexts, the counterfactual policy to a teacher bonus program might well be across-the-board wage increases. These could be as or more expensive than a bonus program and fail to create incentives for better performance. Indeed, research in the U.S. context suggests that the compression of teacher pay scales over time (eliminating differential rewards for performance) was the most important driver of high-ability women out of the teaching profession (Hoxby and Leigh 2004).

Therefore, although teacher bonus programs are costly, they may be more cost-effective than alternative wage policies. But another dimension to the cost-effectiveness of pay-for-performance programs, which is difficult to assess on current evidence, is the cost of distortions that may arise in the medium to long term, such as attempts to game the system. These distortions could be costly to overcome—for example, requiring increasingly elaborate efforts to protect the security of student testing instruments and administration. Or they could generate long-term distortions in system performance (such as "teaching to the test" and neglect of other subjects) that are difficult not only to detect but also to "cost." What is the value of the learning lost if teachers deliver a narrower curriculum? How does this value compare to the value of learning gains in the core subjects (math and language) that are typically tested? Ultimately, the cost-effectiveness of pay-for-performance programs in education may hinge on the social utility assigned to these and other possible tradeoffs. But given the relatively limited developing-country experience with such programs and the even more limited longevity of these experiences, we are still in an early stage of research, trying to build basic data on the extent to which these issues do arise over time, under different pay-for-performance program designs, and in different country contexts.

The Political Economy of Service Delivery Reform

Service delivery failures stemming from weak public sector accountability are, at root, a political economy challenge as much as a technical one. The common thread behind the three strategies highlighted in this book is that they all aim to realign the incentives of education system actors so that higher-quality service provision to citizens is the result. As such, they are reforms that touch the broader political economy of education service delivery. The political dynamics of implementing these types of reforms is not the focus of this book, but it cannot be ignored. First, the political dynamics determine the potential types and pace of reform in a given country context. But, second, an important feature of the accountability-oriented reforms reviewed here is that they themselves can alter the political economy of education service provision.

The politics of public service delivery are complex, even in democracies where citizens can ostensibly hold politicians accountable through the ballot box (Devarajan and Widlund 2007; Keefer and Khemani 2005). Just as complex is the political economy of education reform. Direct incentives to teachers and school personnel in the form of performance pay, SBM programs that extend autonomy at the school level, or programs that empower parents with oversight over teacher performance can face resistance from education bureaucracies and teachers' unions. Indeed, Grindle's 2004 analysis of key education reforms in Latin America during the 1990s showed how reform movements stimulated counterreform movements in country after country. Education bureaucracies and teachers' unions typically favor expanded budgets in efforts to maintain or enlarge the size of the teaching force (Hoxby 1996). For a given budget, unions and bureaucracies will also typically favor investments in teacher-related rather than nonteacher-related investments (Pritchett and Filmer 1999). Reform movements challenge these interests, which tend to resist even experimentation with changes (Hanushek and Woessmann 2007).

Finding systematic ways to overcome these political economy hurdles is challenging. Grindle (2004) found it difficult to identify characteristics that could predict ex ante which reform efforts would be successful in Latin America. In most cases of major reform, the process was characterized by stop-and-go efforts where reform proposals were put forward, faced pushback, in many cases were scaled down, and then only in some cases were successfully put in place. The process was idiosyncratic. But major reforms have taken place. Despite having one of the region's strongest teachers' unions, the Mexican government has been able to introduce stronger accountability for teachers through tests and to decentralize significant decision making to local levels (Álvarez, Garcia, and Patrinos 2007).

Information can play a critical role in breaking the political deadlock. It can expose shortcomings and biases, and its wide dissemination can overcome information asymmetries that perpetuate inequalities (Keefer and Khemani 2005; Majumdar, Mani, and Mukand 2004). Information about outcomes, such as test scores, can become a basis for political competition, either at a national or local level (Khemani 2007). In addition, information can bolster change agents—those who might lead reform efforts.

Strategic issues of sequencing, bundling, and packaging are bound to be important in any reform effort. Brazil's radical 1997 education financing reform—*Fundo para Manutenção e Desenvolvimento do Ensino Fundamental e Valorização do Magistério* (Fund for Primary Education Development and Maintenance and Enhancement of the Teaching Profession, or FUNDEF)—attacked sharp regional disparities in education funding by mandating states to share their resources with municipal education systems (Melo 2007). Despite large scope for political resistance from states that would lose direct control over a substantial part of their revenues, FUNDEF's design cleverly built a countervailing pro-reform constituency. First, the capitation funding formula introduced by the reform created strong incentives for enrollment expansion, which implied hiring more teachers and building more schools—generally the most politically salable reforms. Second, a mandate that 60 percent of the capitation funding go to teacher salaries implied increased salaries in many regions and got teachers on board. Most important, by mandating a shift in resources to municipal school systems, many of Brazil's 5,000-plus mayors became important pro-reform agents. Making this radical reform work required building a sufficiently large coalition of actors who could expect to benefit politically and fiscally from the reform to balance the more concentrated opposition from Brazil's 26 states and the federal district.

Reforms that involve teacher incentives—whether indirectly through SBM or directly through performance pay—are among the most politically sensitive. The reforms need to address issues of intrinsic motivation as well as the level of pay. In the case of contract teachers, they also need to foresee the likely demand for eventual regularization. Clearly some teachers have high intrinsic motivation to teach, and financial incentives that appear to demean that intrinsic motivation may create demoralization and backlash. Likewise, a perception that contract teachers are second-class—doing the same work for less pay and less security—may cause frustration and resistance to grow over time.

It is important to recognize up-front that accountability-oriented reforms implemented at any scale will likely face challenges, from both teachers' unions and education bureaucracies. Working as much as possible to create coalitions for reform—and using information and communications channels to drive home the goals and benefits of the reforms—is critical.

But humility and flexibility may be equally important factors. As documented in this book, not all interventions have produced improvements in learning. Policy makers—and researchers—need to be willing to admit that this is the case and be ready to try alternatives. The policy process should be fed by credible public information on inputs and outcomes so that progress can be monitored transparently. Rigorous impact evaluations managed by third parties can help establish the credibility of implementing agencies in seeking reforms that truly "work" rather than advancing an agenda. It is interesting to note that despite heated controversy around education pay for performance in the United States, randomized trials of individual and group-based teacher bonus programs in three U.S. school districts gained the support of local teachers' unions through the credible promise of methodologically rigorous, third-party evaluations and transparent reporting of results.

Future Directions

Rigorous evaluations of education interventions in the developing world are a relatively new phenomenon, but the number of cases is increasing rapidly. For example, a large and important set of evaluations in Sub-Saharan Africa that have not yet generated results are not reported here. This book will not be the last word on accountability-focused interventions. But our review of the evidence to date suggests that future work should be encouraged along at least two dimensions.

First, given a sound theoretical framework—that is, a logical chain for how an intervention might work to effect change—replication is an important tool for deepening our understanding of what works, where, and why. The number and range of evaluations to date do not support a satisfying synthesis. Replicating successful models in different contexts is necessary to quantify the extent to which programs work under varying circumstances. Replicating interventions that have been successful in small-scale settings at a regional or national level is necessary for confidence about what works "in the real world."

Second, the research discussed here points to the potential benefits of interventions that combine information, SBM, and teacher incentive reforms. There will be a high payoff to research designs that test various combinations and extensions of these approaches. Some of the studies reviewed here had solid crossover designs, and these have played an outsized role in advancing our understanding. It is not easy to organize such research; crossover designs require larger sample sizes and greater supervision. But given the evidence generated to date that reforms that make education actors more accountable for results can motivate increased uptake and more effective use of other education resources, this seems the most promising route to "making schools work."

Note

1. Even percentage-point increases in attendance are hard to compare across settings: attending a school where little learning takes place is not the same as attending a school where a lot of learning takes place.

References

Alcazar, L., F. H. Rogers, N. Chaudhury, J. Hammer, M. Kremer, and K. Muralidharan. 2006. "Why Are Teachers Absent? Probing Service Delivery in Peruvian Primary Schools." Development Economics Department, World Bank, Washington, DC.

Álvarez, Jesus, Vicente Garcia, and Harry A. Patrinos. 2007. "Institutional Effects as Determinants of Learning Outcomes: Exploring State Variations in Mexico." *Well-Being and Social Policy* 3 (1): 47–68.

Andrabi, Tahir, Jishnu Das, and Asim Khwaja. 2009. "Report Cards: The Impact of Providing School and Child Test Scores on Educational Markets." Unpublished manuscript, World Bank, Washington, DC.

Banerjee, Abhijit V., Rukmini Banerji, Esther Duflo, Rachel Glennerster, and Stuti Khemani. 2008. "Pitfalls of Participatory Programs: Evidence from a Randomized Evaluation in Education in India." Policy Research Working Paper 4584, World Bank, Washington, DC.

Banerjee, A. V., S. Cole, E. Duflo, and L. Linden. 2007. "Remedying Education: Evidence from Two Randomized Experiments in India." *The Quarterly Journal of Economics* 122 (3): 1235–64.

Bardhan, Pranab. 2002. "Decentralization of Governance and Development." *Journal of Economic Perspectives* 16 (4): 185–205.

Bardhan, Pranab, and Dilip Mookherjee. 2000. "Capture and Governance at Local and National Levels." *American Economic Review* 90 (2): 135–39.

———. 2005. "Decentralizing Antipoverty Program Delivery in Developing Countries." *Journal of Public Economics* 89 (4): 675–704.

Björkman, Martina. 2006. "Does Money Matter for Student Performance? Evidence from a Grant Program in Uganda." Working Paper 326, IIES, Stockholm University, Sweden.

Borman, G. D., G. M. Hewes, L. T. Overman, and S. Brown. 2003. "Comprehensive School Reform and Achievement: A Meta-Analysis." *Review of Educational Research* 73 (2): 125–230.

Bourdon, Jean, Markus Frölich, and Katharina Michaelowa. 2007. "Teacher Shortages, Teacher Contracts and Their Impact on Education in Africa." Institute for the Study of Labor (IZA) Discussion Paper 2844, IZA, Bonn, Germany. http://ideas.repec.org/p/iza/izadps/dp2844.html.

Bruns, B., D. Evans, and J. Luque. 2010. *Achieving World Class Education in Brazil: The Next Agenda*. Washington, DC: World Bank.

Chaudhury, Nazmul, and Dilip Parajuli. 2010. "Giving It Back: Evaluating the Impact of Devolution of School Management to Communities in Nepal." Unpublished manuscript, World Bank, Washington, DC.

Das, J. 2008. "The Impact of Contracting Out School Management to NGOs and of Transferring Budgets to School Councils." PowerPoint presentation, World Bank, Washington, DC.

De Grauwe, A. 2005. "Improving the Quality of Education through School-Based Management: Learning from International Experiences. *International Review of Education* 51 (4): 269–87.

Devarajan, Shantayanan, and Ingrid Widlund, eds. 2007. *The Politics of Service Delivery in Democracies. Better Access for the Poor*. Expert Group on Development Issues Secretariat, Ministry for Foreign Affairs, Stockholm, Sweden. http://citeseerx.ist.psu.edu/viewdoc/download?doi=10.1.1.133.7367&rep=rep1&type=pdf.

Duflo, E., P. Dupas, and M. Kremer. 2008. "Peer Effects, Pupil-Teacher Ratios, and Teacher Incentives: Evidence from a Randomization Evaluation in Kenya." Unpublished manuscript, Abdul Latif Jameel Poverty Action Lab (JPAL), Massachusetts Institute of Technology, Cambridge, MA.

———. 2009. "Additional Resources versus Organizational Changes in Education: Experimental Evidence from Kenya." Unpublished manuscript, Abdul Latif Jameel Poverty Action Lab (JPAL), Massachusetts Institute of Technology, Cambridge, MA.

Duflo, E., R. Glennerster, and M. Kremer. 2008. "Using Randomization in Development Economics Research: A Toolkit." In *Handbook of Development Economics, Vol. 4*, ed. K. J. Arrow and M. D. Intriligator, 3895–962. Amsterdam: Elsevier.

Duflo, E., R. Hanna, and S. Ryan. 2010. "Incentives Work: Getting Teachers to Come to School." Unpublished manuscript, Abdul Latif Jameel Poverty Action Lab (JPAL), Massachusetts Institute of Technology, Cambridge, MA.

Ferraz, C., and B. Bruns. Forthcoming. "Incentives to Teach: The Effects of Performance Pay in Brazilian Schools." World Bank, Washington, DC.

Gertler, P., H. A. Patrinos, and E. Rodríguez-Oreggia. 2010. "Parental Empowerment in Mexico: Randomized Experiment of the *Apoyo a la Gestión Escolar* (AGE) in Rural Primary Schools in Mexico: Preliminary Findings." Unpublished manuscript, World Bank, Washington, DC.

Gertler, P., H. A. Patrinos, and M. Rubio-Codina. 2006. "Empowering Parents to Improve Education. Evidence from Rural Mexico." Policy Research Working Paper 3935, World Bank, Washington, DC.

———. 2007. "Methodological Issues in the Evaluation of School-Based Management Reforms." Doing Impact Evaluation No. 10, World Bank, Washington, DC.

Glewwe, P., N. Ilias, and M. Kremer. 2010. "Teacher Incentives." *American Economic Journal: Applied Economics* 2 (3): 205–27.

Grindle, Merilee. 2004. *Despite the Odds: The Contentious Politics of Educational Reform.* Princeton, NJ: Princeton University Press.

Goyal, S., and P. Pandey. 2009. "How Do Government and Private Schools Differ? Findings from Two Large Indian States." South Asia Human Development Sector Report 30, World Bank, Washington, DC.

Hanushek, Eric A., and Ludger Woessmann. 2007. "The Role of Education Quality for Economic Growth." Policy Research Working Paper 4122, World Bank, Washington, DC.

Hoxby, Caroline. 1996. "How Teachers' Unions Affect Education Production." *The Quarterly Journal of Economics* 111 (3): 671–718.

Hoxby, C. M., and A. Leigh. 2004. "Pulled Away or Pushed Out? Explaining the Decline of Teacher Aptitude in the United States." *American Economic Review* 94 (2): 236–46.

Jakubowski, M., H. A. Patrinos, E. E. Porta, and J. Wisniewski. 2010. "The Impact of the 1999 Education Reform in Poland." Policy Research Working Paper 5263, World Bank, Washington, DC.

Keefer, Philip, and Stuti Khemani. 2005. "Democracy, Public Expenditures, and the Poor: Understanding Political Incentives for Providing Public Services." *World Bank Research Observer* 20 (1): 1–28.

Khemani, Stuti. 2007. "Can Information Campaigns Overcome Political Obstacles to Serving the Poor?" In *The Politics of Service Delivery in Democracies. Better Access for the Poor*, ed. Shantayanan Devarajan and Ingrid Widlund. Expert Group on Development Issues Secretariat, Ministry for Foreign Affairs, Stockholm, Sweden. http://citeseerx.ist.psu.edu/viewdoc/download?doi=10.1.1.133.7367&rep=rep1&type=pdf.

Kremer, M. E., P. Glewwe, D. Chen, and S. Moulin. 2001. "Interim Report on a Teacher Incentive Program in Kenya." Unpublished paper, Harvard University, Cambridge, MA.

Kremer, M., and A. Holla. 2009. "Improving Education in the Developing World: What Have We Learned from Randomized Evaluations?" *Annual Review of Economics* 1: 513–42.

Lavy, V. 2002. "Evaluating the Effect of Teachers' Group Performance Incentives on Pupil Achievement." *The Journal of Political Economy* 110 (6): 1286–317.

———. 2009. "Performance Pay and Teachers' Effort, Productivity, and Grading Ethics." *The American Economic Review* 99 (5): 1979–2011.

Li, Tao, Li Han, Scott Rozelle, and Linxiu Zhang. 2010. "Cash Incentives, Peer Tutoring, and Parental Involvement: A Study of Three Educational Inputs in a Randomized Field Experiment in China." Unpublished manuscript, Peking University, Beijing, China. http://mitsloan.mit.edu/neudc/papers/paper_223.pdf.

Majumdar, Sumon, Anandi Mani, and Sharun Mukand. 2004. "Politics, Information and the Urban Bias." *Journal of Development Economics* 75 (1): 137–65.

Melo, Marcus André. 2007. "The Politics of Service Delivery Reform: Improving Basic Education in Brazil." In *The Politics of Service Delivery in Democracies. Better Access for the Poor*, ed. Shantayanan Devarajan and Ingrid Widlund. Expert Group on Development Issues Secretariat, Ministry for Foreign Affairs, Stockholm,

Sweden. http://citeseerx.ist.psu.edu/viewdoc/download?doi=10.1.1.133.7367&rep=rep1&type=pdf.

Mizala, Alejandra, and Miguel Urquiola. 2007. "School Markets: The Impact of Information Approximating Schools' Effectiveness." National Bureau of Economic Research Working Paper 13676, NBER, Cambridge, MA.

Muralidharan, K., and V. Sundararaman. 2009. "Teacher Performance Pay: Experimental Evidence from India." National Bureau of Economic Research Working Paper 15323, NBER, Cambridge, MA.

———. 2010a. "Contract Teachers: Experimental Evidence from India." Unpublished paper, World Bank, Washington, DC.

———. 2010b. "The Impact of Diagnostic Feedback to Teachers on Student Learning: Experimental Evidence from India." *The Economic Journal* 120 (546): F187–F203.

Pandey, Priyanka, Sangeeta Goyal, and Venkatesh Sundararaman. 2009. "Community Participation in Public Schools: Impact of Information Campaigns in Three Indian States." *Education Economics* 17 (3): 355–75.

———. 2010. "Community Participation in Public Schools: Impact of Information Campaigns in Three Indian States." Draft, World Bank, Washington, DC.

Patrinos, H. A. 2009. "School-Based Management." Unpublished manuscript, World Bank, Washington, DC.

Patrinos, H. A., J. Guáqueta, H. Bannayan, O. Obeidat, and E. Porta. Forthcoming. "Case Study: Jordan Education Initiative." In *Public-Private Partnerships in Education: The Role of Private Donor Philanthropy in Education Systems*, ed. F. Barrera-Osorio and J. Guáqueta. Washington, DC: World Bank.

Paul, Samuel, 2002. *Holding the State to Account: Citizen Monitoring in Action*. Bangalore, India: Books for Change.

Piper, Benjamin, and Medina Korda. 2010. "EGRA Plus: Liberia." Program Evaluation Report draft, RTI International, Research Triangle Park, NC.

Pritchett, Lant, and Deon Filmer. 1999. "What Education Production Functions Really Show: A Positive Theory of Education Expenditures." *Economics of Education Review* 18 (2): 223–39.

Rau, T., and D. Contreras. 2009. "Tournaments, Gift Exchanges, and the Effect of Monetary Incentives for Teachers: The Case of Chile." Department of Economics Working Paper 305, University of Chile, Santiago.

Reinikka, Ritva, and Jakob Svensson. 2005. "Fighting Corruption to Improve Schooling: Evidence from a Newspaper Campaign in Uganda." *Journal of the European Economic Association* 3 (2–3): 259–67.

———. 2006. "The Power of Information: Evidence from a Newspaper Campaign to Reduce Capture of Public Funds." Unpublished manuscript, Institute for International Economic Studies, Stockholm, Sweden; World Bank, Washington, DC. http://people.su.se/~jsven/information2006a.pdf.

Vegas, Emiliana, and Joost De Laat. 2003. "Do Differences in Teacher Contracts Affect Student Performance? Evidence from Togo." Policy Research Working Paper No. 26955, World Bank, Washington, DC.

World Bank. 2003. *World Development Report 2004: Making Services Work for Poor People*. Washington, DC: World Bank.

ECO-AUDIT

Environmental Benefits Statement

The World Bank is committed to preserving endangered forests and natural resources. The Office of the Publisher has chosen to print ***Making Schools Work: New Evidence on Accountability Reforms*** on recycled paper with 50 percent postconsumer fiber in accordance with the recommended standards for paper usage set by the Green Press Initiative, a nonprofit program supporting publishers in using fiber that is not sourced from endangered forests. For more information, visit www.greenpressinitiative.org.

Saved:

- 9 trees
- 3 million BTUs of total energy
- 850 pounds of net greenhouse gases
- 4,096 gallons of waste water
- 249 pounds of solid waste